An Introduction to SAS® Visual Analytics

How to Explore Numbers, Design Reports, and Gain Insight into Your Data

Tricia Aanderud · Rob Collum · Ryan Kumpfmiller

sas.com/books

contents

about this book

SAS Visual Analytics is a data visualization and analytics application that enables organizations to understand and analyze their most important asset: their data! There is a wealth of information freely available to users on support.sas.com, everything from simple blog tips to in-depth user documentation. All of this information can actually make it more difficult for users to understand how to get the most power from the application, or even know where to start!

Our purpose in writing this book is to provide a single quick-start guide that moves you swiftly through the applications; we aim to teach you the basics so that you can then easily expand that knowledge with some intermediate and advanced techniques. We want to ensure that users understand how to get the most from the application for their organizations.

Is this book for you?

New users or those with some familiarity with SAS Visual Analytics will find this book useful. This book provides a tutorial for new users. It also contains in-depth explanations of data visualizations and how to use them effectively.

If you have the administrative privileges for deploying, configuring, and maintaining your SAS Visual Analytics environment, then we've got you covered here as well. Our goal is to enhance your understanding of how the software works so that you can readily implement proven practices for efficient operation.

Prerequisites

You do not need any previous experience with the Visual Analytics toolset or SAS to use this book. If you are familiar with SAS coding techniques and SAS data handling, you might find some areas of the product easier to understand.

Scope of this book

This book covers the following topics:

- SAS Visual Analytics 7.3 (and later)
- SAS Visual Analytics 8.1

About the examples

Software used to develop the book's content

Reports and explorations for this book were created using the following software:

- SAS Visual Analytics 7.3 (and later)
- SAS Visual Analytics 8.1

SAS Enterprise Guide 7.1 and SAS Studio was used for some data preparation in this book. Most of the data sets were taken from existing sample libraries and no preparation was required. These sources are identified at first use.

The primary references used to write this book were the following sections of the online documentation for SAS Visual Analytics:

- SAS Visual Analytics User Guide, 7.3
- SAS Visual Analytics Administration Manual, 7.3

Example data and reports

You can access an import package for the *Building Your First Report* and *Building Your First Dashboard* chapters in this book by linking to its author page at http://support.sas.com/publishing/authors. Select the name of the author. Then, look for the cover thumbnail of this book, and select Example Code and Data to display the SAS programs that are included in this book.

If you are unable to access the code through the website, email saspress@sas.com.

We Want to Hear from You

SAS Press books are written *by* SAS Users *for* SAS Users. We welcome your participation in their development and your feedback on SAS Press books that you are using. Please visit https://support.sas.com/publishing to do the following:

> Sign up to review a book
> Recommend a topic
> Request information on how to become a SAS Press author
> Provide feedback on a book

Do you have questions about a SAS Press book that you are reading? Contact the author through saspress@sas.com or https://support.sas.com/author_feedback.

SAS has many resources to help you find answers and expand your knowledge. If you need additional help, see our list of resources: https://support.sas.com/publishing.

Subscribe to the SAS Learning Report

Receive up-to-date information about SAS training, certification, and publications via email by subscribing to the SAS Learning Report monthly eNewsletter. Read the archives and subscribe today at http://support.sas.com/community/newsletters/training!

Publish with SAS

SAS is recruiting authors! Are you interested in writing a book? Visit http://support.sas.com/saspress for more information.

about these authors

Tricia Aanderud, Director of the Data Visualization Practice at Zencos Consulting, provides SAS consulting services to organizations that need assistance understanding how to transform their data into meaningful reports and dashboards. She has been a SAS user since 2002, is a frequent speaker at SAS Global Forum and SAS regional user groups, and is the author of two SAS Press books and one self-published book. She has a background in technical communications, process engineering, and customer service. She has a BA in Mass Communications from Eastern Kentucky University.

Rob Collum is a Principal Technical Architect in the Professional Services Division at SAS. For the past twenty years, Rob has enabled the delivery of high-performance solutions that provide substantial value and meaningful impact to SAS customers around the world. He currently works alongside a team of professionals who partner with other divisions to identify, create, and standardize architectural practices for the newest SAS technologies. Rob received a Bachelor's degree in Computer Science from North Carolina State University, is a regular contributor to SAS Global Forum, and has coauthored several SAS certification exams.

Ryan Kumpfmiller works at Zencos Consulting as a SAS and Data Visualization Consultant where he provides consulting services to companies that need support understanding their data and how to get actionable information from it. He has been a SAS user since 2014 and has presented papers at the SouthEast SAS Users Group (SESUG), as well as at SAS Global Forum conferences. Ryan has a BS in Computer Information Systems and an MS in Competitive Intelligence Systems from Robert Morris University.

Learn more about these authors by visiting their author pages, where you can download free book excerpts, access example code and data, read the latest reviews, get updates, and more:

http://support.sas.com/publishing/authors/aanderud.html
http://support.sas.com/publishing/authors/kumpfmiller.html
http://support.sas.com/publishing/authors/collum.html

acknowledgments

Each book starts as a seed in an author's mind. It takes care and nurturing from many dedicated souls to become a finished product. This book is no exception.

First, we want to thank the technical reviewers who challenged our ideas and corrected our words: Michelle Homes, Peter Wiijers, Robert Borst, Ted Stolarczyk, Varsha Chawla, and Rosie Poultney.

Many SAS employees supported, advised, and encouraged this book. The SAS Visual Analytics Product Management team, led by Rick Styll, provided demos, suggestions, and guidance. Chris Hemedinger and Anna Brown of the SAS Visual Analytics Communites assisted with the research and other suggestions.

We also want to thank the SAS Press staff for their flexibility and professionalism. We extend our thanks to Denise T. Jones for production, Kathy Underwood for copyedit, Robert Harris for artwork, and Cindy Puryear for marketing. We would like to especially thank Brenna Leath, our editor, who has tirelessly ensured that the rubber hit the road when it came to getting this book published. *Thank you to all.*

Tricia Aanderud

Writing is a solitary task, but all writers benefit from sounding boards and cheerleaders. Certainly, I would have to give thanks to my brilliant co-authors Ryan and Rob for fulfilling those roles completely. We have truly made another great book!

My colleagues at Zencos were another source of inspiration. They were able to answer technical questions and provide ideas for examples. Ben Zenick and David Septoff helped just by being excited about the project and providing the time off to complete this assignment.

Thanks for my wonderful husband Ken, who brought me coffee, assisted with developing ideas, and encouraged me to write even when I would have preferred to be taking a nap.

Rob Collum

I'd like to express gratitude and recognition to my teammates and colleagues at SAS. Much of my understanding regarding system architecture and software interactions is built upon a solid foundation provided by the rock stars of the Global Enablement & Learning team as well as generous support from the folks in Research & Development. Special thanks to my core team members Simon Williams, Jack May, Edoardo Riva, Stuart Rogers, Erwan Granger, and Mark Thomas, as well as folks from R&D including Brian Bowman, Oliver Schabenberger, Steve Krueger, and Mark Gass.

I'm thankful as well for the team working on this book. Tricia is a firebrand who launched this ambitious project with a clear and definitive vision. She was critical to keeping us – okay, me – on track over the course of this effort. Ryan was a rock, cool and steady, as we thrashed back and forth on content. And Brenna managed some of the most challenging work – coordinating the authors in conjunction with the SAS Press organization – while somehow getting compromises that looked like we each got our own way.

I am also very appreciative of my family who gave me time and space for the occasions I needed to lock myself in a closet to meet key deadlines. They were my reward each time I emerged from reclusion, always ready to engage, play, and remind me why I'm working so hard.

Ryan Kumpfmiller

Completing this project was quite the ride that spanned over many months. It took a lot of dedication and was finished only by the professional and personal support of everyone around me.

I'd like to thank everyone at Zencos for all of their assistance. This could not have been done without Ben Zenick and David Septoff. They were supportive from day one and eager for us to pursue this project. I would like to especially thank Ivan Gomez and Ben Murphy for their expert advice and guidance.

I'm also very grateful to have so many supportive friends and family in my life. Their excitement and curiosity about the project always kept my motivation going. They were understanding when I needed time to myself and there for me when I needed to wind down after long days.

Lastly, I'd like to thank my incredible co-authors Tricia and Rob. Tricia was always there to make sure our writing was on track and we never had to go very far for a question with Rob's technical expertise.

introduction

At SAS Global Forum in 2012, SAS Institute CEO Dr. James Goodnight introduced an application that offered not only a way to quickly process data, but to make analytics approachable to business users. There was an industry revolution taking shape, and data was becoming a mainstream topic.

From a simple laptop at a small desk, Dr. Goodnight described the importance of speed in analysis, simplifying statistics, and producing data insights. The laptop was connected to the servers in Cary, NC, over 600 miles away. The dataset he had placed in the application contained billions of rows. Neither fact seemed to concern him. His focus was on the task at hand, which was discovering the mysteries within the data. With a few swift mouse maneuvers, a gorgeous analytical graph instantly appeared. The application had determined the best way to analyze the data. There was no coding required. There was no waiting required. This stunning application was called SAS Visual Analytics.

This book is being written during an interesting period for the evolution of SAS Visual Analytics. As we signed our publishing contract, SAS announced that the application would undergo a metamorphosis. It would become part of the newly announced, cloud-based SAS Viya product and sport a redesigned user interface. As we were creating examples, writing content, and taking screenshots, SAS R&D was completing product verification and adding some final touches for the new release.

Within the application, the changes are largely found in the user interface organization and appearance. The larger change was to the in-memory storage solution. In the previous releases, the in-memory component is called the SAS LASR Analytic Server. In the new release, the component is called the Cloud Analytic Server (CAS). Both servers are similar in that they use the server random access memory (RAM). The differences are found in how this task is achieved.

If you understand how to use an earlier release, you can adopt the new release with minimal effort. This book is largely based on SAS Visual Analytics 7.3, but does include guidance for the SAS Viya release. This chapter provides an introduction to and overview of the applications. The second part of the chapter provides an overview of the book.

Application introduction

SAS Visual Analytics provides a complete platform for analytics visualization, enabling you to identify patterns and relationships in data that were not initially evident. Users of all skill levels can load data, search for analytic patterns, and create robust reports and dazzlingly interactive dashboards.

The speed of the platform is based on a high-performance, in-memory analytic engine. Large data tables are loaded into the server RAM, which allows nearly instant calculations and data display. The application supports an out-of -the-box web server, so organizations can easily share analyses and reports through a web browser or a mobile device.

SAS Visual Analytics is available in two deployments: non-distributed and distributed. The non-distributed version is a single server deployment and the distributed deployment works across multiple servers. The difference is the amount of data that can be processed. There is no difference in the user interface.

Understanding in-memory data storage

A key feature of SAS Visual Analytics is the in-memory data storage. To use in-memory data, the application loads the data from the file system in the server's random access memory (RAM). With the data loaded in RAM, data queries, calculations, and analyses are done instantly. The SAS LASR Analytic Server handles this functionality.

The LASR Analytic server represents a huge shift in how analytics are applied to large volumes of data. By using a massively parallel processing architecture, the LASR Analytic server can distribute your data in chunks across multiple machines and keep all of that data persistently loaded in RAM, which enables the server to process your analytic jobs at lightning speed. This means that the LASR server delivers analytics results at previously unattainable levels of performance.

Understanding the application

Many new users are confused about how the applications work together. The following figure shows each application and how data travels through each application.

Figure 1 Application overview

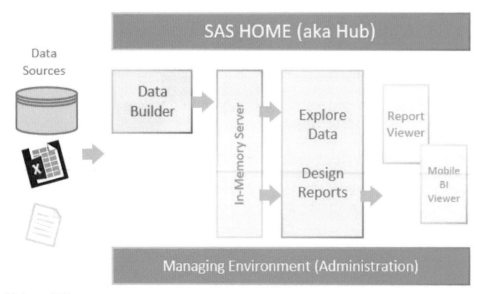

Here's a brief overview of each application and its purpose. Each of these applications is discussed in full in later chapters.

- SAS Visual Analytics Homepage (SAS Home/Hub)

  This application is the entry point to the tool. You can access content and the other applications based on your assigned role.

- Report Viewer/Mobile BI Viewer

  The application enables you to view content such as reports or stored processes. The Mobile BI viewer works similar to the Report Viewer but it runs on your mobile device or tablet.

- Data Builder

  This application enables you to load data from a data source to the SAS LASR Analytic Server. Your data can be in a database, a spreadsheet, or even in a social media engine. This application is used by data administrators and content builders. In the SAS Visual Analytics 8.1 release, the Data Builder was redesigned to focus on data wrangling. This change allows non-technical users a more intuitive way to join data tables and massage their data.

- LASR Analytic Server

  The LASR Analytic Server provides the in-memory storage engine. Perhaps the biggest change between the releases was the introduction of SAS Viya. In addition, the server name changed from the LASR Analytic Server to Cloud Analytic Server (CAS).

- Visual Designer/Visual Explorer

  The Visual Designer enables you to build interactive reports and a dashboard. The Visual Explorer enables you to explore new data sources and create advanced analytics. The content can be shared with Visual Designer. Once saved, this content is available to the Report Viewer application. In the SAS Visual Analytis 8.1 release, the Visual Designer and Visual Explorer were combined into one application. With the combined applications, users can explore data and create visualizations in the same application.

- Administrator

  This application enables you to load data and to manage and monitor the SAS LASR Analytic Server. This application is used by administrators. In the SAS Visual Analytics 8.1 release, the Administrator functionality was merged with the SAS Environment Manager. The SAS Environment Manager was released with SAS 9.4. It offered a way to monitor the SAS platform. Moving the SAS Visual Analytics Administrator to SAS Environment Manager was part of broader long-term plan to have a central location to administer the system.

How to use this book

This book is divided into four parts that focus on different areas of the application.

- **Part 1 Getting Started**

  Learn the basics of SAS Visual Analytics by creating a new report. You can learn how to quickly load data to create beautiful reports. Next, you can create a dashboard using some of the additional product features.

- **Part 2 Customizing Your Data Visualizations**

  Once you understand the basics, then you can learn more about using the other data objects and working with advanced analytics.

- **Part 3 Administration and Data Loading**

  The SAS Visual Analytics solution provides a remarkably powerful and dynamic set of software tools with which you can accomplish astounding feats of large-scale digital data manipulation and analysis. It's important to understand how those software tools function and interoperate so that you can get the best and most efficient operations out of them.

- **Part 4 SAS Visual Analytics 8.1**

  This part of the book takes you into the newest release of SAS Visual Analytics, which is on SAS Viya. These chapters introduce you to the new environment and show you how to navigate and use the Visual Data Builder and Visual Analytics applications.

part one

getting started

This part provides a tutorial for SAS Visual Analytics. You will learn how to how to access content through SAS Home. Then you will build a simple report. In the next chapter, you will learn the basics for creating a performance dashboard. After completing those chapters, you learn how to load data with the Data Builder.

- Chapter 1 Accessing Content

    This chapter explains how to use the SAS Home page, which provides a gateway to the application features and content. You are guided through the home page features and some of the Report Viewer features.

- Chapter 2 Building Your First Report

    The chapter is a tutorial for Visual Designer (also known as Report Builder). It shows you how to build a simple report and provides an overview of the basic product features. Topics include interface overview, adding data, creating a simple report, and how to control the report look and feel.

- Chapter 3 Building Your First Dashboard

    This chapter is a tutorial for the advanced features in the tool. You are shown how to create a performance dashboard that explains how to think about the data, determine the best layout, and use extra features.

- Chapter 4 Using the Data Builder

    This chapter shows you how to massage and load your data into the SAS LASR Analytic Server.

accessing content

SAS Visual Analytics has a central entry point called SAS Home, or in older releases, *the Hub*. You can think of it as the central access point. From SAS Home, you can open content or other tools within the application. What you can do from the homepage is based on the role that the administrator assigned to you. When you want to view a report, the content is displayed in the Report Viewer.

This chapter starts with the methods to access content and define the default roles. Then you are guided through the homepage features and some of the Report Viewer features. The information in this chapter is intended to provide a quick overview. SAS Institute has a collection of training videos in the SAS Visual Analytics Video Library at support.sas.com.

Methods of accessing content

Users can access SAS Visual Analytics content through a web browser on a PC or through a mobile device, such as an Apple iPad. A key feature of SAS Visual Analytics is its built-in web functionality. When users enter the application, they access the homepage, which provides access to the content and other product features. Your site can allow guest access through a public portal. A public portal or kiosk allows access to pre-determined content without requiring any credentials.

Accessing content with a web browser

Users can access SAS Visual Analytics from any of the popular web browsers, such as Google Chrome, Mozilla Firefox, or Apple Safari. Users might have access to all product features and content or limited access based on the permissions and capabilities assigned by the system administrator.

Accessing content through the public portal

You might want to make your data available to the public. The public can be anything from your customer base to the entire world. The United Nations has the ComTrade public portal that you can visit from the SAS Visual Analytics demo site. The site allows you to explore the data and analysis without entering any credentials. The following figure shows the UN ComTrade site.

Figure 1.1 SAS Visual Analytics in a public kiosk

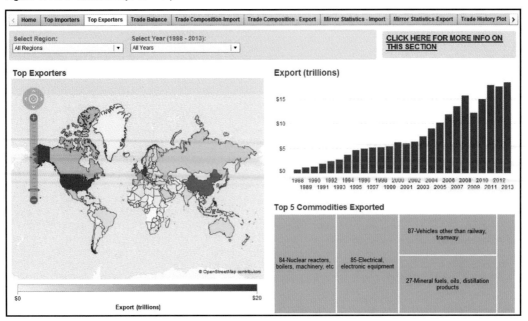

You can also use this technique on your intranet where employees can access the reports and use the data discovery techniques without having an additional login. This is built-in functionality that can be configured. Your site administrator can customize the security to ensure that only the reports you want available can be seen. Refer to the SAS Visual Analytics Administrator's Manual for more information.

Accessing content with the mobile bi app

You can also access reports from a mobile device. The mobile device management is built-in functionality. As an administrator, you can allow your users to access the portal either within a VPN or with just a login. You can adjust the mobile security to ensure the safety of your data. The data is only shown on the device when the user is connected to your network.

There are several example reports available when you download the free SAS Mobile BI app from iTunes store or from Google Play for Android. For SAS Visual Analytics 8.1, the mobile app became available for Windows 10. See the References section for additional information about features and administration.

Accessing content from Office Analytics

If your site has Office Analytics licensed, users with authorization can include SAS Visual Analytics reports in their Microsoft Office content.

Understanding roles

Your capabilities from SAS Home are based on the role the SAS Visual Analytics administrator assigned to you. The roles exist to define how users interact with the application. For example, a user assigned the consumer role reviews reports or analysis. In contrast, they don't need to access the advanced functionality. While the report builders are creating content, they obviously require more permissions and capabilities. Here are the default roles with capabilities:

Consumer	Views the reports, analytics and dashboards for content. May use a desktop or mobile device to consume the reports. Consumers might be internal or external to the organization based on how SAS Visual Analytics is configured.
Content Builder	Creates content like reports, explorations, and dashboards for consumers. This role might produce the data sets or use those made available from the Data Administrator.
Data Administrator	Schedules and loads data tables into SAS Visual Analytics. Makes data from multiple data sources available to the application.
Platform Administrator	Manages the SAS Visual Analytics environment and platform which includes controlling the folder structure, user accounts, and access to the content.

Depending on the organization size, some users might fill more than one role. In a smaller organization, one person might be responsible for creating content and administering the system. In larger organizations, there might be entire departments devoted to each role.

For more information about managing roles and their capabilities, refer to the SAS Visual Analytics Administration Guide for your release.

Accessing SAS Visual Analytics

Users can access SAS Visual Analytics content and applications through the SAS homepage. You can think of it as a central entry point. From a web browser use the following URL to access the homepage, where server and port are specific to your site:

http://<server:port>/SASVisualAnalyticsHub

This URL is case sensitive. If you are unsure of the server and port, contact your SAS site administrator. In almost all cases, a login user ID and password are required.

Transformation of the homepage

Starting with SAS Visual Analytics 7.2, there were two versions of SAS Home. Between SAS Visual Analytics 7.1 and 7.2, the homepage went through a metamorphosis. The homepage was converted to use HTML5 from Adobe Flash. The new look, based on HTML5, was called Modern mode. The previous homepage was called Classic mode. The Modern mode does not support all the same features as the Classic mode.

Note: All of the following figures show how the homepage appears when accessed by a content developer who has data administration rights. This user can view reports, create reports, and explore data.

Figure 1.2 Classic mode homepage in release 7.3

Figure 1.3 Modern mode homepage in release 7.3

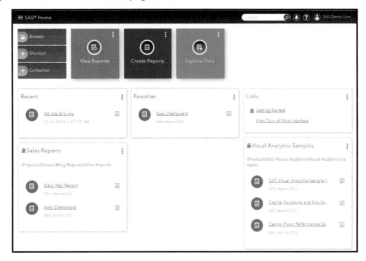

For SAS Visual Analytics 8.1, the homepage content was rearranged but contains the same functionality. This layout was introduced to make it easier for new users to understand. One difference was that the term *collection* changed to *content tab*.

Figure 1.4 Homepage in SAS Visual Analytics 8.1

Understanding SAS home

No matter which mode you are using, the homepage has the same basic functionality. The main areas of the homepage enable you to access applications within the product and to access content, which are described below. Here's how the homepage appears when accessed by a consumer. This user can view reports.

Figure 1.5 Modern mode homepage in SAS Visual Analytics 7.3

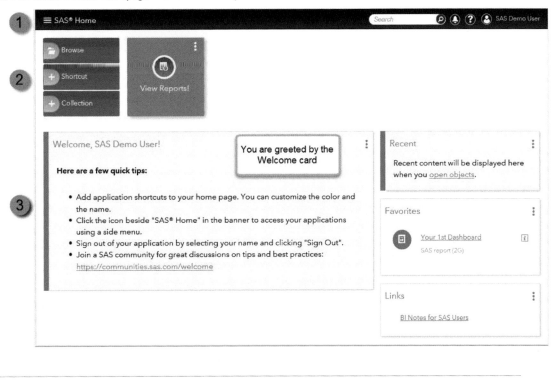

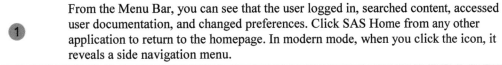

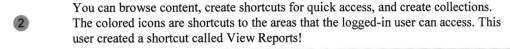

1	From the Menu Bar, you can see that the user logged in, searched content, accessed user documentation, and changed preferences. Click SAS Home from any other application to return to the homepage. In modern mode, when you click the icon, it reveals a side navigation menu.
2	You can browse content, create shortcuts for quick access, and create collections. The colored icons are shortcuts to the areas that the logged-in user can access. This user created a shortcut called View Reports!
3	You can manage the content in these areas. You can see recent content, create bookmarks for your favorite content, access links to external content, and access collections. Click the title to open the report in the Viewer.

The homepage is configurable. You can control which collections are shown, what items are in your favorites, and any shortcuts. Refer to the user documentation or training videos for more details.

Opening a report

If you need to find a report, exploration, or dashboard that is not showing on the homepage, you can find it by searching or browsing. If you know where the report is located, then you can navigate to it.

To navigate to a report called Casino Floor Performance Sample:

1. Click **Browse**. The Open window appears.
2. Navigate the folder structure until you find the report that you want to view. The report is located in SAS Folders ▶ Products ▶ SAS Visual Analytics ▶ Visual Analytics Samples.

   As you select each folder, the contents appear to the right. In the following figure, you can see how each folder level opens. Notice that the path or breadcrumbs are shown in the upper left corner so that you know where you are.

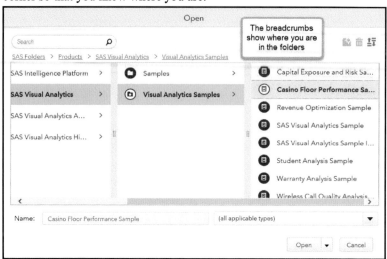

3. Click the object name to open the report in the Report Viewer.

Creating a shortcut

If a certain application is used more frequently, the user might want to create a shortcut. Shortcuts are shown at the top of the homepage and create quick access to the applications. To create a shortcut to the Report Viewer:

1. Click **Shortcut**. The Add Application Shortcut window appears.
2. In the **Application** drop-down list, select **Report Viewer** from the list.
3. You can keep the default name or type a name that is meaningful to you. Examples might be **View Reports!** or **View Content**.
4. Select the shortcut color.

5. Click **Save**. The shortcut appears on the top.

Creating a collection or content tile

A collection enables you to organize similar content. Sometimes the folder structure can be difficult to navigate for consumers. As the number of reports and content grows, it is more confusing trying to provide the path or understand how to find related content that might be stored in multiple locations. You can create a collection that is displayed on the homepage for easy access. You can also choose to share your collections with others. The advantage to collections is that you can organize similar content spread across multiple folders in a convenient location. When organizing content for storage, a content builder might want reports organized by topic or department. A report consumer who is less familiar with the structure just wants an easy way to see the report and other similar information. A collection is an easy way to ensure that the content is easy to find.

Ideas for collections

A collection can be based on a specific topic or around a user role. These reports might exist in several folders, but the report consumer would not be any wiser.

- Create a collection for a **project**. If your organization was exploring how to enhance revenue, the collection might include reports about current revenue and analysis of the past quarter's product sales.

- Create a collection based on **roles**. Line managers could see content related to their department content. Employees at a higher level could see reports across the organization.

- Create a collection based on a **time frame**. Place reports from last year or last quarter in a collection.

- Create a collection based on an **area of focus**. Place reports based on a customer or company issue. If there is a field issue, you might need reports from several departments.

While working on this book, we wanted to have the content examples available to all the authors. Each author had created example content, but it was spread across different folders. The solution was to create a collection called Final Examples. Here's how to add a collection called Final Examples.

1. Click **Collections**. The Collection window appears.
2. To create a new collection:
   a. In the Name field, type a name for the collection. This name appears on the homepage but can be edited later.
   b. Use the Location drop-down list to locate where you want to store the collection folder. This is not where the content is stored, only the metadata object.
   c. Click the **Publish this collection for all users** check box to ensure that others can see this collection. If you want to keep it private, leave the check box empty.

d.   Click **Save** when finished. The collection card appears on the homepage. You can now add content to the collection.

3.   On the right side, click the card control icon and select **Edit**.

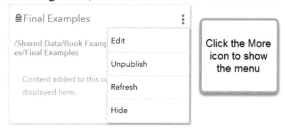

4.   Click the + sign to add content to the collection. When prompted, browse the folder structure to add the reports that you want. You can add as many reports, stored processes, or other items as you want. The link is just a shortcut to your content.

In this example, a link to the **Your 1st Dashboard** object was added to the collection. Notice that you can use the arrows to change the order. Select the object and click the trash can icon to discard the link.

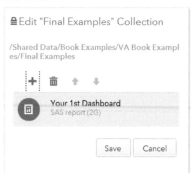

5.   Click **Save** when you are finished editing the collection. This updates the collection on the user homepage.

Using the report viewer

The SAS Visual Analytics Report Viewer enables you to interact with reports and other SAS Visual Analytics content. When you open a report, the content opens in the Report Viewer. The Information panel on the right provides details about the objects. You can add or review comments. If the report has alerts set, you can subscribe to the alerts. The following figure shows a report opened in the Report Viewer. The Report Viewer is also used on mobile devices and works in a similar manner.

Figure 1.6 Report Viewer

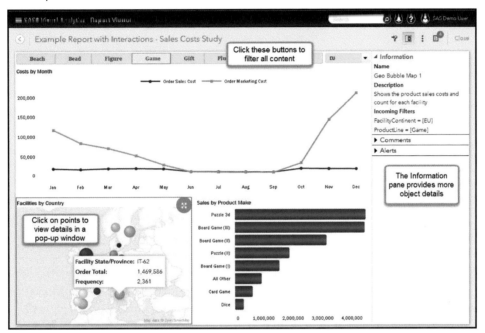

As shown in the preceding figure, when you click on the button bar or drop-down control objects, SAS Visual Analytics immediately changes the data to reflect the new view. Some data objects control other objects, so if you click on a line chart dot, the bar chart and the map filters the data to show that view.

Working with new consumers

Consumers are the primary users of the Report Viewer. It has many features that can get overlooked by new users. Many new consumers benefit from watching the videos in the SAS Visual Analytics Video Library. Some organizations make their own videos to explain how to navigate the structure and use some of the more common reports and dashboards.

Navigating a report

You can use the Report Viewer options to navigate the report. This topic provides an overview of some of the features you can use.

Opening other sections

Click the arrow if you want to see reports you recently had open. If the report has multiple sections, you can click the Section icon to view the other sections. In later releases, the term *section* has been changed to *page*. Instead of a drop-down list as shown in the following figure, the pages are across the top.

Figure 1.7 Open other report sections

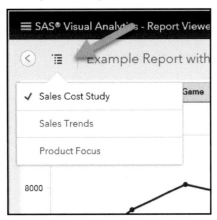

View additional report information

When viewing a report, the user might not understand the report purpose or what filters have been applied. In the following figure, you can see an example of a report with the Information panel displayed. The Information panel contains overall report information. When the user clicks on an object, it provides additional information about that object.

Click the **Information** icon to open the Information window. This window provides expanded information about the report and each object. Click an object to learn its name and view the description. If there are any display rules in use, you can view those. Open the **Comments** area to search, view, and add comments.

Figure 1.8 Use the information panel to view details

Other report viewer options

Click the **Control** icon for additional options. You can browse for other reports, edit the existing report, refresh the report content or print the report. If you want to email, click the **E-mail...** selection. A link to the report is added to an email message for the user.

Figure 1.9 Control menu

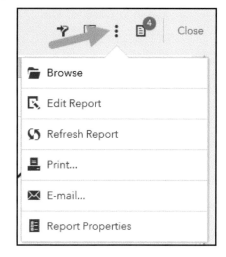

References

Bailey, David, I-kong Fu, and Anand Chitale. 2014. "Share Your SAS Visual Analytics Reports with SAS Office Analytics." *Proceedings of the SAS Global Forum 2014 Conference*. Paper SAS27402914. Cary, NC: SAS Institute Inc.

Nori, Murali. 2015. "HTML5 and SAS Mobile BI—Empowering Business Managers with Analytics and Business Intelligence." *Proceedings of the SAS Global Forum 2015 Conference*. Paper SAS1722-2015. Cary, NC: SAS Institute Inc. Available at: http://support.sas.com/resources/papers/proceedings15/SAS1722-2015.pdf.

SAS Mobile BI Video Library. Available at: http://support.sas.com/documentation/onlinedoc/mobile_bi/videos.html.

SAS Visual Analytics Video Library. Available at: http://support.sas.com/training/tutorial/. [SAS Library Note: the actual link is to a tab (http://support.sas.com/training/tutorial/#s1=2) on the aforementioned URL]

chapter two

building your first report

The SAS Visual Analytics Designer (the Designer) is the SAS Visual Analytics application that enables you to build reports and dashboards. The Designer can be accessed through the web application. Once the content is prepared in the Designer, it can then be viewed on the SAS Visual Analytics Viewer or through the SAS Mobile BI application. You can also import and access data directly from the Designer.

One of the benefits of the Designer is that you don't have to create code when you build reports, which can be a huge help to analysts who might not be fluent with SAS code. Tables, graphs, and other objects are all controlled through a drag-and-drop functionality. All object properties can be set using screen options. Even creating new variables involves going through a guided interface!

In this chapter, we go through how to access and navigate the Designer. From there, you are guided through creating an initial report that includes using basic objects, creating new data items, and setting up interactions between objects.

Accessing the designer

You can access the Designer through either a direct link or by navigating SAS Home. The following figure shows you which spots on the Hub lead you to the Designer.

Figure 2.1 How to get to the Designer from the Hub

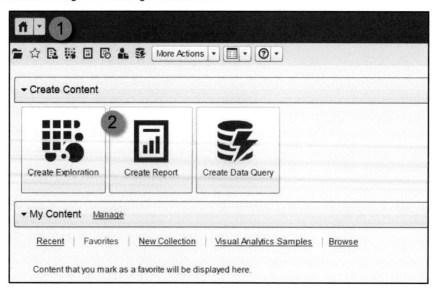

You can use the drop-down list ① to link to the applications on the system, including the Designer. The **Create Report** tile ② under **Create Content** also links you to the location.

You can also directly link to the Designer if you know your server and port number. The link is structured as follows:

http://<server:port>/SASVisualAnalyticsDesigner

Introducing the designer layout

When you navigate to the Designer, you are brought to the main screen, which consists of three distinct areas that are used for development.

Figure 2.2 Areas of the Designer

The left pane is used as an inventory for data, objects, and reports. The middle area is the canvas where reports are designed and structured. The right pane contains multiple tabs, which enable control over the objects.

Using the canvas

The canvas is the user's workspace for creating reports. It is broken up into multiple tiers that include prompts as well as sections.

Figure 2.3 Tiers of the canvas

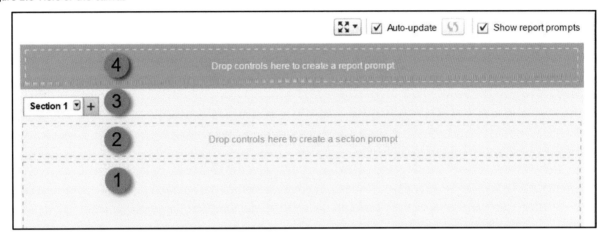

The letters A, B, C, and D represent the tiers of the canvas. As you go up the canvas, each tier has a responsibility to what is below it. Here is how they are set up:

1 Body - This is where the report objects can be placed and then get populated with data items.

2 Section Prompt – This tier acts as a filter to the body. Control objects can be positioned here to regulate what data shows up in the objects in the body.

3 Sections – Here is where the sections of the report are displayed as tabs. Each report can have multiple sections. Every section has its own independent section prompt and body.

4 Report Prompt – Similar to the section prompt, this prompt controls data across sections in the report. Any control object placed here filters the entire report.

Using the left pane

The left pane of the designer is where you can access an inventory of objects, the data sets that you are working with, and even other reports. This area is where you begin when starting to build reports. In order to start developing a report, you need both data and objects. The object is the chart, table, or control that must be associated with data in order to display information.

The window pane is set up with four tabs for each of the actions. You can turn on or off which ones show up in the top bar by clicking the drop-down list in the top right corner of the panel as shown below.

Figure 2.4 Left pane of the Designer

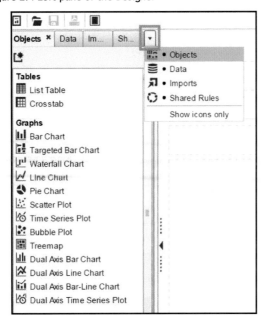

The **Objects** tab is where you can drag the various objects to the body of a report. This tab is broken into the categories of objects that include tables, graphs, controls, containers, and others. All of the objects can go into the body of the canvas, but only control objects can go into the prompt areas. (See Sections ② and ④ from Figure 2.3).

The **Data** tab is where you can import data and see all of the data items for each source. By clicking the **Select a data source** drop-down menu on the **Data** tab, you can access the Add Data Source window where you can import data or access any of the data sets in the LASR library. Once a data set is brought in, the data fields populate the body section of the tab. These data fields are also drag-and-drop enabled once objects are put onto the canvas. When any of the data items are selected, their properties populate at the bottom. You can manipulate how the data appears on the canvas by changing these values.

The last important part of the **Data** tab is the drop-down arrow ▾ at the top. This is where you can create new data items and perform other manipulations to your data that help make better reports. These options are covered later in this chapter as well as in later chapters of this book.

The **Import** tab can be used to bring in other reports created in SAS Visual Analytics. If there was a particular object, section, or whole report that one user wanted to add to their current report, they can find that item and then drag it to their report.

The **Shared Rules** tab is where you can create display rules for gauges that can apply to multiple gauges in a report. This can be very helpful in dashboards where gauges are often used. A shared rule makes it easy to apply a display rule across the ones that you want. Display rules and gauges are covered further in Chapter 3.

Using the right pane

The right pane is where a user can control the attributes of the report, sections, and objects. Attributes include titles, look and feel, filtering, and other customizations. Each one of the tabs can be used on an object, but only some of them can be used on the whole section or report.

Figure 2.5 Tabs on the right pane of the Designer

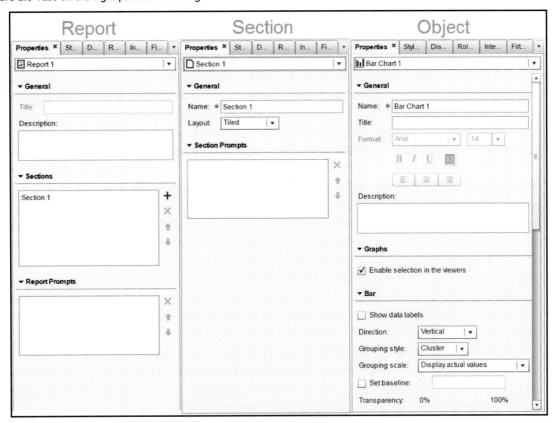

The **Properties** tab is the only one that has options for an object, section, or report. Depending on which one you have selected, the options within the tab are different. At the report tier, you can change the title, set a description for the report, and control the section and report prompts of the report. From the report tier, you can change to the section tier of the tab by selecting any of the sections. The **Properties** tab on the section tier consists of the title, the layout, and control of the section prompts.

The layout gives you a choice of tiled or precision. Tiled is much more user friendly in that as you add each object, the canvas just continuously splits the rectangles in half. Then you can adjust the split afterward. Precision gives you complete control over each object on the canvas. You can change the height and width as well as stretch and shrink as you can with a picture in a document. This gives you a lot more control over the layout of the canvas but should only be used after you're more familiar with the application.

At the object level, the **Properties** tab can vary depending on the object selected. There are always the settings of name, title, and description. Title is what shows up on the canvas, and name is how the object is referenced across the report. The rest of the options can include anything from selecting axis settings, determining if and where to put a legend, or how to handle grouping of data items.

Figure 2.6 Report and object level Styles tabs

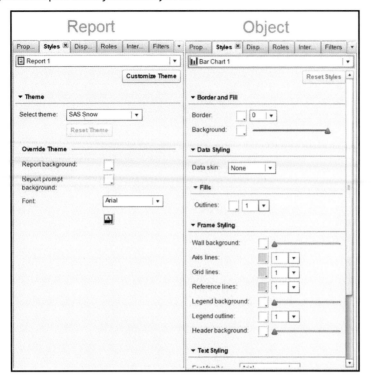

The **Styles** tab is another tab that has options for both the report and object tiers. At the report tier, the **Styles** tab enables you to control the theme of the report. Default report themes are available from SAS, or you can override them with color selections of their own. On the object level, the **Styles** tab is similar to the **Properties** tab in that it can change depending on the object that is selected. This is where text, data, backgrounds, and frames can be styled to your preference.

Branding matters!

This is something to do after your reports are created, but also to think about while you are developing. In the preceding topic, we mentioned that you can create color selections of your own for the report theme. Having a set color scheme for all of your reports gives them a unified look and feel. If you are presenting them within an organization, you could even use the brand colors of the organization. Clicking **Customize Theme** in the section launches you into the Theme Designer, which lets you go even more in depth!

The rest of the tabs only have options for objects, and the choices available can also change depending on the object. The **Display Rules** tab enables you to add conditions to the object so that data or other elements change colors based on certain values. The **Roles** tab is where the data fields are controlled. Some objects can require multiple measures, and this is where they can be set (as opposed to dragging them to the object). The **Filters** tab works similarly to the control objects such that a user can limit data based on a certain value for a data field, except this is just on a singular object. Interactions are a way to have objects and sections relate to one another. This can be done as filtering or brushing and is covered later in this chapter. Finally, the **Ranks** tabs is a way that you can see categories in an object based on the ranking of a certain measure (for example, top 10 products based on revenue).

Building your first report

The right preparation can save you many hours of work, and with experience this is something that you start doing naturally over time. However, when you're just getting started with this process, there are a couple things to consider before you start developing.

- **What do you want to know?**

  Putting data fields into charts and looking at the counts can give you some insight into your data, but this is just scratching the surface of what the application can do. It is good to think ahead of time about what data fields you are really interested in exploring. Could there be actionable insight if you compared, say, store sales by product lines over time? Making a list of these thoughts is good to keep you on track to get the answers that you are looking for.

- **Do you have the right data?**

  Whether you are importing data off your local machine or pulling from a database, it is important to have the fields that you want in the right format so that you can start to look at the questions that you are trying to answer. Sometimes sources might need to be joined or transposed before adding the data into the application so that everything is available to the user in the correct way. Also, some data calculations might need to be done in the application, so all of the elements of each calculation have to be in the source data. For example, if you wanted to look at profit by items sold, you would need both their sale price and what it costs to make them in the source data.

Now these aren't necessary steps, but they can save you a lot of time and possible rework if thought about before diving in. For our first report, we are going to look at a toy store company. We are exploring their customer behavior. Some of the things to look for are how the purchases of the customers change weekly, monthly, and yearly. Not only that, but does this change according to product line or geographic area? Also, in which areas of the company are customers providing us with the most profit? This report is built using the VA_SAMPLE_SMALLINSIGHT data set that is shipped with SAS Visual Analytics.

So what we're going to do is set up four graphs and one control in a section to try to get answers to the questions above. We are going to look at the breakdown of sales by product line, where the transactions are coming from, and in what months or weekdays they are occurring. We also are setting up filtering of objects through interactions so that we can drill down into the data to get more insight. Here's the report that you build by the end of this chapter:

Figure 2.7 Final result of our first report

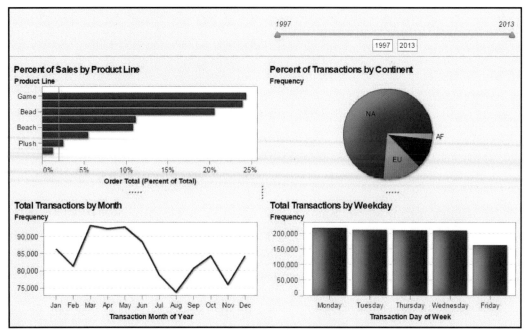

Adding a data source

A data source can be anything that contains information in a structured form. This can be spreadsheets, text files, database tables, and so on, just as long as there is a way for the application to understand how the data is to be brought in. For example, if you wanted to bring in a spreadsheet, there is the option for which worksheet, start row, and columns to bring in. With a TXT file, there are similar options such as choosing which delimiter is used to separate the data.

There are also multiple areas to which you can bring in a data source to the application. There is an option to bring in data locally, which is from your personal computer. You can also pull in data from a server. This can be SAS data sets on a SAS server or database tables on a server that is not from SAS. To get data from a server that is not from SAS, software must be licensed for it and the administrator must grant access. There is also social media data such as Twitter, Facebook, or Google Analytics where you can pull information that is publicly available.

To add a data source to the report:

1. The left pane is where you can add data sources to the report. When you click on the square with a + sign in the **Data** tab, the Add Data Source window appears. Everything in the data sources table is what is currently on the SAS LASR Analytic Server and available to the user.

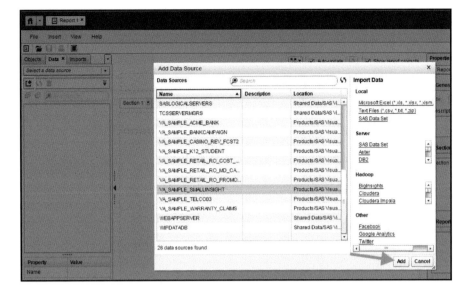

2. Find the VA_SAMPLE_SMALLINSIGHT data set. If you do not see it, then talk to your system administrator about getting the Visual Analytics sample data loaded onto the system.

3. Select the VA_SAMPLE_SMALLINSIGHT data set and click **Add**. The data source appears in the Data pane and is ready to use.

Working with data sources

After you click **Add** in the Add Data Source window, the data set populates into the **Data** tab. Each of the category data items has a number after it. This is the number of distinct values each data item contains. For example, there is an 8 after Product Line, which says that there are 8 different product lines across all of the data that was brought in.

Figure 2.8 Bringing in a data source to the Designer

The data items are divided into three sections when brought in which are Category, Measure, and Aggregated Measure. There are others such as hierarchies and geography items that can be created. Those are covered in later chapters.

Category	Categories can be a combination of character, dates, geography, and numeric data items. This is also the default section if the application cannot recognize a number or date as it comes in.
Measure	Measures are values that can be used in computations. These are numeric data items that have a numeric format applied to them. Frequency is a default measure that shows up for every data set and represents 1 for every row of data.
Aggregated Measure	Aggregated measures are numeric values that are computed using predefined conditions. This includes averages, sums, percentages, and so on, of a certain field. Frequency percentage is a default aggregated measure for every incoming data set.

Incoming columns from a data set are going to fall into the Categories or Measure areas. Aggregated measures other than frequency percentage must be created. You can create aggregated measures as well as other data items by clicking the drop-down menu at the top of the tab below the data set.

Figure 2.9 Adding new data items

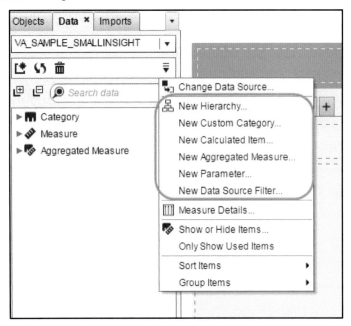

In this menu, there are various options to create new items for the data set.

New Hierarchy is a way to relate data items to one another in a parent-child hierarchical manner so that you can drill down into specific areas. This works well for one to many relationships such as a product line to its individual products.

New Custom Category creates a new category field that is a grouping based on a previous field. For example, test scores could be grouped into their respective letter grade (A, B, C, D, or F).

New Calculated Item is a way to create new data items in the application by using a combination of data items in the data set as well as logical and arithmetic operators. This is covered later in this chapter.

New Parameter is a way to create a data item that can pass values based on selections within objects.

New Data Source Filter is a way to place a condition on the data set that keeps the rows that you require. For example, if you wanted only the sales for the United States, then you could use a Data Source Filter to keep all rows where Facility Country/Region equals US.

Data item properties

The last thing to cover in the **Data** tab is how you can change the properties of the data items.

Figure 2.10 Property options for data items

Property	Value
Name	Transaction Date
Classification	Category
Format	MMDDYYYY
Aggregation	None
Sort Options	Click here to change the value

At the bottom of the **Data** tab is a two-column table that contains the metadata of each data item. **Name** is how the data item title is going to appear on the canvas, so this is where you can change the name to something that is easier to understand for the viewer.

Classification is the section of data types that each item can fall into. Depending on the value, this is where the user can switch categories from measures and vice versa.

Format is how the values of the data item appear on the canvas. This is important for measures since you can change whether the numbers show up as decimals, percentages, currency, and so on.

Aggregation is another property that applies to measures. You can specify a measure as a sum, average, count, among many other options.

Sort Options identifies whether there was a custom sort on the data item or not.

Creating new data items

For our report, we are going to create two new data items for our data set, a new date and a derived item.

Change the data item format

We want a new data item that is just the year so that we can easily look at the data by years.

Here are the steps:

1. Right-click **Transaction Date** and select **Duplicate Data Item**.
2. Click **Transaction Date** (1) to select it.
3. In the Properties area, change the name to **Transaction Year**.
4. Change the **Format** to **Year**.

What we did here was create an additional data field in the Designer so that we would have the data in two different formats. This did not add an extra field to our underlying data set. It just appears that way on the data tab.

Working with SAS dates

In the preceding example, we took a data item with a full date and created a new data item with just the part of the date (year) that we wanted just by changing the format of it. This can be done since SAS date types are so versatile. There is no need to use a function or follow any process. By changing the format, the underlying full date is still there, but only the part that you want will be shown. This can be done with many date formats including Day of Week, Month, and Month-Year.

Using a derived data item

Derived data items are common predefined aggregate measures built into the application to make it easier for you to create new actionable variables. Similar to the data item that we just added above, these are not new fields in the data set. They are just calculations defined so that when you use them in the report, the application already knows what calculation to perform on the original data field. In the following steps, we are going to create an aggregate measure through one of the derived item options.

1. Right-click **Order Total** in the **Measures** section. Select **Create** and then **Percent of Total**. All of the options in this menu are default aggregate calculations that can be used with measures.

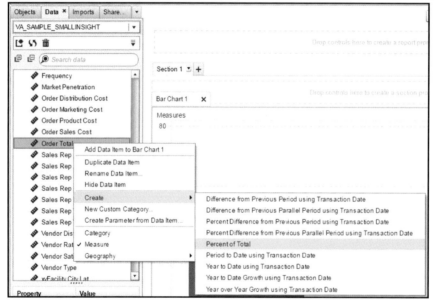

2. On the **Data** tab, go down to the aggregated measures section, and you see **Order Total** (Percent of Total) at the bottom.

Working with the layout

Now that we have our variables set up, we can start to bring objects into the canvas and design the report. There are two ways that you get objects into the canvas. One is through the **Insert** menu on the top toolbar. The other way is to drag the object from the **Objects** tab in the left pane.

Starting the layout

The report uses four objects in the canvas area.

1. For our first object, we are going to drag a bar chart by dragging the Bar Chart text under Graphs on the **Objects** tab to the canvas.

2. The next object is going to be a pie chart. As you drag the object, notice how the application starts to guess how you would like your objects split on the canvas, either horizontally or vertically. Split this one vertically with the pie chart going on the right side.

3. Our third object is a line chart. This goes under the bar chart.

4. The final object is a bar chart that goes under the pie chart. Your canvas should look like the following figure afterward.

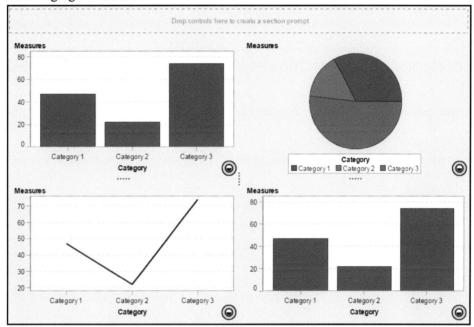

When an object is placed on the canvas, it always has the red circle located in the lower right corner of the canvas. This is simply a warning to indicate that there is no data specified for the object yet. Some objects require only one data item; but others can require multiple measures and categories. Until that minimum is met, the object does not populate with the data and the red circle remains.

Populating your objects

As with adding objects, adding data to the objects can be done in two ways. One is through the drag-and-drop function using the **Data** tab in the same way that you can drag objects with the **Objects** tab. The other way is through the **Roles** tab in the right pane. When clicked on the object, the **Roles** tab displays all of the possible locations for data items within the object.

Here's what to do for our report:

1. On the **Data** tab, find **Product Line**.

2. Drag it to the first bar chart in the top left corner.

3. Notice how the **Roles** tab is updated with **Product Line** as the Category.

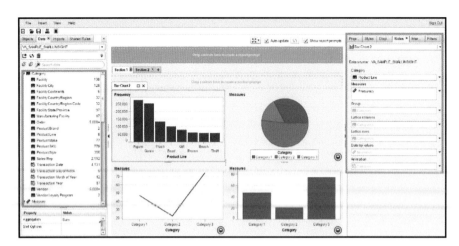

Once **Product Line** is dropped or selected, the chart automatically populates as you can see in the above picture. Some objects only need one data item. When that is the case, they default with Frequency as the measure. Frequency is just a count of every row. However, for our example we are going to use the aggregate measure, Order Total (Percent of Total), that we created earlier. You can do that by clicking the **Measures** drop-down list on the **Roles** tab, selecting **Replace Frequency**, and then finding the **Order Profit** (Percent of Total).

Improving the data object appearance

Now that our first chart is made, we can change the appearance of it by using the **Properties** and **Styles** tabs in the right pane. The **Properties** tab is where we can change the context of what appears on and around our bar chart. The reason to make changes to the appearance is so that the end viewer can get more context around what they are looking at and to make it more visually appealing when viewers first glance at the report and objects.

Limit chart junk!

There are ways that you can improve the appearance of objects in your report and also ways that you can actually make it harder to interpret. In *The Visual Display of Quantitative Information,* Edward Tufte writes about how to avoid using chart junk. He explains how chart junk is any decoration of graphics that does not give the viewer any additional information. This can be grid lines, tick marks, unnecessary labels, and so on. Using all those extra lines that do not say anything just makes it harder for the viewer to know what to look for.

Changing the properties

Here are a few things that you can change to improve the appearance for the end viewer.

- Under **General**, change **Name** and **Title** to **Percent of Sales by Product Line**.
- Change to bold and change the **Title** to 16 pt font.
- Under **Bar**, select **Horizontal** for the **Direction**.
- Under **Reference Lines**, click **Create new reference line**. Use a value of 0.02 and click **Add**.
- Under **Grid Lines**, uncheck the **Show grid lines** box.

Changing the appearance

The **Styles** tab is where we can change the look and feel of the chart. Here are some examples:

- Under **Data Styling**, change the **Data skin** to **Matte**.

- Under **Data Colors**, change the first box under **Fill** to the color of your choice.

Most of these changes were just for you to get used to using the various options available for the objects, but a few of them have more meaning.

> **Making your visualizations more appealing**
>
> In *Information Visualization*, Colin Ware describes through the perceptual process of how our eyes interpret an image. Pattern perception is a key component for visualizations since we want to find discrepancies and trends in the data. When we apply any of the data skins to an object, the data display of the object is given a certain texture and shading that makes the data portion more appealing to the eye. This can speed up pattern recognition because the viewers' eyes will gravitate more to the data instead of other areas in the report.

Adding a reference line

The reference line is good to use to benchmark the data against some number.

Figure 2.11 Bar chart with a reference line added

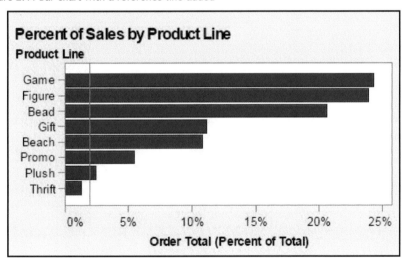

So, for our example, corporate has come to us saying that they want to see if all of the product lines are pulling their weight of sales. We set the reference line as a benchmark at 2% to see if any product lines fall under that amount. Since we have added the reference line, the grid lines can get a little confusing, which is why we unselect them.

Adding data to other objects

Now that we have completed our first object, it is time to fill in the rest of our objects with data and get them to look the way we want.

Here's the steps to create the additional objects:

Pie chart (top right corner)

1. **Name and Title**: Percent of Transactions by Continent (Bold and 16 pt font).
2. Under **Data Labels**, check **Show Category Labels**.
3. Uncheck **Create Other** slice for minimal values.
4. Uncheck **Show Legend**.
5. **Data Skin**: Matte.
6. **Roles**:
   Category: Facility Continents
   Measures: Frequency

Line chart (lower left corner)

1. **Name and Title:** Total Transactions by Month (Bold and 16pt font)
2. **Data Skin:** Matte
3. Roles:
   Category: Transaction Month of Year
   Measures: Frequency

Bar chart (lower right corner)

1. Name and Title: Total Transactions by Weekday (Bold and 16pt font)
2. **Data Skin:** Matte
3. Roles:
   Category: Transaction Day of Week
   Measures: Frequency

When you are all finished, your report should look something like this:

Figure 2.12 Report with all chart objects and data items added

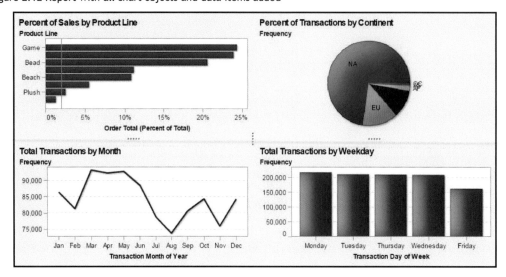

Within this graph, we have created a report that displays an overall analysis of the purchases from our customers. We can see which products our customers are spending the most on, where in the world those transactions are coming from, and a breakdown of the months and days of when they occurred. This, however, is just a static view of the data. After looking at this report, you might want to know the geographic breakdown for just the beach product line or the months in which customers buy the most games. In the next section, we start to connect the objects together so that this report becomes dynamic and you can access the discovery part of their data analysis.

Working with data objects

For every report where you are doing analysis, you want to not only pack the most data you can onto the screen but also give the user multiple views of the data. Being able to filter data by certain conditions gives the user the ability to see the data from a different point that might interest them or bring about an idea. That could be within a certain date range, by a category, or some other condition that they see fit. Being able to break down the data in this way gives more power to you to see more visualizations about their data, which could lead to additional insight about what they are exploring.

Within the Designer there are multiple ways to filter data including using a Data Source Filter; adding a filter in the **Filter** tab for an object; applying a control in the prompts sections; and setting up interactions in the **Interactions** tab. The Data Source Filter can be found on the left pane **Data** tab. When you click on the drop-down menu there is an option to create a **New Data Source Filter**. This is a filter that you can place on the whole data set before even working with it. Once set, all of the data items that a user can drag to objects are pre-filtered with that set condition. We are going to use the other ways to filter data in our report; the steps are in the following sections.

Using the Filter tab

Another way is to use the **Filter** tab on the right pane when working with an object. Here, you can select certain data items and filter out values so that certain rows never get displayed by the object. When you get to the tab, you have the option of selecting any data item in the data set through the drop-down list or selecting advanced in the drop-down list and creating your own filter.

In our report, we know that we're going to close our Oceanic and Asia facilities since they're becoming unprofitable and even though it is a small amount, we want it out of the continent breakdown. Here's what do to do for our report:

1. Go to the **Filters** tab in the right panel.
2. Make sure that **Percent of Transactions by Continent** is selected in the first drop-down list.
3. Click the second drop-down list and select **Facility Continents**.
4. Click **Add Filter**.

5. Uncheck **AS** and **OC**. You should be able to see the pie chart update without those continents in the canvas.

Filtering with report and section prompts

If we want to give the end viewer control over what is being filtered, there are two ways to do that. One way is through the report and section prompts that sit at the top of the canvas. You can put control objects in these areas of the canvas, which then control what data filters down into the sections and objects. The report prompt filters data for all of the sections. The section prompt filters data for all of the objects in the individual section. Each of the control objects that can be used in a prompt are listed below:

Object	Description	Best used with …
Drop-down List	Lists all of the possible values in a drop-down menu.	Categories with many different values
Button Bar	In a ribbon form, lists all of the values of a particular category.	Categories with only a few different values
Text Input	Similar to a search field, this is a text box that enables you to enter text.	Descriptive categories where you might want to search for a keyword
Slider	Best used when you want to filter based on a chronological range. Works best with dates.	Dates

*The Drop-down List control cannot be used in the section prompts.

Adding a slider object

For our report, we are going to add a slider to the report. This can be done through a drag-and-drop operation just like all of the other objects.

Here's how you do it for this report:

1. Under **Controls** on the **Objects** tab, drag the Slider to the section prompt of the canvas.
2. Add Transaction Year as the Measure/Date in the **Roles** tab.

3. The object then populates with the minimum and maximum values from our data field as shown below:

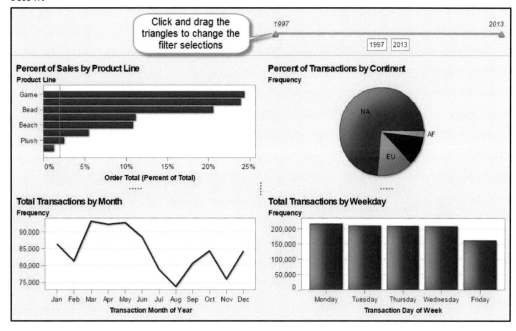

You can then modify the triangles on the slider to get the range that you want to see. If the triangles are put on the same year, then the data is filtered for just that one year. After the triangles are set, you see the data within the objects change to how they have filtered the report. Remember that this filters all of the data in a section.

Adding object interactions

The other way to let the user do filtering in SAS Visual Analytics is to build interactions between objects. Earlier in the chapter, the **Interactions** tab was mentioned as a way to connect objects and sections together. For this section, we are just going to focus on connecting objects together. But you can also connect objects to other sections, reports, info windows, or even set-up external links. This can be done by going to the **Interactions** tab of an object in the section and clicking the **New** drop-down menu. Here is where you can find the ways to set up links to areas outside of the section.

Create an interaction

Here's the steps to create an interaction in our report:

1. Make sure that our initial "Percent of Profit by Product Line" bar chart is selected. The **Interactions** tab can be used for every object, so we want to make sure that we are setting the one for the bar chart.
2. On the **Interactions** tab, select **New** and then **Interaction** in the drop-down list.

3. Stick with the first selection but change the drop-down list so that it reads **Percent of Sales by Product Line filters Percent of Transactions by Continent**.

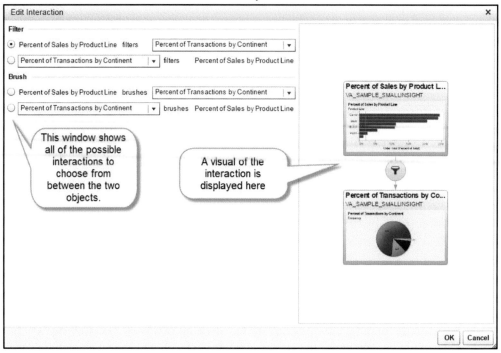

4. Click **OK**.

When we click OK, the connection is set up between the two objects. You'll notice the data change in the pie chart if you click any of the product lines in our first bar chart.

The Filter works just like any other way of filtering would. If the connection is established between the objects and a value is selected, then all other values are filtered out of the proceeding object. Brushing, on the other hand, highlights the values instead of hiding them. Since we are working with aggregations, the brush option would not really work and is better used with individual data points such as scatter plots.

Using the interactions view

One interaction is nice to use, but with many objects in a report, you might want to have multiple interactions set up so that the end viewer can really dig deeper into their data. Another, and more visual, way to add interactions is to use the **Interactions View** button. When you click this button in any object, you notice that it brings up all of the objects in your section. You can see the one that we have already set up by the filter icon and arrow between the two objects. We can easily create more filter interactions here by positioning the cursor over an object and then clicking and holding to draw a line to the other objects. Here are the additional interactions to set up for our report:

- Percent of Profit by Product Line filters Total Transactions by Month

- Percent of Profit by Product Line filters Total Transactions by Week

- Percent of Transactions by Continent filters Total Transactions by Month

- Percent of Transactions by Continent filters Total Transactions by Week

- Total Transactions by Month filters Total Transactions by Week

Your web of interactions should look something like this at the end:

Figure 2.13 Interactions view

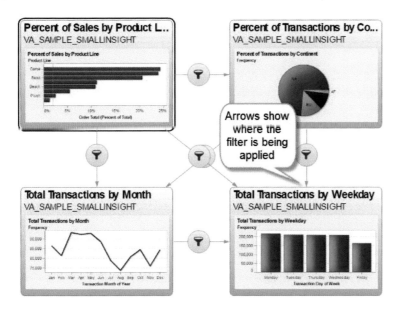

The filter cannot go each way from object to object, so we have to be strategic with how we set up all of the interactions. For the sake of this report and as a good visualization practice, we keep all of the interactions set up in a simple manner, left to right and top to bottom. In this way, anything selected from the top left object filters the rest of the objects, the top right filters the bottom ones, and so on, from there. With this setup, everything eventually funnels to the final object in the bottom right. Now you can go back into your report and check for yourself how everything works.

Saving the report

Now that we are all done with the development of the report, we want to save it before doing anything else. Saving works like most other applications, and you can just select the **File** menu in the top toolbar and then click **Save As**. This brings you to the Save As window that gives you your SAS file locations to save.

Figure 2.14 Save As window

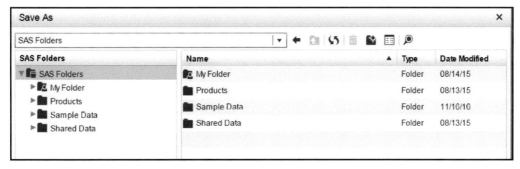

Under SAS Folders, you have a few options to choose from. My Folder is a location specific to your account for the application. Anything that you put in here cannot be seen by anyone else. All of the other folders are public, which means that other people on the system can access them. Until your reports are finalized, you might want to keep them in My Folder so that no one edits them by accident.

Reviewing the report

Our report is complete! We have thought about what we wanted to learn from this report, set up all the objects and data for it, and then customized it with connections and filters so that we can get multiple views of our data. After all that developing, now we can move into the data analysis part and see whether we can find out anything interesting in the data.

Users can go about finding their analysis in any way they want, but it's also important to go back to the questions that we wanted to answer before we started developing the report. We had an interest in learning about our customers' buying behavior and where we were getting the most profit from them. Here's some intriguing findings that can be found in this report.

- Struggling Thrift Product Line

  The Thrift product line only makes up 1.27% of sales and that decreases to 0.40% over the last five years (2009-2013). Being such a small part of the business, this product line needs more investigating to find out if it is even profitable enough to be worth keeping up.

- Customers do not go for Plush on Fridays

  Most of the product lines either get a little higher (Bead, Gift, Beach) or lower (Game, Figure, Promo) with sales on Fridays compared to the rest of the week. This can be attributed to the purpose that each line serves. For example, people tend to go to the beach more on the weekends. So Friday would be a major shopping day for that line. However, the Plush product line sees an 80-85% drop on Friday sales, which is an extreme difference compared to all of the other lines. What could cause customers to only buy Plush toys Monday through Thursday?

- Beach items only sell in the summer

  Of course, there would be some seasonality with the beach line, but it turns out to be very dramatic. From October to March, there is little to no sales for beach items; and in the Europe stores, they do not even attempt to sell anything in those months. This requires some further inventory analysis to make sure that we are selling all of our beach products off before those months come each season.

These actionable insights are just a sample of what can be found in that single data set. By setting up a report and using SAS Visual Analytics to dive into the data, we can analyze data much quicker compared to querying a table or scrolling through a spreadsheet. Not only that, but with the click of a button, you can have almost any view of the data that you want. With this chapter we have just scratched the surface. In the next chapter, we dive into dashboards and show some additional features that you can work with in the designer.

References

The following sources provide more information about the topics discussed in this chapter:

SAS Institute Inc. 2015. *SAS Visual Analytics 7.3: User's Guide*. Cary, NC: SAS Institute Inc.

Tufte, Edward R. 2001. *The Visual Display of Quantitative Information*. Cheshire, CT: Graphics Press.

Ware, Colin. 2013. *Information Visualization: Perception for Design*. 3rd ed. Waltham, MA: Morgan Kaufmann.

chapter three

building your first dashboard

When asked to design a dashboard, you must spend some time with the users understanding their needs and goals. Many users ask for a dashboard and use the term in a generic way to mean a web-based report with charts and graphs that can link to other web pages. A dashboard is more than a report because it involves conclusions.

In *Effective Dashboard Design*, La Grouw notes that you can differentiate a dashboard and a report by their core attributes. A report does not lead users to a conclusion; it simply presents facts that allow users to make their own judgments. Consider Figure 3.1. The chart on the left tells the viewer what sales were for each month. The viewer sees that sales improved by year end after taking a sharp decrease in the spring. This chart shows useful facts, but what we do not know is whether it is a good thing.

Figure 3.1 Difference in reports and dashboards

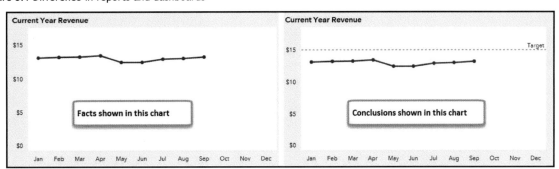

A dashboard can provide context for facts, and thus provide the basis to form a conclusion. Effective dashboards can help a user quickly understand what is happening and what needs to happen next. In the preceding figure, consider the chart in the right pane. The viewer can draw a conclusion from the chart, which is that the team is not meeting their goal. Presenting the facts in this way provides an immediate understanding of what is happening, and indirectly suggests the follow-up action.

Dashboards help users understand if a process or project is running smoothly. Typically, metrics are centered on some performance aspect, such as strategic objectives, time lines, or quality result. Keep in mind, the information does not present the next level of detail, which is what or why events are happening.

Is it a dashboard or a scorecard?

In the early 1990s, when the terms *performance dashboard* and *balanced scorecard* were introduced, there were fewer vendors able to support either method. Scorecards tend to be tabular in nature, whereas dashboards tend to contain graphical elements, such as gauges or line charts. Since their introduction, the terms have somewhat become synonymous. Both terms generically refer to presenting actionable data on a web page.

In *Information Dashboard Design*, the author Stephen Few defines a dashboard as a "visual display of the most important information needed to achieve one or more objectives." The word *objective* is a key in this definition because it implies a performance measurement. There are no set rules for what a performance dashboard must contain other than focusing on visualizing organizational objectives.

A scorecard or balanced scorecard is a management system framework that was popularized in the book, *The Balanced Scorecard* by Doctors Robert Kaplan and David Norton. This methodology encourages organizations to monitor performance against financial and nonfinancial strategic goals. This method tends to focus on progress instead of performance.

Dashboard building process

The dashboard building process requires that you identify the organization objectives. Place the objectives in a pleasing layout with accurate data that viewers can easily understand. In this topic, you will learn a dashboard building process.

Understanding your customer

We are going to continue the work from the *Building Your First Report* chapter with the Toy Company. This is a large international company with multiple products and a large sales force that is spread across the world. The Sales vice president has requested a dashboard to track sales targets, profitability, and approval ratings. The main users of the dashboard are the three regional sales managers. The company has several issues that include decreasing profits and poor customer approval ratings. This dashboard should help the organization improve profitability, sales targets, and customer service.

When designing the dashboard, keep your user's skill level, use case, and purpose in mind. Let's think about the audience for this dashboard. We know these users are not seeking detailed statistical analysis. Their goal is much simpler. They want to monitor their organization. Most of the time these particular users are traveling and plan to use their tablets to consume the information.

The main goal is for the user to have a takeaway. We want the vice president to know whether the organization is on target; and, likewise, we want the regional managers to know what is going wrong so that they can address the issues. You can train users to understand a dashboard. So, do not shy away from a more complicated visualization if it will help the user understand or compare what is happening.

Establishing objectives

After studying the issues from the previous year, the management team has set the following key performance indicators (KPIs). These KPIs are intended to improve overall sales performance and increase customer approval. The following table explains the selected KPIs and how these should be measured.

Key performance indicators	Explanation
Achieve regional sales target of 40% by end of year.	Many of the sales reps consistently fail to reach their targets, which affects the regional sales target. The management team wants to compare the Sales Rep target to their actual values to determine which Sales Reps need help. The CEO set a minimum goal of 40% for each region.
Achieve profitability of 60% for all regions by year end.	One of the regional managers discovered that many of the sales reps were giving massive discounts to improve their approval ratings. This action interferes with the company's ability to meet revenue goals. In many cases, the ratings did not improve because of other factors that the management wants to monitor. The management team wants to ensure the sales reps understand that profitability is equally important to satisfaction. The CEO set a minimum goal of 60% for each region.
Improve Regional Approval ratings by established target by year end.	Many customers complained that the order details were incomplete and that sales reps were not helpful in resolving issues. These complaints caused decreased sales and ratings in the regions. It was different for each region, so individual targets need to be created for each region. The ultimate goal is to move from an average of 55% approval to consistently above 60%.

Determine supporting information

With each KPI, you should provide supporting charts and information. The Sales Vice President set the KPIs based on desired improvements. The regional managers realize the KPIs require some organizational changes. They need to understand which sales reps need more coaching or if the targets are set too high.

The regional managers asked to have additional charts created on the dashboard. Some of the suggestions were to see the actual sales against the target and to track the target achieved against the profitability. They want to compare the differences between the product lines and the sales reps. Since the ratings were important to the vice president, it would be useful to see the best and worst ratings for each sales rep. Maybe some customers were more difficult to please and the ratings were not fair.

Planning the data and data objects

For this dashboard, the sales database contains the records. The management team knew this data was available because they had used it for several years. When an established data collection method exists, this makes the job of creating a dashboard easier.

Getting data for your dashboard

If your organization does not use a database to store data, there are some other options. You can maintain the information in a spreadsheet or a SAS data set. In those cases, the measures can be summarized so that there is less effort in updating and storing the data.

Determining the best way to present the measures is your next step. The choice is obvious in some instances. When you are presenting KPIs, the gauge is a natural choice. In many cases, the controls are obvious as well.

Base your selections on good data visualization practices and what works best for your audience. Keep in mind that there might be multiple ways to show the measurement without one being better than the other. It might take several iterations to find the perfect way to show the measurements. For a more detailed discussion of data visualization techniques, refer to the chapter *Visualizing your data*.

The following table lists the measurement, the required data, and the data objects the team chose for this dashboard after several iterations.

Measurement	Required data items	Data object chosen
KPI 1 – KPI 3	KPI 1: Regional Sales Target as percentage KPI 2: Regional Profitability Ratio KPI 3: Regional Approval Rating as percentage	Gauge A gauge is perfect to show KPIs. It shows how measurement is tracking against the goal.
Sales Reps with Actual Sales against Target Sales	Sales Rep Actual Sales in currency Target Sales Goal in currency	Targeted Bar Chart This data object shows the individual measurements and targets for each sales rep.
Sales Reps with Sales Target Achieved against Profit Ratio	Sales Rep Total Sales Profitability ratio	Bar-Line Chart This object enables you to compare the total sales against the profitability ratio. A dual-axis line chart would have also worked.
Sales Reps by region and date with ratings	Region Date Sales Rep Best approval rating Worse approval rating Average approval rating Profit Ratio	List Table with display rules A detailed listing of information was requested. The list table works best for this information.
Filters: Regional Month/Year Product Line Sales Rep Picklist	Regions Date Product line Sales Reps	Button Bar Drop-Down List List Text Input List These control objects allow the user to filter what they see.

Creating a mock layout

The dashboard layout signals to the user which elements are the most important. In this case, we know the KPIs are of primary concern. Thus, they will receive a starring role in the layout. The regional managers had suggested some supporting information to allow some exploration that we can incorporate.

Considering your layout

The first instinct is to put everything on a single page. In the following figure, this layout placed all information on the same page.

Figure 3.2 Dashboard layout

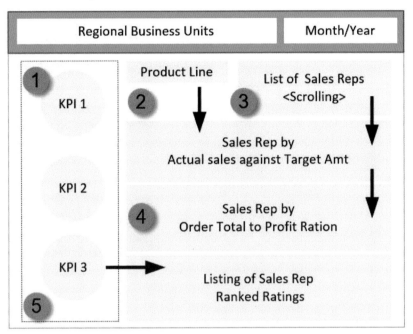

There are several issues with this layout, indicated by the following numbers:

① When the KPIs are along the side, they appear equal to the exploration information. These KPIs should have a starring role.

② The center of the layout has a big gaping hole.

③ Some regions have 20-30 sales reps. For the regional managers to select sales reps to view, they must scroll through a long list. That does not seem very useable. The list needs to be in a vertical position.

④ The graph and list table appear crowded in our mock layout! Imagine how it will look on the screen. We need some color to help the user know which items are related.

⑤ The arrows indicate which data object controls the other data objects. Without these arrows, the user would assume the top controls filter everything below, including the table. There's no reason to have the detailed list table on this page; it can move elsewhere.

Creating a workable layout

After playing with the data objects, you are able to determine which objects belong together. Instead of creating multiple dashboards, this dashboard has a single layout to support the vice president and regional managers. The management team can check the KPIs for the entire organization. Then, using the filters, they can compare each region and multiple dates if desired.

In the bottom area, the regional managers can use the filters to compare product lines and individual sales reps. A second page called Sales Rep Ratings enables the regional manager to drill down to more detail about the ratings. Color is added to help the eye quickly spot differences.

Figure 3.3 Determining interactivity

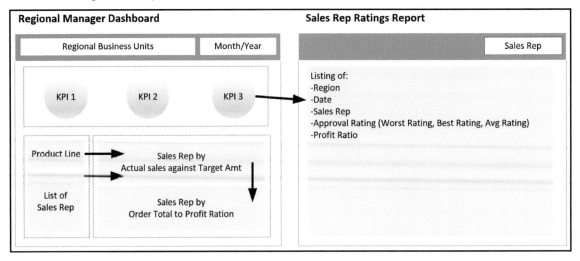

Tips for more useable dashboards

The most successful dashboards use a clean, minimal look. As Edward Tufte would direct us, *"Let the data talk."* Avoid using logos or other decorative elements on your page. You must be careful that your design choices do not distract your user from understanding the main messages. The design should instead be the *sex appeal* that attracts the user's eye!

Here are some additional tips to make your dashboard easier to use:

- If your dashboard is internal to the organization, there is little reason to have the logo on it. If it's required to be there, keep it small and near the right top or bottom. This keeps the logo from appearing to be the central focus.

- Add a first page or section to your dashboard that contains any supporting information that the users might need. This information might link to related websites, explain how to access the dashboard, or provide housekeeping information. The content might contain topics such as when the data is updated or the counting rules.

- Ensure that your dashboard is fast. This might require pre-summarizing data, rethinking calculations, or using different visualizations. Users do not like extensive wait times. This process might take some experimentation to determine the optimal load and display time.

- Minimize the navigation and click paths that a user needs to get information. If the users have to navigate multiple screens for an answer, they might look for other organizational sources.

One final note: In these past few pages, you might have the impression that the dashboard design process is a few simple steps. In reality, it took several weeks of planning. There were multiple layout iterations considered before this one was selected. SAS Visual Analytics makes the process easier, but you still must know what you want to achieve and ensure that your data supports the desired outcome. After the dashboard is complete, it most likely will continue to change as the organization grows and improves.

Building the dashboard

After the preliminary work is complete, you can build the final product. Here are the two layouts that you are going to create in this topic. The first layout is the Regional Manager Dashboard, and the second layout is the Sales Rep Report.

Figure 3.4 Regional manager dashboard and sales rep report

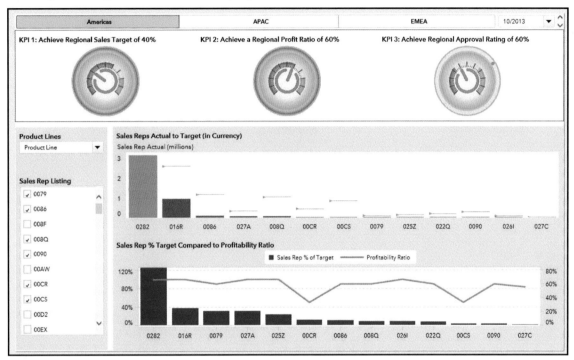

Adding the data objects

With the layout planned and measurements identified, you can determine the required data items. In some cases, the data source might already exist. If you have to create the data source, it's useful to know what items are needed. Some of the data items can be created within SAS Visual Analytics to keep your data source as small as possible.

In this case, we are using the VA_SAMPLE_SMALLINSIGHT data source. This data source lists each order from January 1997 to October 2013. For each order, we know the sales rep, the order amount, the transaction date, and several other factors that you might expect to find with an order. SAS Visual Analytics enables you to aggregate the measures so that you can sum the order total by several categories. You can use region, country, product line, or even sales rep. The aggregation also makes it easy to build measurements and use filters to quickly get results.

The following table lists the requirement measurements identified in the Establishing objectives topic on page 38, the data item that you can use with your data object, and any special steps that you need to use the data item.

Required measurements	Data items from data source	Special steps
Sales Rep User ID	Sales Rep	No changes needed
Product Line	Product Line	No changes needed
Sales Rep Actual Sales	Sales Rep Actual	No changes needed
Sales Rep Target	Sales Rep Target	No changes needed
Orders from the past 3 years represented by Month and Year	Transaction Date	Use a format to change this data item to month and year.
Regional Territories based on continents	Facility Continents	Create a Custom Category based on this data item to use in Button Bar
Sales Rep Target Achieved	Sales Rep % of Target	This data item must be an average across all sales. Change the aggregation method.
Sales Rep Approval Rating as average, minimum, and maximum	Sales Rep Rating	Using this value create some additional aggregations.
Profitability Ratio	Order Total Order Product Costs	Create an aggregated measure based on the gross margin. Gross margin is the order total minus order product costs.
Regional Approval Target	None	Create a parameter based on a new calculated item called RegionalRatingTarget.

Creating new data items

From the preceding table, you can see several new data items that need to be created. This topic explains how to create the data items.

Working with data items

It is easy to be confused when your data source contains more data items than you need. You can filter the list to keep it manageable and to reduce confusion. In the following figure, you can see the data items listed in the Data pane are the ones checked in the Show or Hide Data Items window.

To show or hide data items:

1. Click the **Data** menu drop-down list.
2. Click **Show or Hide Items**.
3. In the **Show or Hide Items** window, check the data items that you want to appear.

Figure 3.5 Showing and hiding data items

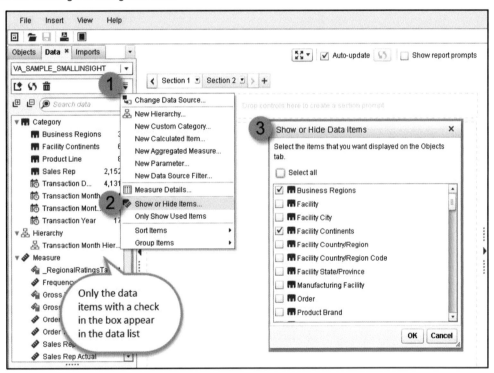

Applying a format

The drop-down list on the Regional Manager section contains a drop-down filter that uses a date variable. It appears as the month and year value, but you only have the transaction date value that is based on a daily value. If you think that you need to add more data items to the source data—you don't. You can change the format so that the data item appears as Month-Year.

To create the new data item, duplicate the Transaction Date data item by right-clicking and selecting **Duplicate Data Item**. A new data item appears.

Select the new data item so that it is active in the Property area. Its name is displayed in the **Name** field.

   ① Change the name to Transaction Month, Month Year, or a name that makes sense for your report.

   ② Change the Format to **MMYYYY**. Notice that the count changes from 4,131 to 191. This count indicates the format is applied.

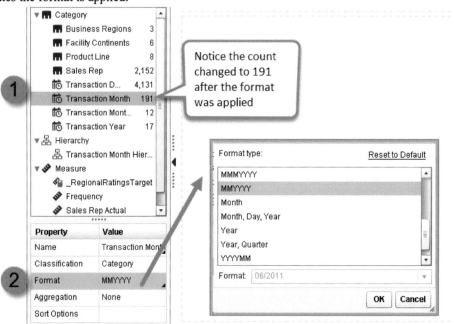

Date formats

If you are not familiar with SAS programming methods, then you might not understand a format. Formats are handy! You can turn a date value such as 01FEB2016 into several other values.

* If you apply the Year format, the data item appears as 2016.

* If you apply the Month format, the data item appears as Feb.

* If you apply Quarter format, the data item appears as 1st Quarter, 2016.

The underlying data does not change, but the appearance is changed. This enables you to build charts based on different groupings, such as year, month name, or quarter. Formats can also be used to change a value from dollars to other money formats, such as Euro or Yen.

Creating custom categories

The dashboard uses a button bar to filter the data. The button bar is based on the business regions called APAC, EMEA, and Americas. The business regions are based on the facility continents. However, these values do not exist in the data source. You can create this data item using a custom category. A custom category enables you to assign labels to groups of values in an existing category or measure.

To create the new data item, do the following:

1. Select **Data ▶ New Custom Category**.
2. Select the **Facility Continents**.
3. In the **Name** field, type Business Regions. You can use any name that is not already in use. The name that you choose is what appears in the data items list.
4. In the Label1 area, type **APAC**. From the values list, drag **AS** and **OC**.
5. Click **New label** and type **EMEA** in the Label2 area. From the values list, drag **AF** and **EU**.
6. The remaining continents belong to the Americas. Instead of creating another label, click the **Group remaining values as** button and replace Other with **Americas** in the field. This assigns any values left to that values.

   Your window should appear similar to the following figure when you are finished.

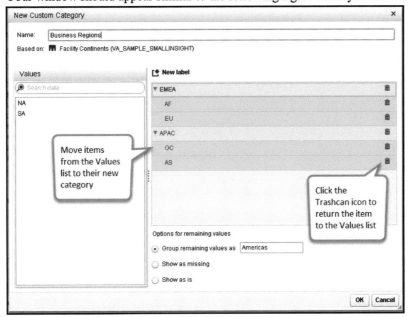

Dealing with remaining values

When creating custom categories, consider if the data values will change in the future before assigning the remaining values. In the preceding example, you created two custom categories and then assigned the remaining values as Americas. In this case, the region values are controlled by the organization. But consider other situations. For example, what if the North Pole or South Pole were added as a data value? Would it still make sense to default the remaining values to Americas?

Changing the aggregation method

The regional managers want to review the best, worst, and average approval rating for each sales rep. By changing the aggregation method, you can find this value quickly. The default aggregation is SUM for all data items, and the same is true for Sales Rep Rating. Using this data item, you can create your two new data items: one for minimum rating and one for maximum rating.

These data items are aggregated based on the categories applied. In the following example, the Sales Rep Rating, Sales Rep Rating (Min), and Sales Rep Rating (Max) are shown. In the top table, the values are an aggregation across all business regions for all years. In the bottom table, the yearly aggregation was added and the data filtered for 2009. Compare the two tables to see how the values changed based on the category applied.

Figure 3.6 Measures

Overall Approval Ratings

Business Regions	Sales Rep Rating (Min)	Sales Rep Rating ▲	Sales Rep Rating (Max)
APAC	20%	51%	100%
Americas	20%	53%	100%
EMEA	20%	55%	100%
	Minimum: 20%	Average: 53%	Maximum: 100%

Approval Ratings for Year

Business Regions	Transaction Year	Sales Rep Rating (Min)	Sales Rep Rating ▲	Sales Rep Rating (Max)
APAC	2009	20%	48%	80%
Americas	2009	20%	53%	100%
EMEA	2009	38%	57%	100%
		Minimum: 20%	Average: 53%	Maximum: 100%

When used as the Overall Approval Ratings at the top, the values are similar across the regions. However, in the second table when adding the year, the individual values have more variation. The point is that the same measure was used, but it quickly changed value based on the category applied. The aggregation method prevents you from needing to create a separate data item for each level because the values update based on the category.

To create the new data items:

1. Right-click the **Sales Rep Rating** and change the aggregation method to **Average**.
1. Right-click the **Sales Rep Rating** data item and select **Duplicate Data Item**.
2. Select the new data item. In the Properties area, change the name to Sales Rep Rating (Min) and the aggregation method to Minimum. This value represents the worse rating the sales rep received.
3. Right-click the **Sales Rep Rating** data item and select **Duplicate Data Item**.
4. Select the new data item. In the Properties area, change the name to Sales Rep Rating (Max) and the aggregation method to Maximum. This value represents the best rating the sales rep received. You should have two new data items in your list.

Create calculated items

You can add calculations based on your own formulas. Typically, a calculated data item is an expression, such as *cost * quantity*. For this dashboard, we need to measure gross profit. Gross profit is based on the Order Total minus the Product Cost. You can calculate items based on date or character values. You can also use IF/THEN logic to create new data items.

Creating your own measures

Calculated items and aggregated measures enable you to add new data items to your data source. SAS Visual Analytics calculates these data items in real time. Not only does this save data preparation time, it also helps the dashboard be more dynamic because the user is getting answers on demand.

The Calculated Item window has three main areas: Data Items, Operators, and Work area. From the Data Items area, you can access data items in your data source or other calculated items that you have created. From the Operators area, you can make changes to your data item. For example, you can add, subtract, or compare data items. In the Work Area, you apply operators to your data item. For example, in the following figure, the EMEA Target value is created by testing if the business region equals EMEA. This calculated item can be used in a data object or as part of another calculation.

Figure 3.7 Creating a calculated item

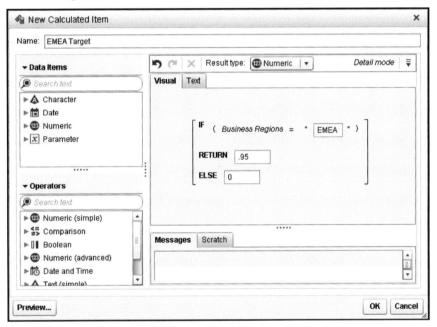

To create a new calculated items:

1. Click **Data ▶ New Calculated Item**. The New Calculated Item window appears.
2. In the **Name** field, type Gross Margin. You can use any name not already in use. This name appears in your Data Item list.
3. In the **Operator** field, type the minus sign (-). Drag the x – y object to the work area.
4. In the **Data Items** area, select **Order Total** and drag it to the first empty box.
5. In the **Data Items** area, select **Order Product Cost** and drag it to the second empty box.
   Your window should look similar to the following figure. You can click **Preview** in the left corner to review your calculation.

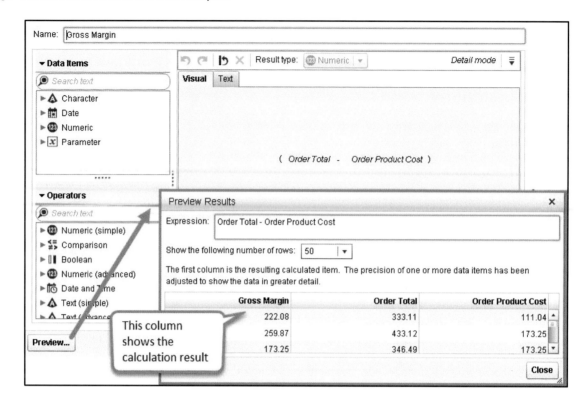

Creating aggregated measures

Aggregated measures are difficult to understand when you first start. These data items are similar to the calculated items. You can create logic, do calculations, and return complex formulas. It is often not obvious how the two data items are different. There is an easy way to think of each one. Calculated items go across the rows while aggregated measures go down the columns. In the following figure, Gross Margin was created as a calculated item and as an aggregated measure. Notice that the aggregated measure contains the overall result of *Order Total - Order Product Cost* across all regions and years.

Figure 3.8 Calculated item versus aggregated measure

Business Regions	Transaction Year	Order Total	Order Product Cost	Gross Margin (Calculated Item) ▲	Gross Margin (Aggregated Measure For All)
EMEA	2013	5,136,734	2,402,293	2,734,441.07	14,102,088
EMEA	2010	6,382,054	2,916,960	3,465,093.60	14,102,088
EMEA	2012	7,373,542	3,493,781	3,879,760.83	14,102,088
EMEA	2011	7,839,377	3,816,584	4,022,792.17	14,102,088
				14,102,087.67 Total: 14,102,088	

Aggregated measures calculate values *across and down* a column. This amount is the total sum for all rows.

Calculated measures use values across the rows.

Aggregated measures are calculated in two ways. You can create the data item so that it recognizes the category and uses a *BY group* calculation or uses an overall calculation. In the following figure, additional aggregated measures were added that use the BY group option. You can see that the Gross Margin (Aggregated Measure By Group) reacts to the Transaction Year and shows the individual values. In fact, it does not have a value different from the Gross Margin (Calculated Item). This is why new users are often confused by the two different methods.

Figure 3.9 Aggregated measurement types

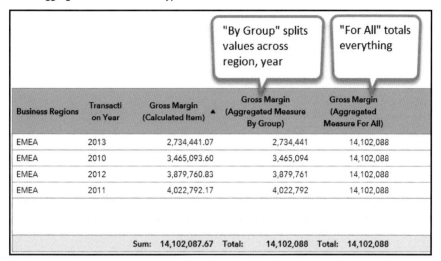

Business Regions	Transaction Year	Gross Margin (Calculated Item) ▲	Gross Margin (Aggregated Measure By Group)	Gross Margin (Aggregated Measure For All)
EMEA	2013	2,734,441.07	2,734,441	14,102,088
EMEA	2010	3,465,093.60	3,465,094	14,102,088
EMEA	2012	3,879,760.83	3,879,761	14,102,088
EMEA	2011	4,022,792.17	4,022,792	14,102,088
	Sum: 14,102,087.67	Total:	14,102,088 Total:	14,102,088

When showing overall values, it is smarter to use an aggregated measure. However, that doesn't mean that it is always the best approach. You might need to experiment to get the result that you want.

For the dashboard, you need an aggregated measure that has the Profitability Ratio. This aggregated data item is based on the Gross Margin data item. The formula is Total Sales divided by Gross Margin. Use the following instructions to create the aggregated measure.

1. Click **Data ▶ New Aggregated Measure**. The New Aggregated Measure window appears.
2. In the **Name** field, type Profitability Ratio.
3. In the **Operator** field, type the divide sign (/). Drag the x / y object to the work area.
4. In the Data Items area, select **Gross Margin** and drag it to the first empty box.
5. In the Data Items area, select **Order Total** and drag it to the second empty box.
   Your window should look similar to the following figure.

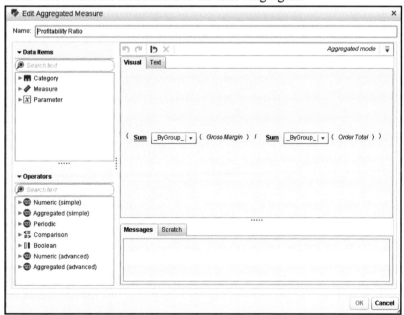

6. Click **OK** to create the aggregated measure.
7. In the Properties area, change the **Format** to **Percent**. Adjust the Decimals value to 0.

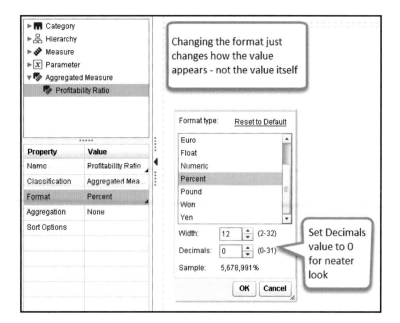

Creating the layout

After creating your data items, you can start on your dashboard layout. The following figure shows two pages and the data objects for each. This layout is based on the example shown in the *Building the dashboard* topic.

Figure 3.10 Creating the layout

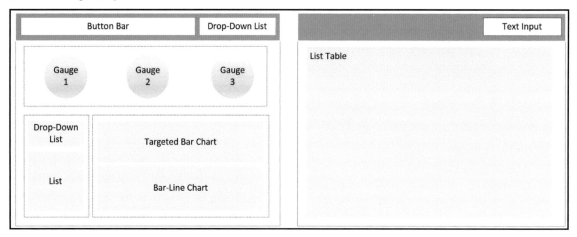

Adding sections or pages

Sections (also called pages) provide a way to organize report content. When you open a new report, there is one section. You can create multiple sections for your reports.

1. Start a new report.
2. Right-click the **Section 1** tab and select **Rename**. Type Regional Manager Dashboard.
3. Click the + button to add a new section.
4. Right-click the **Section 1** tab and select **Rename**. Type **Sales Rep Report**.

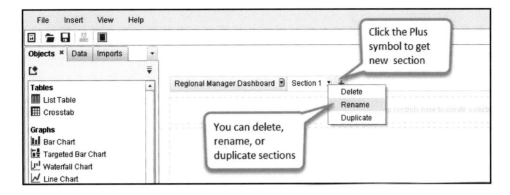

Adding containers

Containers provide a way to group data objects. You can change the color and size of containers to show the data objects that belong together. This dashboard uses three containers: one for the gauges, one for the prompts, and one for the graphs. The containers have different colors to show how they are related to each other. The top container is a darker gray, and the two bottom containers are the same color of gray.

Figure 3.11 Container layout

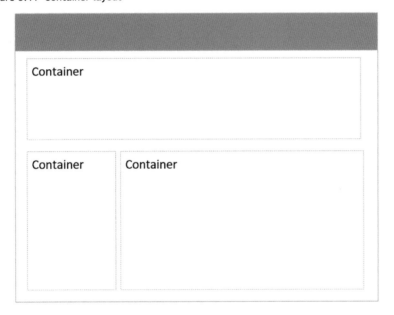

To add a container:

1. From the Objects pane, drag the Container data object to the work area. The container uses all available the space.
2. Select the container object.

3. From the Style menu, change the border color to blue and the line to 3.

4. Add the second container object beneath the first. You might need to add a container to the left and then drag it under the other container. The mouse pointer turns into a green + sign when you move it on top of the left margin. The step might take several attempts the first time you try it.

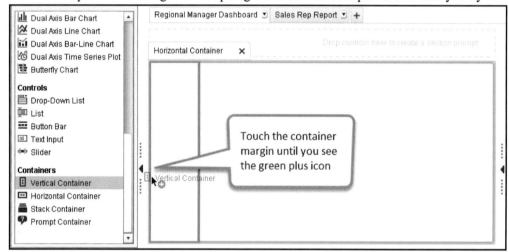

5. Change Container 2 to a .50 transparency. Select the first gray as the background color.

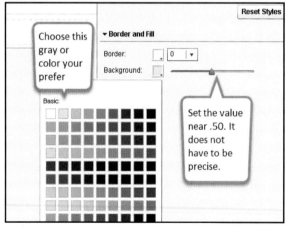

6. Add the third container by right-clicking container 2 and selecting **Duplicate Container**. Position the container so that it uses 75% of the bottom half as shown in the layout example above. It doesn't have to be exact.

Your layout should look similar to the following figure:

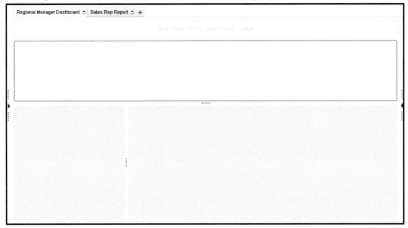

Adding section filters

Using a section filter, you can filter all data objects within a section. The dashboard has two section filters on the Regional Manager section and one on the Sales Rep Ratings section.

Figure 3.12 Adding the section filters

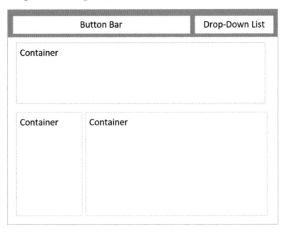
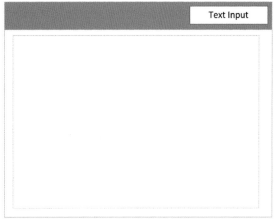

To create the section filters:

1. Add the Button Bar control to the regional manager section.
   a. In the Roles pane, select **Business Region as the Category** and remove Frequency from the **Frequency** field.
   b. In the Style pane, change the **Background selection color** to light blue. The setting turns the active button a different color so the user knows which selection is made.

2. Add Drop-down list data objects to the regional manager section.

    a. In the Filter pane, add a **Filter on Transaction Month** and set the begin date to January 2012. This prevents earlier dates showing.

    b. In the Roles pane, select **Transaction Month** as the Category and remove Frequency from the **Frequency** field.

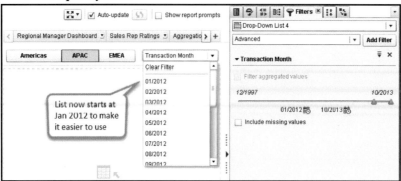

3. Switch to the Sales Rep Ratings section.

    a. Drag the text input control to the section filter area.

    b. In the Roles pane, select **Sales Rep as the Category** and remove Frequency from the **Frequency** field.

Working with data objects

You can now add the data objects to the containers. Container 1 has three data objects, Container 2 has two filter items, and Container 3 has two data objects.

Using gauges in a container

There are five different gauges available in SAS Visual Analytics. Some of the gauges can be shown as horizontal or vertical, so it appears that there are more choices. A gauge requires a measurement and display rules. You can add a target if you want. Refer to the *Visualizing your data* chapter for more details about gauges and display rules.

Display rules use color to show the user the ranges for each measurement. For these gauges, the display rules are set to indicate different values. All gauges use a traffic light (red/yellow/green) method to indicate good or bad. The lower measurements are red and the over goal measures are green. The following figure shows the same gauge in different traffic light values.

Figure 3.13 Dashboard gauges

SAS Visual Analytics does not limit the scale or the colors on the display rules.

To add the gauges, do the following:

1. Drag the Gauge data object to Container 1.
   a. On the **Properties** tab, change the Name to KPI 1 and the Title to KPI 1: Achieve Regional Sales Target of 40%.
   b. On the **Roles** tab, add the Sales Rep % of Target as the Category. Change the aggregation to Average or Maximum.
   c. On the **Properties** tab, set the Width to 33. This indicates the percentage this data object is allowed to use.
   d. On the **Properties** tab, set the Gauge Type to Speedometer.
   e. On the **Style** tab, set the Data Skin style to Modern.
   f. On the **Display Rules** tab, set the following values. Enter the values for green first and then work your way up.

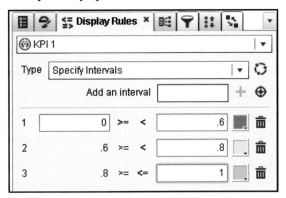

2. Right-click the first gauge and select Duplicate KPI 1.
   a. In the **Properties** tab, change the Name to KPI 2 and the Title to KPI 2: Achieve Regional Profit Ratio of 60%.
   b. In the **Roles** tab, add the Profitability Ratio as the Category.
   c. In the **Display Rules** tab, set the following values:

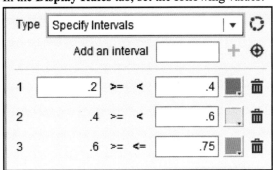

3. Right-click the second gauge and select Duplicate KPI 2.
   a. On the **Properties** tab, change the Name to KPI 3 and the Title to KPI 3: Achieve regional approval rating of 60%. Set the aggregation to Average.
   b. On the **Roles** tab, add the Sales Rep Rating as the Category.
   c. On the **Display Rules** tab, set the values the same as ones for KPI 2.

Using parameters for targets

The Sales vice president wanted each business region to have an individual target for KPI 3. The target is a stretch goal based on the previous year's sales goal. Since we want each one to be different, we need to add a parameter so the gauge knows to read the value from a calculated item.

Understanding parameters

Parameters allow the data objects to change based on user selection. When the user selects the region, the tool uses the target value for the gauge updates based on that selection. In the following figure, the user selected APAC which sets the target on dashboard gauge to 59%. The target is represented by the dot. If the user selects EMEA, the target is changed and the gauge updated.

Figure 3.14 Using parameters for targets

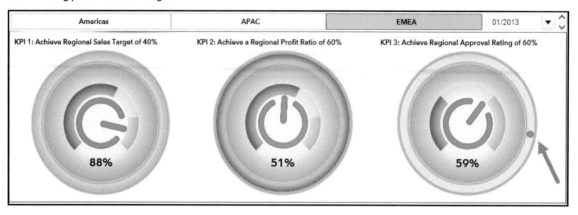

Parameters can be used with filters, calculated items, and aggregated measures. The parameter value is set globally for the section. This means that when the user makes the selection, the filter only contains that value until another selection is made.

Creating a parameter

You need three items to set a target:

- Parameter data item to contain the value of the Business Region filter. This value is populated when the user clicks a button on the button bar.

- Calculated data item that contains the target value for each business region. You present these values when you create the calculated data item.

- Gauge with the target value set.

To add the parameter to the gauge:

1. Create the parameter:
   a. Select **Data ▶ New Parameter**.
   b. In the **Name** field, type RegionalSelection.
   c. In the **Type** field, select Character.
      Your window should look similar to the following figure:

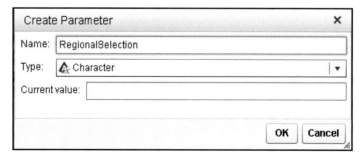

   d. Click **OK** to create the new parameter.

e.   Select the Button Bar and add the new parameter to the **Parameter** field.

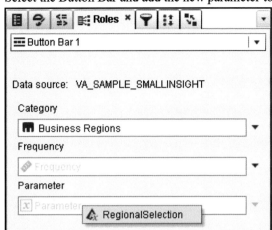

2.   Create the Calculated Item. There are multiple ways to create this formula.

a.   Select **Data ▶ New Calculated Item**.

b.   In the **Name** field, type _RegionalRatingsTarget.

c.   On the **Visual** tab, drag the IF … ELSE operator to the Work area. Then drag a second IF … ELSE operator into the **Else** field.

d.   Drag the = operator to each condition box.

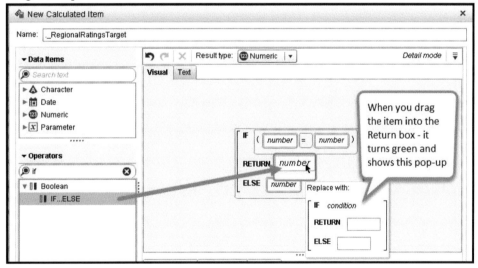

e.   Drag the RegionalSelection parameter into the first condition field. Then type EMEA in the second box.

f.   In the **Return** field, type .69.

g.   Drag the RegionalSelection parameter into the first condition field. Then type APAC in the second box.

h.   In the **Return** field, type .59.

i. In the **Else** field, type .62. There are only 3 regions, so this value is for the Americas. Your formula should look like the following:

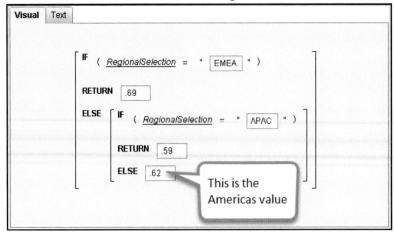

Some users find it easier to type formula on the **Text** tab as shown in the following figure. It might be easier to cut and paste or work with complex formulas using this method.

```
IF ( 'RegionalSelection'p = 'EMEA' )

  RETURN 0.69

  ELSE (
     IF ( 'RegionalSelection'p = 'APAC' )
     RETURN 0.59

     ELSE 0.62

     )
```

3. Click **OK** to create the data item.

4. In the Format area, change the aggregation method to Mean. The default aggregation is Sum, which causes the value to display as the aggregation for all rows. If you select mean or max, then you get a single value for the row.

5. Select the KPI 3 gauge. On the **Roles** tab, add the _RegionalRatingsTarget as the Target.

    A dot appears on the gauge and moves each time a different region is selected. The parameter causes the value to change when the user makes a different selection.

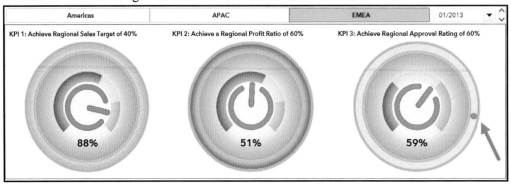

Adding data objects to a container

The dashboard has two data objects in Container 3. These data objects provide more details than the gauges and help the user understand more about the data.

Using a targeted bar chart

A targeted bar chart enables the user to see how close or far a category was from a goal. For this dashboard, we want to show each sales rep with her actual sales against the target. The target is represented by the gray bar above each bar. The closer the bar is to the box, the closer the sales rep was to meeting the target value.

All sales reps are expected to achieve 80% of their target. This chart includes a display rule, so the bar turns green when the target was achieved. Otherwise the bar remains red.

Figure 3.15 Targeted bar chart show individual performance

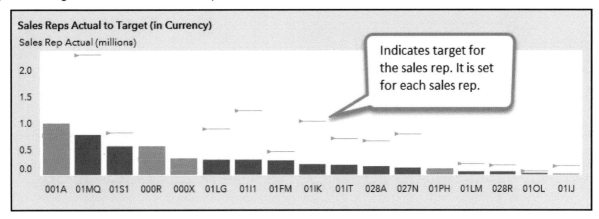

To add a targeted bar chart:

1. Drag the Targeted Bar Chart to the Container 3 object.
2. On the **Properties** tab, change the Title to Sales Reps Actual to Target (in Currency). Change the font to bold.
3. On the **Roles** tab, set the following:
   a. In the **Category** field, add Sales Rep.
   b. In the **Measure** field, add Sales Rep Actual.
   c. In the **Target** field, add Sales Rep % of Target.
4. On the **Display Rules** tab, select **New**. An Add Display Rule window appears.
   a. Select the **Expression Details** tab.
   b. In the Column field, select **Sales Rep % of Target**.

   c.   Type .8 in the **Value** field.

   d.   Change the Style color to green.

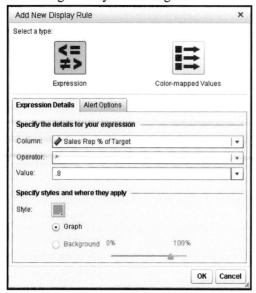

5.   On the **Styles** tab, change the first data color from blue to red. This causes all bars to be red unless the Display Rule overrides the color and sets it to green.

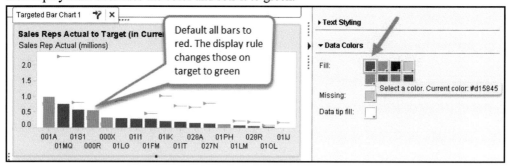

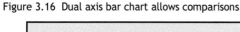

Using a dual axis bar-line chart

A bar-line chart mixes a line and bar chart. The line chart uses the left and right axes for its values. For this dashboard, the bar represents each sales rep total sales. The line represents the profitability ratio. This is just additional information that shows high sales does not translate to a large profit. Managers might want to review the data to determine if heavy discounts have been given.

Figure 3.16 Dual axis bar chart allows comparisons

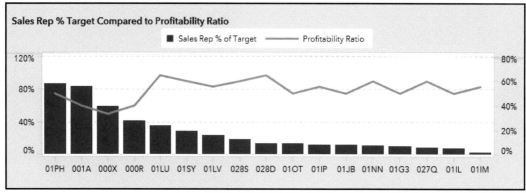

To add a dual axis bar chart:

1. Drag the Dual Axis Bar-Line chart to the Container 3 object.
2. On the **Properties** tab, change the Title to Sales Reps Sales with Profitability Ratio. Change the font to bold.
3. On the **Roles** tab, set the following:
   a. In the **Category** field, add Sales Rep.
   b. In the **Measure** (bar) field, add Order Total.
   c. In the **Measure** (line) field, add Profitability Ratio.
4. On the **Styles** tab, change the color so it is easier to see the data:
   a. In the Fill area, change the first data color to light blue.
   b. In the Line/Marker area, change the second data color to black or dark blue. The line is on the second measure and uses the colors in the second box.

Adding controls to a container

The dashboard uses Controls to enable the Regional Managers to explore the data based on product line or sales rep. These controls are then made interactive with the data objects in container 3. In the following figure, you can see the planned interactions for the controls and objects. The drop-down list and list controls interact with the Targeted Bar Chart. The Targeted Bar Chart passes the filtering to the Bar-Line chart. For more details about interactions, refer to the *Creating your first report* chapter.

Figure 3.17 Establishing interactivity between objects

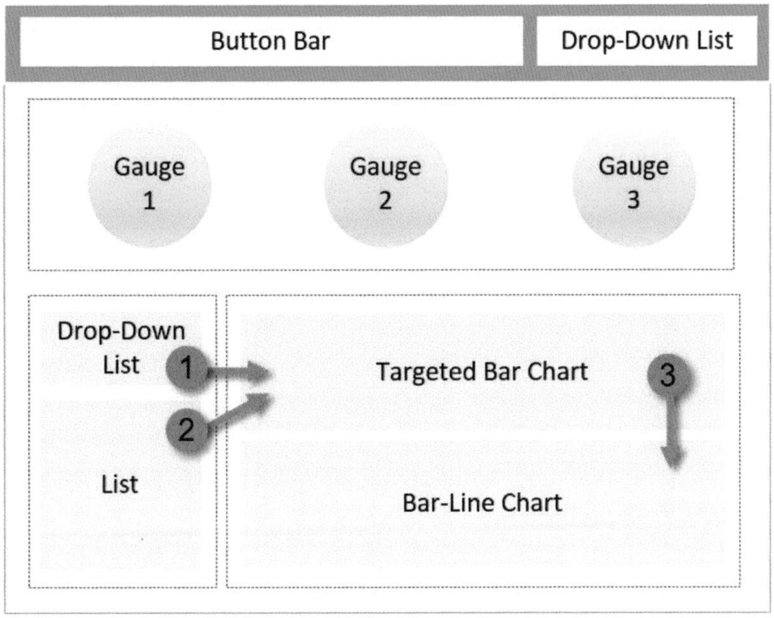

To add the controls and set up the interactions:

1. Add a Drop-Down List to Container 2.
   a. In the Roles tab, assign Product Line to Category. Remove the Frequency value.
   b. In the Properties tab, set Title to Product Line and the Height to 20.
   c. In the Interaction tab, set the control to filter the Targeted Bar Chart.

2. Add a List to Container 2 under the other control.
   a. In the Roles tab, assign Sales Rep to Category. Remove the Frequency value.
   b. In the Properties tab, set the Height to 75. This allows some white space beneath the controls.
   c. In the Interaction tab, set the control to filter the Targeted Bar Chart.
3. Add an interaction to the Targeted Bar Chart.
   a. Select the Targeted Bar Chart.
   b. In the Interaction tab, set the Targeted Bar chart to filter the Bar-Line Chart.

Adding a list table

The Sales Rep Report uses a list table to contain some detailed approval ratings metrics. The table can be filtered by the Text Input control in the section filter area. A display rule is used to highlight the sales reps with low ratings. Refer to the *Visualizing your data* chapter for more details about working with list tables.

Figure 3.18 Using display rules with a list table

					Sales Rep
Sales Rep Ratings by Region and Month					
Business Regions	**Transaction Month** ▼	**Sales Rep**	**Sales Rep Rating (Min)**	**Sales Rep Rating**	**Sales Rep Rating (Max)**
EMEA	10/2013	028D	39%	39%	39%
EMEA	10/2013	027Q	60%	60%	60%
EMEA	10/2013	01SY	41%	41%	41%
EMEA	10/2013	01PH	48%	48%	48%
EMEA	10/2013	01OT	100%	100%	100%
EMEA	10/2013	01NN	40%	40%	40%
EMEA	10/2013	01LV	40%	40%	40%
EMEA	10/2013	01JB	47%	47%	47%

To add a list table:

1. Drag the List table to the Work area.
2. On the **Properties** tab, change the Title to Sales Rep by Region and Month.
3. On the **Roles** tab, add the following data items to list table:

4. On the **Style** tab, make the following changes to enhance readability:
   a. Click the **Wrap text** check box to allow the headings to go on 2 lines.
   b. Change the **Background color** on the Column headings to light blue.
   c. Change the **Font** to Bold.
5. Click the Sales Rep Rating column and select **Add Display Rules**. You want any average ratings below 40% to be highlighted with a different color background.
   a. Set the value to .4.
   b. Change the background color to red or orange. You can also change the text color or font.

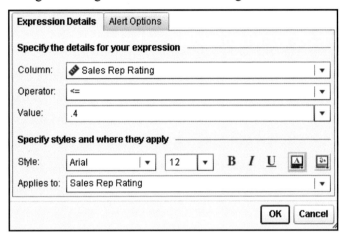

Linking to another section

The Sales Rep Ratings section uses a table to contain some detailed approval ratings metrics. The managers can click the KPI 3 to get the regional details for each sales rep. This action is called linking. You can link to other sections or other reports. When a parent section links to a child section, the filtered values are passed to the data objects in that section. In this case, the list table is filtered based on the selections for Gauge 3.

Figure 3.19 Linking objects to sections

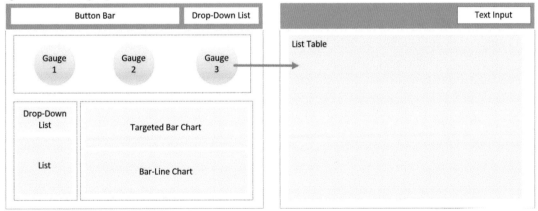

Understanding section linking

When an object is linked to another, a special symbol appears on the section. Click the icon to see which section has linked to the tab or click the Link icon to return to the section. In the following figure, notice that the list table is filtered for APAC. The link icon shows the list is filtered from the Regional Manager dashboard.

Figure 3.20 Applying section filtering

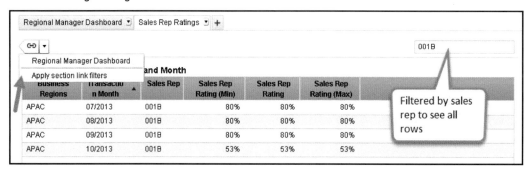

You can investigate a single sales rep. In the following figure, you would type the sales rep user ID in the control field. This action filters the list table. To see more than a specific month, uncheck the Apply section link filters.

Figure 3.21 Removing filtering

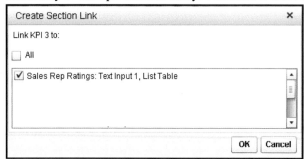

Applying section linking

To set up the link from the dashboard gauge to list table:

1. Right-click Gauge 3 (KPI 3) and select **Add Link ▶ Section Link**.
2. In the Create Section Link window, select the section where you want to link.
   There may be multiple sections and you can link to more than one.

Other dashboard enhancements

In this chapter, you created a pre-designed dashboard. This topic contains some additional ideas and methods for enhancing a dashboard.

Adding text boxes

In some cases, a dashboard might contain data or formulas that might confuse new users. You might want to provide commentary about the dashboard or a link to a helpful website. You can do this with a text object. The Sales Rep Report provides ratings, but it doesn't explain how the data was collected or what the colors mean. Let's add a text box that explains the ratings colors and provides a link to an example survey.

Text boxes contain text or a link to an external location, an existing report or report section. You can control the appearance of each text item. You can also use the **Properties** tab to add a border or change the background color.

To add a text object:

1. Drag a Text object to the work area.
2. In the text box, type your text. You can control the format of individual text items. In the example, the heading text is larger. The color names were highlighted in the figure below as an example of some changes you can make.
3. To add a hyperlink, highlight the text that you want to have the link, click the Link icon, and type your link in the box. In the example, a link was added to an example survey.

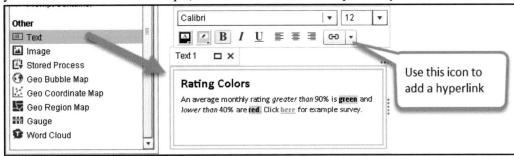

Adding artwork

You can add images to your dashboard, such as an icon or a logo. For this example, we are adding a link to the SAS training videos and using an image. Here's an example of how the image would look after adding it to the Sales Rep Report.

Figure 3.22 Using image and text objects in your report

Sales Rep Ratings by Region and Month

Business Regions	Transaction Month ▲	Sales Rep	Sales Rep Rating (Min)	Sales Rep Rating	Sales Rep Rating (Max)
EMEA	01/2011	01HY	60%	60%	60%
EMEA	01/2011	028P	56%	56%	56%
EMEA	01/2011	000Y	40%	40%	40%
EMEA	01/2011	000C	85%	85%	85%
EMEA	01/2011	01KH	52%	52%	52%
EMEA	01/2011	01NG	78%	78%	78%
			Minimum: 20%	Average: 53%	Maximum: 100%

Rating Colors

An average monthly rating *greater than* 90% is **green** and *lower than* 40% are red. Click **here** for example survey.

Watch Training Video

There are three supported file types (JPG, PNG, and GIF). When you add the image, it is stored with your report. It can be re-used in other reports and dashboards.

To add a new image:

1. Drag the Image object to the work area. An Image Selection window prompts you to use an existing image or load one from your local machine.
2. Click the **Load from local machine** option and click **Browse** to locate the image file.
3. Click the **Save image to the repository** to select where the image is stored.
4. Select the image scale if you need to control the final size. This setting is also available on the **Properties** menu.
5. Add any text in the Tooltip text. When the user hovers over the image, this text is displayed.

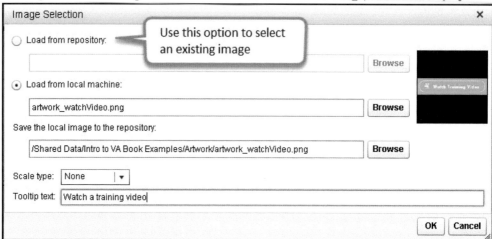

6. Click **OK** to return to the work area.
7. To add a link, right-click the image and select the **Add Link** choice. You can link to an external or internal location.

Embedding a stored process

From SAS Visual Analytics, you can embed a stored process in your report or link to a stored process from a data object. When embedding a stored process in your report, you can take advantage of existing stored processes or add other SAS-based reports.

SAS Visual Analytics has a stored process object that enables you to place the stored process within the report. However, the stored process does not interact with the other elements of the report. For example, you cannot use the report or section filters on the stored process or use the prompt choices to interact with other objects.

When embedding a stored process in SAS Visual Analytics, the data can be located on the SAS Visual Analytic server or from other locations. You can use the tables loaded in the SAS LASR Analytics Server, but it's better that you avoid the practice. If you use data from the SAS LASR Analytic Server, it must be transferred from the in-memory location to a local SAS session. For smaller tables, the performance would hardly be noticed, but larger tables might take a long time to download and overwhelm the SAS session.

SAS Visual Analytics ships with some sample stored processes. In this example, you will embed a sample stored process in the existing dashboard.

1. Create a new section in your report.
2. Drag the Stored Process object to the work area.
3. When prompted, navigate to the SAS Folders > Products > SAS Intelligence Platform > Sample folder and select the Sample: Multiple Output Formats stored process from its metadata location.

The stored process runs and the results appear in the section.

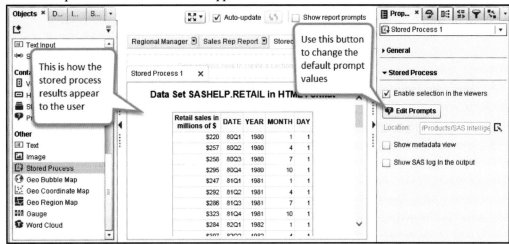

When the stored process has prompts, you can change the prompt values from the Properties pane. Click the **Edit prompts** button to select the different prompt values. The choices you select are saved with the stored process and become the default for all users. However, the user can change the values in the Report Viewer.

Extending stored processes

You can also link to a stored process from a data object. You can pass parameters to the stored process. This technique is often used when you want the user to download a larger data set for more analysis.

Summary

This chapter was focused on helping you learn how to use the tool to create a dashboard for a fictional company. The design process presented was to demonstrate the overall process and how each step would work. Much of the process might have appeared as if the designer was working alone with some minimal management direction.

If you build a dashboard and no one uses it, it can be frustrating or disappointing. The main reason this situation occurs is because the users do not find the dashboard useful. It might be because the dashboard contains measurements that no one uses. Or the data used within the dashboard is inaccurate. It's also possible that the dashboard is too difficult to use. Many of these symptoms point to a designer who didn't work with the end user.

The only time you should build a dashboard alone is when you are prototyping an idea. Many managers do not realize the need for a dashboard until they can see a working model. You can then have a conversation with the managers about what is happening in their organizations that is creating so-called *pain points*. You want to know about the pain points because this is where the opportunity for change and process control presents itself.

As you build the dashboard, you want to present layout ideas to the end users. This enables the team to become excited about what you are doing and guide you to help them get the best end result. Even after you finish the dashboard, it is a good idea to watch the users interact with it. You want to ensure that they are able to understand the information pathways and how to answer the questions they have.

Keep in mind that creating a dashboard is a highly iterative process. While some dashboards may be needed for a short time period, most dashboards are used for several years within organizations. This doesn't mean the content changes. Ensure that you have documented your process well enough for someone else to understand the design and intended use.

References

Aanderud, Tricia, and Angela Hall. 2012. *The 50 Keys to Learning SAS Stored Processes*. Raleigh, NC: Siamese Publishing.

Aanderud, Tricia, and Michelle Homes. 2014. "SAS Admins Need a Dashboard, Too." *Proceedings of the SAS Global Forum 2014 Conference*. Paper 1247-2014. Cary, NC: SAS Institute Inc.

Aanderud, Tricia. 2016. "Five Secrets for Building Fierce Dashboards." SESUG 2016: *Proceedings of the SouthEast SAS Users Group*. Paper RV-185. Cary, NC: SAS Institute Inc.

Bodt, Mark. 2014. "The Many Ways of Creating Dashboards Using SAS." *Proceedings of the SAS Global Forum 2014 Conference*. Paper 1269-2014. Cary, NC: SAS Institute Inc.

Few, Stephen. 2013. *Information Dashboard Design: Displaying Data for At-a-Glance Monitoring, Second Edition*. Burlingame California: Analytics Press

Grouw, Gail La. 2012, *Effective Dashboard Design: Design Secrets to Getting More Value From Performance Dashboards*. Seattle, Washington: Self-published through CreateSpace Independent Publishing Platform.

Kaplan, Robert S. and David P. Norton, D. 1996. *The Balanced Scorecard: Translating Strategy into Action*. Boston, Massachusetts: Harvard Business School Press.

Tufte, Edward R. 2001. *The Visual Display of Quantitative Information*. Cheshire, CT: Graphics Press.

chapter four

using the data builder

The Data Builder is the SAS Visual Analytics application that lets you extract data from various sources, prepare data, and load data sets into the SAS LASR Analytic Server or other locations. If you recall from previous chapters, the LASR Analytic Server is where your data is placed before you can use it in the report building sections. Using the Data Builder, you have more flexibility with preparing and importing your data into the LASR Analytic Server. The Data Builder can also be used to create staging tables or load tables into the Hadoop Distributed File System (HDFS).

With the Data Builder, you can build queries around the data and then you can run those queries to manipulate and move the data to output locations. Data can be accessed through local files, databases, SAS data sets, and so on. While building your query, you have the option to perform minor data manipulation such as adding new data items, summarizing data, and even joining with other tables. The Data Builder does this through a user interface that is building SQL code in the background.

When SAS Visual Analytics moved from version 7.3 to 8.1, there was an overhaul to the Data Builder in regards to the interface (switch to HTML5) and functionality. This chapter focuses on the main aspects of the Data Builder and the capabilities of 7.3, Chapter 13 takes you through the 8.1 version and all of the updates that come with it.

Using the Data Builder

So why should you use the Data Builder instead of just importing the whole data set? For this, you must remember that LASR Analytic Server works on temporary memory. Therefore, any conditions, simple calculations, groupings, and so on, are just place holders. The real data is computed each time you interact with the data set. By doing some initial data prep in the Data Builder, you can polish your data set and have it ready before it even goes into the LASR Analytic Server.

The Data Builder should also be considered when you are trying to work with multiple data sets or append data sets in the LASR Analytic Server. There is access to tables in the LASR Analytic Server, and you can also import data from local files, servers, databases, and social media. With tables already in the LASR Analytic Server, there is functionality in the Data Builder to construct a query that appends to that table every time the query is run. When you want to join tables, queries can bring in multiple tables so that you can connect them as needed through a user interface or SQL code. You can even create an entire star schema if needed.

Additional SAS products for data preparation

There are many capabilities with the Data Builder, but it is important to remember that this tool works best with simple data preparation. If you need to transpose, remodel, or perform complex calculations with your data, then you want to consider SAS Enterprise Guide, SAS Studio, and SAS Data Integration Studio.

Creating a data query

A data query is your means to create a new table from a data source and then load it into a source. At its roots, a data query is a SAS program that connects you to your sources so that you can pull data from them. Then, the query performs everything necessary behind the scenes so that you can load into the LASR Analytic Server, send the query to HDFS, or create a staging table. In the Data Builder, queries also must be saved before you can use them. Once you save a query, you can then use it in another query or execute it to load data.

How does the Data Builder work?

Above, we mentioned how data queries are like SAS programs. They can function like that because they are metadata objects. Source tables first need to be registered in metadata before you can use them in a query. The Data Builder uses SAS Folders as its source for importing tables. This comes from the SAS Management Console; tables are only available in the SAS Folders if they have been registered in metadata.

When tables are registered in metadata, the query then knows the exact location, file type, and names of columns in each table. Along with the source tables, a query also contains information for column properties, aggregations, and possible criteria for joining tables. The query also has the information to register the resulting output table in metadata.

With that information known, you can then start the process of creating a query. Here are the basic steps for creating a query:

1. **Select the source data**

    This is where you find and add your data sources that are registered in the metadata.

2. **Prepare the source data**

    In this step, you clean and combine your data. If you have multiple tables, then you need to define where they are joined. For individual tables, you can remove rows by declaring conditions for the data or you can remove columns by not including them in the output.

3. **Shape the Output Table**

    Here is where you can add any columns that you would like . These columns can include aggregations or other calculations in your data.

4. **Determine the Output Location**

    You have your table ready to go, but now you need to decide its name and where it is going. Tables can be saved to the LASR Analytic Server and other locations that are defined in the metadata such as other SAS servers or HDFS.

5. **Preview and Save**

    Once you have your output table ready, you can preview your data. The preview gives you a small snapshot of your data. If you like what you see, you can save your query. You cannot run a query until it is saved. Queries can also be saved at any time; they do not need to be complete.

6. **Run the Query**

    When you click ▶ to run the query, the code that was developed behind the scenes executes and your output table is placed in its new location.

Before you begin

The tables used in queries can come from just about anywhere. This can be local files, server data, database tables, or social media data.

However, these tables need to be registered in metadata in order for you to access the data in the Data Builder. An administrator can use SAS Visual Analytics Administrator or SAS Management Console to register tables in metadata for you.

You also have access to LASR tables when adding tables to your query. LASR tables can be used as source tables for a query, but it is not recommended. The workspace server is used to process the query (not the SAS LASR Analytic Server). This can overwhelm the SAS session if the LASR table is large, resulting in reduced performance. It is best to use the access to the LASR table for appending only. Once you have initially added data into your query, you can always decide to add more tables or remove what you have.

Connecting to other databases

When you are trying to import from a database, one of the SAS/ACCESS products for the database must be licensed and configured on the SAS Workspace server. You might need to provide credentials as well when trying to access the data.

Opening the Data Builder

You can access the Data Builder through either a direct link or by navigating from SAS Home.

Figure 4.1 Getting to the Data Builder

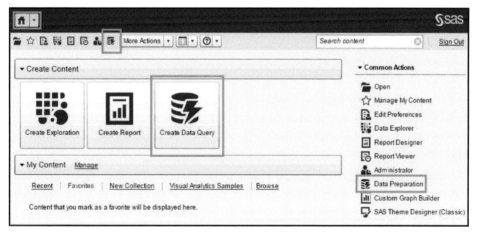

Within SAS Home, you can access the Data Builder with any of the links and icons that have the (database/lightning) symbol. Also, the main drop-down list in the top left corner has an option of Data Preparation that links you to the Data Builder as well.

You can also directly link to the Data Builder if you know your server and port number. The link is structured as follows:

http://<server:port>/SASVisualDataBuilder

Understanding the Data Builder layout

After you navigate to the Data Builder, you see a screen that contains three different areas that help you through the query building process.

Figure 4.2 Data Builder layout

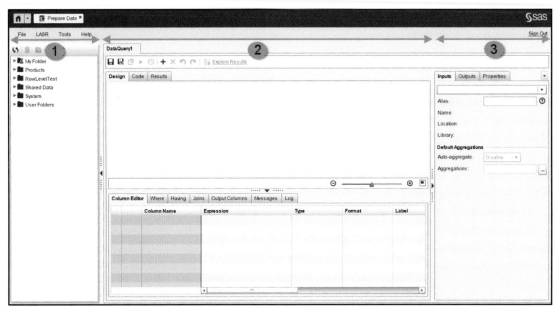

At the top of the page, there are two toolbars, which are used to navigate to other sections of the applications and access common tasks.

The left section ① is the navigation pane; this section displays tables and data queries in the SAS Folders tree. This is where you can see what is registered in the metadata. The toolbar contains icons for working with the files and creating new folders and queries.

The middle section ② is the workspace that enables you to build data queries. The toolbar at the top contains icons for working with the query. The lower pane enables you to manage the attributes of the query. The upper pane is active for the **Design** tab and the **Code** tab in the workspace. When you preview or run your query, the output shows in the **Results** tab.

The right pane ③ enables you to manage the properties of the query, the input data, and the output data. This is where you select how you want the output handled and where it goes.

Building your first query

For our first query, we are going to use the EMPINFO and SALARY tables that are available in SAS Enterprise Guide. We want to look at a few things with this data. First, we want to make sure that our dedicated employees (25+ years at the company) are being compensated properly. Also, we want to check which locations have the employees who tend to stay with the company the longest. The EMPINFO table contains information about all employees such as address, phone numbers, age, department, start and end dates, and so on. Salaries of employees are located in a separate table for privacy reasons.

Creating the query

To create a new query:

1. Locate your data source in the left section and drag it into the Design tab. EMPINFO was selected and you can see the data source contents once it is in the work area.

2. Add a second data source called SALARY. The Data Builder suggests a join by drawing two lines between it. You can click the **Joins** tab to modify the join. Here is where you can change the join type or data fields under Join conditions. Join Type can do inner, outer, left, and right joins. For this example, we are keeping the inner join.

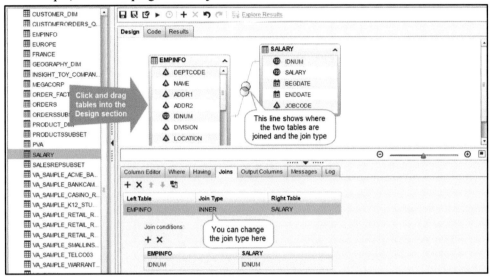

3. In the tables that are laid out in the design tab, click data items to add to the Column Editor. For our query, we are going to use Name, ADDR2, IDNUM (EMPINFO table), SALARY, and BEGDATE. The Column Editor keeps track of the data items that are going into the new table. You can view all of the items currently selected by clicking on the Column Editor in the bottom section.

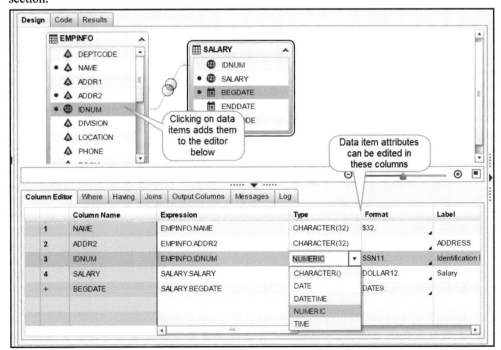

You can change data items by clicking the columns and making selections. By default, there are no columns in the output table until you specify them. If you want an entire table, you can right-click inside the table and select Add All Columns.

4. Make changes to the data items in the column editor. For our query, we are just going to change our labels to Employee Name, Address, ID Number, Salary, and Begin Date.

    The Type column changes the SAS data type for each item in the output data set. Format changes how the data is displayed. Label changes how the column heading is shown. If you leave the label field blank, the Column Name becomes the default header for the column.

5. Determine the output name and location for query in the Outputs tab to the right. For this we are just going to change the table name to Emp_Salary

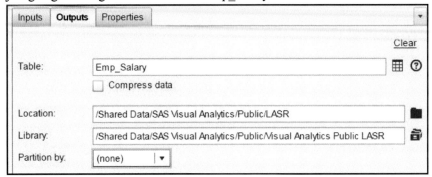

The Location and Library options indicate where your output data is going to be registered in metadata. The Location is where the table's metadata definition is stored, and the Library is the output table's SAS library (in this case, the LASR Analytic Server). We want our data to go to LASR, and the Location and Library should be defaulted to LASR and Visual Analytics Public LASR, respectively. If it is not, you can find them by clicking on the file icons on the right side. The Partition By option is a way to put an index on one of the columns for more efficient data access. This should only be used in performance tuning after creating the query.

6. Save the query with a **Save As** to put it in your selected location. We name this query EmpInfo Salary Join. You cannot run a query until it has been saved.

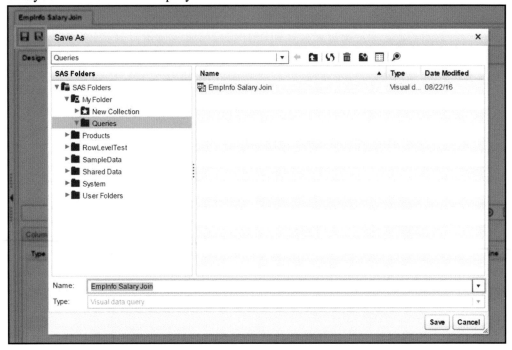

After you save the query, it shows up in the metadata folder structure on the left side where you put it. When you save the query, we can see the metadata object in the LASR Analytic Server.

You can view what is in the LASR Analytic Server by clicking the home menu in the top left corner and selecting **Administrator**. The Emp_Salary table has a red square for its status because there is not yet data associated with it, just its definition.

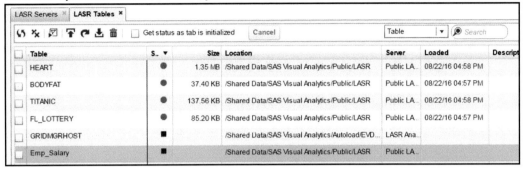

7. Click ▶ in the menu bar of the Data Builder and then select **Run**.

The ▶ icon opens to a drop-down menu that gives you the option to preview or run the query. The **Preview** option runs the query and loads the first 100 rows into a temporary table so that you can review the output. The **Run** option loads the full data set into its output location. Both options show the data in the **Results** tab.

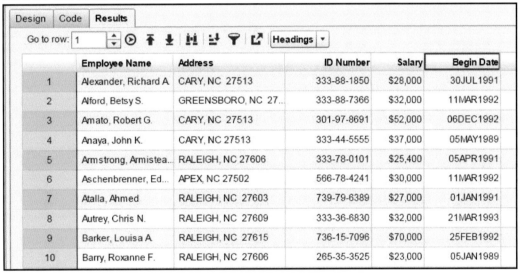

You can see the labels of the columns by clicking the **Headings** drop-down menu. Now, if you go back into the Administrator, you can see your data loaded with a green circle as its status.

Modify the query

Once you add all of the columns from the source tables that you want as output, you also have the ability to create new columns based on the data from the source tables. Notice that there are categories for character, numeric, and date in the type field. This is how each data item will be classified in the output table. If there is a data item that is not correct, you can change it.

You can also create custom calculations by using SAS functions on the input data tables that you have brought in or add new categorical data based on ranges or values in your data. SAS functions are a way to use the SAS language within the query to take action on data items. They can be used to parse out strings, manipulate dates, change case on characters, along with many others actions.

Adding a numeric calculation

One of the things that we want to look for is employees that have at least 25 years of experience. We have brought in BEGDATE, which is the date that they started, but we still need to calculate the time. A custom expression can help us out.

To add a numeric calculation using functions:

1. In the Column Editor, click the plus sign icon on the last row to add a new row. Give the data item a name, type, and label.

2. In the **Expression** field, click the icon at the end of the field.

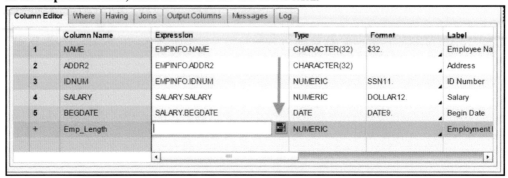

3. Calculate the employee's length of time with the company using TODAY() – BEGDATE.

    The expression window has a tabbed panel on the left and the SQL expression on the right. You can choose to type the SQL statement or double-click from the Fields and Functions on the left. The columns from the input tables are under fields. You can find the Today function under Date/Time Manipulation in Functions.

    Note: With SAS date functions such as Today(), SAS handles them by converting dates to integers based on 0 = January 1st, 1960. Any dates before then are treated as negative integers.

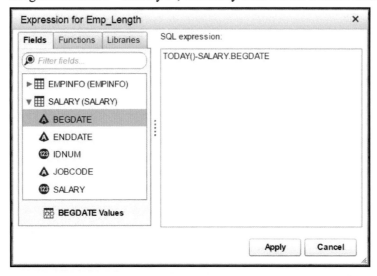

4. Click **Apply** to return to the Column Details window. Here you can click **Verify** in the top toolbar next to the **Save** and **Save As** icons. The verify feature checks your code for any syntax errors.

5. Click **Preview** to see the results.

	Employee Name	Address	ID Number	Salary	Begin Date	Employment.
1	Alexander, Richard A.	CARY, NC..	333-88-1...	$28,000	30JUL1991	9155
2	Alford, Betsy S.	GREENS...	333-88-7...	$32,000	11MAR19...	8930
3	Amato, Robert G.	CARY, NC..	301-97-8...	$52,000	06DEC19...	8660
4	Anaya, John K.	CARY, NC..	333-44-5...	$37,000	05MAY1989	9971
5	Armstrong, Armiste...	RALEIGH,...	333-78-0...	$25,400	05APR19...	9271

The result is shown in days. It would be easier to understand if it was in Years. Let's modify the formula so that the result shows in years.

6. Edit the expression in the Expression field. In the expression field, divide by 365. Then change the format to 8.

Note: A format of 8. shows the numeric field with up to 8 digits and no decimals. Adding a digit after the period allows for any decimal digits up to that digit.

7. Run the Preview to see the results.

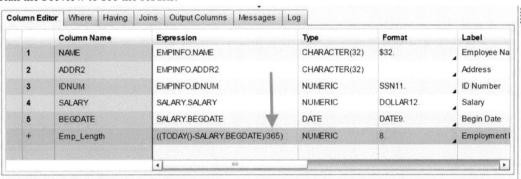

	Column Name	Expression	Type	Format	Label
1	NAME	EMPINFO.NAME	CHARACTER(32)	$32.	Employee Na
2	ADDR2	EMPINFO.ADDR2	CHARACTER(32)		Address
3	IDNUM	EMPINFO.IDNUM	NUMERIC	SSN11.	ID Number
4	SALARY	SALARY.SALARY	NUMERIC	DOLLAR12.	Salary
5	BEGDATE	SALARY.BEGDATE	DATE	DATE9.	Begin Date
+	Emp_Length	((TODAY()-SALARY.BEGDATE)/365)	NUMERIC	8.	Employment I

Column Editor | Where | Having | Joins | Output Columns | Messages | Log

	Employee..	Address	ID Number	Salary	Begin Date	Employm...
1	Alexander...	CARY, NC..	333-88-1...	$28,000	30JUL1991	25
2	Alford, Bet..	GREENS...	333-88-7...	$32,000	11MAR19...	24
3	Amato, R...	CARY, NC..	301-97-8...	$52,000	06DEC19...	24
4	Anaya, Jo...	CARY, NC..	333-44-5...	$37,000	05MAY1989	27
5	Armstron...	RALEIGH,...	333-78-0...	$25,400	05APR19...	25

Result of the new formula

Adding a character data item

We want to plot the states to view our dedicated employees' general locations. Our ADD2 data item has the city, state, and ZIP code of their addresses, but we're only concerned about the state. Using the expression window, we can also use functions on character data to create new columns.

To add a new character column using functions:

1. Add a data item and open the Expression Window.
2. On the **Functions** tab, go to String Manipulation and double-click the SCAN function.
3. On the **Fields** tab, select EMPINFO.ADDR2. This is your string.

Note: The SCAN function in SAS delimits a string into sections based on a certain character and extracts the section that you want. In the SQL expression, the SCAN function is shown as SCAN(string, section to extract, 'delimiter').

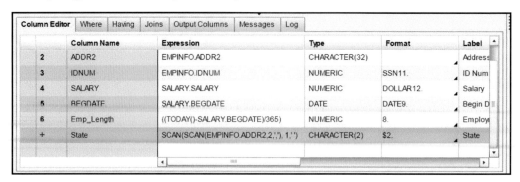

Since our address field is shown as "City, State, Zip" we are going to have to use a SCAN within a SCAN to extract our two letter state.

4. Preview your data again. You can see that now you have the State data field.

	NAME	ADDR2	IDNUM	SALARY	BEGDATE	Emp_Len...	State
1	Alexander...	CARY, NC..	333-88-1...	$28,000	30JUL1991	25	NC
2	Alford, Bet..	GREENS...	333-88-7...	$32,000	11MAR19...	24	NC
3	Amato, R...	CARY, NC..	301-97-8...	$52,000	06DEC19...	24	NC
4	Anaya, Jo...	CARY, NC..	333-44-5...	$37,000	05MAY1989	27	NC
5	Armstron...	RALEIGH,..	333-78-0...	$25,400	05APR19...	25	NC

Here are some other useful SAS functions for your data prep.

*For all available SAS functions, please visit support.sas.com.

STRIP(var)	Removes leading and trailing blanks.
TRANWRD(var, target, replacement)	Replaces specific text (target) with text of your choice (replacement).
COMPRESS(var, text)	Removes elements (text) from your character string.
SUBSTR(var, start position, length)	Extracts a substring from your character string. You can identify the spot (start position) and how many characters to extract (length).
CAT(var1, var2, … varN)	Combines strings. Other variations let you identify a delimiter or how to handle blank spaces. CATS trims all leading and trailing blanks.
UPCASE(var)	Converts all characters in the string to uppercase. LOWCASE and PROPCASE are also functions that can be used to change case.
PUT(var, format)	Changes variable type from numeric to character.
INPUT(var, informat)	Changes variable type from character to numeric.

Filtering the data

There are two ways to filter the data in a data query. Behind the scenes, this is a SQL query, so the WHERE and HAVING clauses are used to filter out what you do not want. A WHERE clause specifies conditions on the input data to filter out before anything is even processed or calculated. The HAVING clause filters out values after processing, which allows it to handle both input data and any aggregate functions or new columns.

Limit data before processing

It is best to use the WHERE clause for all input data and the HAVING clause just for new fields since you are calculating on fewer rows by filtering out any unnecessary data beforehand with the WHERE clause. This can help processing performance since you are minimizing the data beforehand.

Adding a WHERE clause

We only want active employees. The easy way to get this information is to just get those who did not have an end date. From there, we can use a WHERE clause to filter out those with an end date.

To add a where filter:

1. Go to the **Where** tab. This tab enables you to add the WHERE clause.
2. On the **Fields** tab, drag the ENDDATE data item to the SQL expression box.
3. Click the ENDDATE values at the bottom of the **Fields** tab to see a list of values to filter. Click the missing (.) check box.

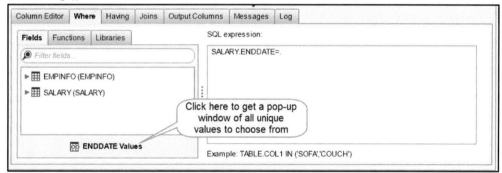

4. Preview the result.

Adding a HAVING clause

Going back to our original reason for querying this data, we only want to see employees with around 25 or more years of experience. We can use the HAVING clause to filter those rows out after we have already made the calculation for the dates since the HAVING clause works as you are exiting the data source.

To add a HAVING clause:

1. Go to the **Having** tab.
2. Find the Emp_Length data item. On the **Fields** tab, this time you have an Output Columns section. Expand it to see the columns set for output. Drag Emp_Length to the SQL expression panel. Notice how it used the formula instead of the column name.

3. Add the >= 25 at the end of the formula.

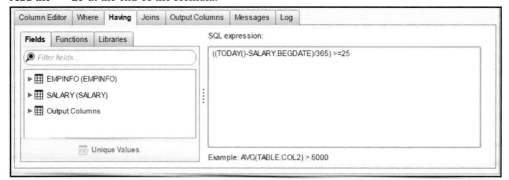

4. Run Preview. Now you see only rows with Emp_Length at or longer than 25.

Create a summary data query

In the previous example, we explored how the Data Builder gives you the ability to combine, filter, and calculate on incoming data sources. Using the power of SQL, the Data Builder can easily summarize data for you. This means taking a certain measure and calculating a statistic on all of the rows of the data set. The Data Builder has a standard set of aggregate functions that you can use on the **Inputs** tab.

When using these aggregate functions, you can also base these statistics on a certain data item in the data set and only aggregate on the distinct values of that data item. This is referred to as using a Group By.

Here are the basic summary statistics available in the Data Builder:

- Count
- Average
- Sum
- Minimum
- Maximum
- Standard Deviation

Steps to summarize data

For this example, we are going to use the same tables in the previous query. We want to look at salaries based on the company's locations as well as the gender of employees working at each location. For this, you start a new query, drag the EMPINFO and SALARY tables into the Design tab, and then add LOCATION, GENDER, and SALARY to the column editor.

To add aggregations to the data query:

1. On the **Inputs** Tab, select **SALARY** as the table from the top drop-down list.
2. In the Default Aggregations section, under the **Auto-Aggregate** field, select **Enable**.

3. Click the **…** button in the Default Aggregations field and select the Pick aggregations.

4. Go to the **Output Columns** tab in the bottom section. Notice how the **Salary** field has now been broken into all of the aggregations that we specified in the previous step. Now preview the data.

	SALARY_SUM	SALARY_STD	SALARY_MIN	SALARY_MAX	SALARY_COUNT	SALARY_AVG	LOCATION	GENDER
1	$14,184,400	$38,603	$12,000	$500,000	$308	$46,053	Cary	M
2	$14,184,400	$38,603	$12,000	$500,000	$308	$46,053	Cary	F
3	$14,184,400	$38,603	$12,000	$500,000	$308	$46,053	Cary	M
4	$14,184,400	$38,603	$12,000	$500,000	$308	$46,053	Cary	M
5	$14,184,400	$38,603	$12,000	$500,000	$308	$46,053	Cary	M

You can see here that for each of the aggregations for Salary, we are getting the same number in each row. This is how an aggregation is done without a Group By. All of the rows are calculated on, and a new column is added for the calculation with the same value being issued for each row. This can be useful in some instances, but it is not what we're looking for in this data set.

5. Go back to the Column Editor on the **Design** tab. Under Aggregations, click the button for Location or Gender, select **Group By**, and then **Apply**.

6. Run the preview.

	SALARY_SUM	SALARY_STD	SALARY_MIN	SALARY_MAX	SALARY_COUNT	SALARY_AVG	LOCATION	GENDER
1	$376,000	$26,344	$16,000	$80,000	$8	$47,000	Austin	F
2	$677,000	$17,413	$13,000	$80,000	$16	$42,313	Austin	M
3	$4,234,500	$24,795	$12,500	$183,000	$94	$45,048	Cary	F
4	$8,545,400	$46,015	$12,000	$500,000	$182	$46,953	Cary	M
5	$38,000		$38,000	$38,000	$1	$38,000	Chicago	F
6	$184,000	$53,003	$24,000	$122,000	$3	$61,333	Chicago	M
7	$31,000		$31,000	$31,000	$1	$31,000	L.A.	F
8	$65,500	$7,425	$27,500	$38,000	$2	$32,750	L.A.	M
9	$33,000		$33,000	$33,000	$1	$33,000	Maryland	M

This time we only get 9 rows of data. That's because we grouped by Location and Gender. Therefore, we get only one row for each of the combinations of Location and Gender available in the data. Then for each one of those combinations, the aggregations are computed. Each of the numbers for the aggregations are based on just the rows that match that Location and Gender.

Updating the code

When you are working in the Data Builder, the application is building SAS and SQL code behind the scenes to develop each query. You can see the results of each of your options by going to the **Code** tab that's right next to the **Design** tab. An example is shown below in the following figure.

Figure 4.3 Data Builder layout

```
Design    Code    Results

All Code  |  Preprocess  |  Postprocess

🔒 ↺

 1 /** QUERY **/
 2
 3 %LET VDB_GRIDHOST=sasbap.demo.sas.com;
 4 %LET VDB_GRIDINSTALLLOC=/opt/TKGrid;
 5 options set=GRIDHOST="sasbap.demo.sas.com";
 6 options set=GRIDINSTALLLOC="/opt/TKGrid";
 7 options validvarname=any validmemname=extend;
 8
 9 /* Register Table Macro */
10 %macro registertable( REPOSITORY=Foundation, REPOSID=, LIBRARY=, TABLE=, FOLDER=, TABLEID=
11
12 /* Mask special characters */
13
```

Each time you make an addition, change, or selection in the Data Builder, the tab contents are updated with the corresponding code. If you scroll through it, you see LIBNAME statements, PROC SQL statements, macros for registering tables, and so on. This is all written in the SAS language, so it is possible to copy this code and run it in SAS Enterprise Guide or use it in a batch process.

The Preprocess and Postprocess links are to blank editors of code where you can put additional SAS statements that run before or after the query runs. For example, if you had another library that you wanted the query to write to, you could have a SAS statement that sends it there as well. You can use the Validate icon at the top to check your SAS statements as well.

Important note!

You can even change the code within the data query by clicking on the lock just below **All Code**. You must remember that once you do unlock the code for editing, you are no longer able to use the **Design** tab. All updates to the query must then be made within the code editor. The only reason to do this would be when you have to make a customization to the query and are comfortable working within the code. Even the Validate option is disabled when you switch to custom modifications.

Scheduling a query

The Data Builder also lets you automate queries through a scheduling feature. This is useful when you have reports that need the data refreshed hourly, daily, monthly, and so on. Within the scheduler, you can also choose if you would like to run it just once or make it a recurring event.

The scheduling feature works by creating a job, deployed job, and deployed flow that get stored in the same location as the query. The job takes care of the data query processes. A deployed job is then created from the job, which places that job into a deployed flow. This is all then scheduled on the scheduling server from the Data Builder. (See the *SAS Visual Analytics: User's Guide*.)

Figure 4.4 Schedule window

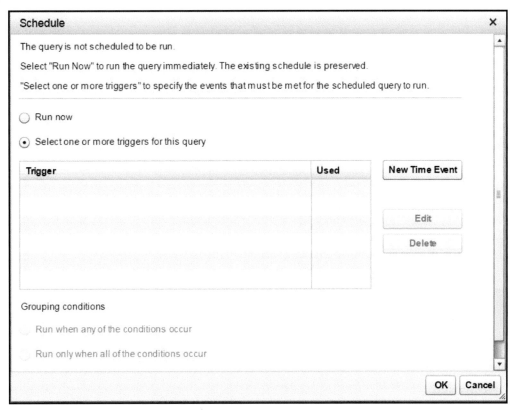

In Figure 4.4, you can schedule a job by clicking the clock icon in the top toolbar of the query. Once the icon is clicked, a schedule window appears.

In this window, you can either **Run now**, which immediately executes the query, or you can **Select one or more triggers for this query**, which is where you can create a Time Event.

A Time Event enables you to schedule the query at a future time and also decide whether you want this to recur on an interval. For this example, we are going to create a Time Event that runs the query at 6:00 AM every weekday.

Figure 4.5 New Time Event window

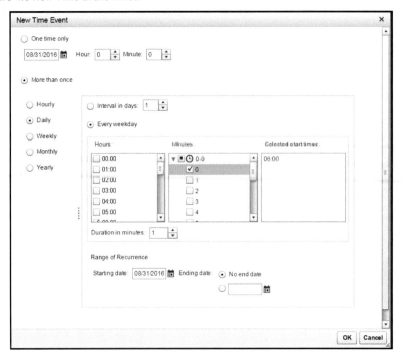

After running this more than once and on a daily schedule, the options appear in the central window to decide on the time. **Interval in days** lets you choose to run it on different days. So if you wanted to run it every other day, you would select that choice and increase the number to 2. We want this to run every weekday, so that is what is selected. In the next window, you can choose the time. **Duration in minutes** at the bottom is where you can declare how long to wait on dependencies if they are involved in your process. So if this query is waiting for another job to complete or file to be created before processing, you can set the number of minutes that it waits for that condition to be met. Then at the end, you can choose when this scheduled query starts and ends.

References

SAS Institute Inc. 2016. *SAS Visual Analytics 7.3: Administration Guide*. Cary, NC: SAS Institute Inc.

SAS Institute Inc. 2015. *SAS Visual Analytics 7.3: User's Guide*. Cary, NC: SAS Institute Inc.

customizing your data visualizations

Once you have completed the basics of SAS Visual Analytics, it is time to dig into the advanced features. In this part, you learn more about creating functional and useful data visualizations. The first two chapters provide in-depth learning for the basic data visualizations along with guidelines from industry experts. The last chapter shows you some of the more advanced statistical objects and features available in the application and how to apply them.

One of the best features of SAS Visual Analytics is the ability to create advanced analytical objects. After reading this chapter, you will be able understand the concepts even with only a limited understanding of the statistics.

- Chapter 5 Visualizing Your Data

  This chapter walks through the simple data objects like line, bar, and pie charts. It explains how to use each object and provides tricks for overcoming the common issues that intermediate users face as they create reports.

- Chapter 6 The Where of Data

  Prepping your data is important to get the geography to work, so guidelines and tips will be provided for that. The chapter discusses the map objects as well as how to use location analysis.

- Chapter 7 Approachable Analytics

  Business users are often intimidated by statistical objects. This chapter covers how to use them along with the analytical features that are found in the Data Explorer. This chapter shows how easy it is to turn data into insights!

chapter five

visualizing your data

No matter which data visualization object you are using, there are still a few rules that apply to all of them. In *Looking Good in Print*, Roger Parker has many examples of how newbies and professionals create ineffective ads, wedding invitations, and newsletters because of a failure to understand how people consume visual information.

Parker provides several makeovers to show what a difference a clean design, a color change, or removing words can make. While he is often re-doing something that was uninspired, he is also careful to note that design is not about a right or wrong technique. It is about *effective* communication. A cardboard sign that reads Yard Sale in a faint, small font is just not as effective as one with large letters and an arrow pointing where to go. A careful person could see the smaller sign and arrive at the sale, but the clearly written sign could draw more attention to itself and capture more customers. Thus, the well-designed sign is more effective.

This is good advice to keep in mind as you read this chapter and select your own visualizations. Think about the most effective way to communicate your message instead of the prettiest, coolest, or even easiest. In this chapter, you learn about the basic data objects, review usage guidelines, and some tips for overcoming common situations.

Elements of an effective data visualization

When crafting a report or a data visualization, keep in mind your message, your audience, and your technique.

Your message: know your point

It seems obvious to start with a statement like "Know your point" or "Make sure you understand your message." Why would someone assemble a data visualization otherwise? The problem introduces itself when you mix a fancy data visualization application with your everyday business analyst. The result is a data visualization that says, "Hey, look what I can do!" It is easy to find cool ways to display the data without considering if it leaves the audience with an ineffective message.

This is where data storytelling enters the picture. The data visualization must either answer a question, clarify a point, or reveal relationships within the data. After seeing the data visualization, the reader should have a takeaway. The takeaway can be as simple as an insight or as complex as a determining what additional paths to explore.

Definitely, analysts should be encouraged to find new ways to display data, but the method should enhance their message and not focus on the software. Think of what your data visualization is trying to communicate to your audience before you create it.

How do I know my data visualization works?

Write your question on the top of the graph and then explain to yourself how the data visualization supports your point. You might be surprised if the data visualization cannot answer the question that you are posing.

Your audience: know who is listening

If someone is inexperienced with a bar chart, then data in a box plot will really take some explaining. The audience might miss your point if they are confused about the data visualization technique. However, if your audience is willing to learn, it might be worth your time to educate them. In general, save your sophisticated data visualization for an advanced crowd.

You also need to consider how well the audience understands the underlying data. If you are showing contact center data, those audience members who are more familiar with the department or topic require less education than someone who walks in off the street. Audience members "in the know" expect issues about inadequate staffing or increased call volumes. Because they understand more about how the data is collected, they're more likely to understand advanced data visualization.

Your technique: follow the KISS principle

Probably you have heard the Keep It Simple Stupid (KISS) principle stated hundreds of times—probably because it is true. Keep your message and chart simple. Audiences can be quickly overwhelmed when there is too much data, visual clutter, or information in the data visualization. They can easily miss your point, which is to direct their attention to what is important.

Keep your message simple and straightforward by removing any unnecessary visual clutter. Your job is to direct the viewer's attention to what is important about the message. The following guidelines can be applied to the majority of your data visualizations and will be discussed further in this chapter:

* Set your X-axis as 0.

* Limit the number of categories shown at once.

* Avoid over-labeling the elements—it creates chart junk.

* If you use an Other category, it should be a small percentage of the data.

Data visualization experts, such as Few and Tufte, remind us that users should not be distracted by the presentation method. Instead, users should be focused on the numbers and the message. Your goal is to simplify the data visualization so that the users can see what you see.

Keep it simple stupid is not an insult

If you were an average mechanic working in combat conditions, you would value an engine whose design team followed the KISS principle. This principle is most often attributed to Kelly Johnson of Lockheed Skunk Works. He led a team who designed spy planes. "Stupid" does not refer to the user, but to the design. It should be so obvious what was wrong with the engine that even someone with an average understanding could repair the engine.

Line charts

Line charts enable you to see trends over time. They have a much more direct purpose than any other chart type. Variations of line charts include area plots, time series charts, and even Pareto charts.

This topic uses the consumer complaint database from the Consumer Financial Protection Bureau (http://www.consumerfinance.gov). This database tracks complaints that are received by financial institutions.

Interpreting the results

In the following figure, you can see the arrival rate for consumer complaints. There is a line for each product. This data visualization provides the following takeaways and follow-up questions:

- During 2013, consumer complaints decreased by half but then started rising again in early 2014. Wonder what caused the decrease and then the increase?

- At the start of 2014, complaints about credit reporting doubled and remained high. Is it possible that not all bureaus were reporting complaints prior to 2014?

- Complaints about bank accounts remained consistent. Wonder if everyone is accurately reporting this data?

The line chart makes following the trends easy. For a two-year period, you could understand how complaints arrived and have some ideas about where to explore next.

Figure 5.1 Line charts display trends

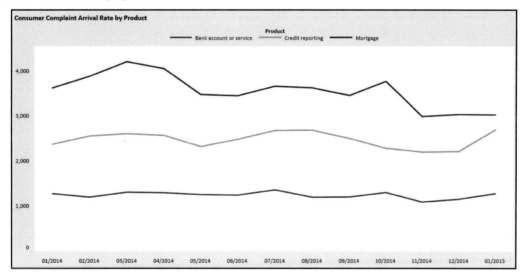

Line charts: guidelines

When producing these charts, keep the following tips in mind:

- X-axis is an ordered time series value, such as year, month, hour, or even minute. Y-axis is a measure such as a count, average, or percentage.

- Use a line to connect each data point. It is easier to understand the trend when the points are connected. The eye glides down the line to understand the trend.

- Indicate missing values with a 0 or a note on the object. If you did not have data for the summer of 2013, then you would want to ensure the viewer understood that the data was missing. Otherwise, your chart might take a huge leap forward, and the viewer would draw the wrong conclusion.

Use 0 as y-axis value

If you need to infuse your chart with some drama, then play with the y-axis value. Consider the following graphs and how much more dramatic the trend seems when we changed the y-axis value. The reported product issues are arriving at a dramatic pace, indicating a product with many issues. When we place the y-axis back at 0, it is easier to understand that there is a flow to the arrival that might even be seasonal.

Figure 5.2 Adding drama to a line chart

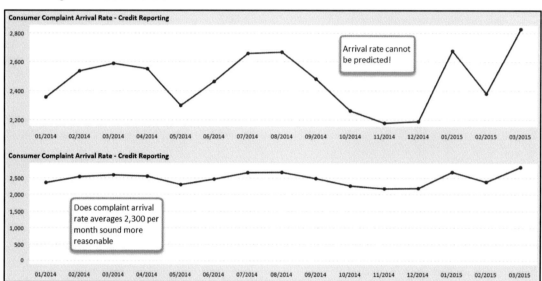

To control the axis values:

1. Select the data object and select the Properties pane.
2. In the Left Y Axis area, type 0 in the **Set fixed minimum** field.
3. You can change the maximum value for the axis by typing a new value in the **Set fixed maximum** field.

Remember the KISS principle

The cognitive psychologist George Miller, in "The Magical Number Seven Plus-or Minus Two," asserts that most people can keep only about five to seven items in their working memory at once. When a chart becomes too busy or has too many lines, it is more difficult for the viewer to absorb the information. Time to apply the KISS principle!

In the following chart, only 11 lines are showing, but you will spend a lot more time studying it as compared to the chart in Figure 5.1. One takeaway is that some products receive few or almost no complaints. If your message is "there's only a few products with issues," then use this chart to emphasize that point. If your point is to show the growth difference in the main areas, use the chart in Figure 5.1.

Figure 5.3 Keep your categories simple

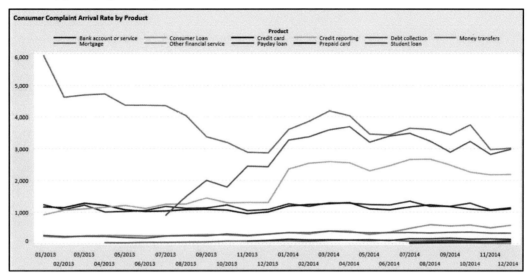

A remedy for this situation is to add a filter that enables the viewer to control how much information is displayed at once. Viewers might only be interested in certain products or want to compare certain products.

Be careful with stacking area plots

SAS Visual Analytics provides three options for a line chart appearance, shown on the **Properties** tab:

- Overlay filled: Shows each line with the filled area behind it.

- Overlay unfilled: Shows a line. This is the default overlay.

- Overlay stacked: Shows all the groups and places one on top of the others. Thus, the data is stacked. This enables the viewer to see how each category contributed over time

If your line chart contains a grouped data item, you can use the overlay filled and overlay stacked choices.

Figure 5.4 Overlay stacked line chart

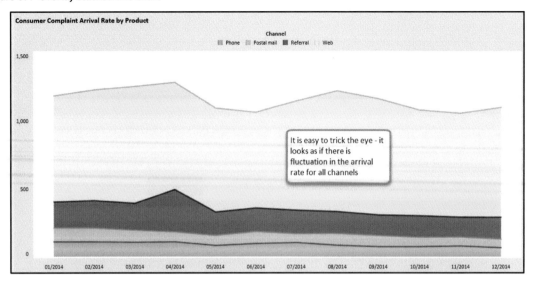

When you are working with stacked area plots, you can easily confuse users if they don't understand your message. The problem lies in how you want to emphasize the parts to the whole. In this example, the data visualization shows an area plot grouped by complaint channel to help the viewer understand which channels drove the overall trend. The question was "Which channel contributed the most to the arrival rate in 2014?"

What if the title was a more generic one—such as "Arrival Rate by Channel?" causing the reader to focus on the arrival rate fluctuations. Although it appears that Phone and Postal mail had a lot of variation, it is not true.

In the following figure, the grouped data item was moved to the Lattice Row role. When you divide the channel into a lattice chart, a different story emerges. In this story, the web channels contribute the most to the trending with the web channel driving everything by the year-end, as shown in the following figure.

Figure 5.5 Use the lattice feature to understand individual categories

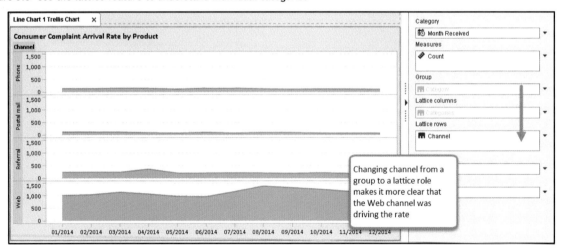

The point with this illustration is not that the stacked area plot is bad but instead the question is, "Was it effective?" This example is to help you understand how a data visualization was misinterpreted despite our best intentions.

Line charts: tips and tricks

Here's some tips and tricks to help you work with common situations in line charts.

Tip 1: Dealing with a long timeline

When you have a long timeline that you want to show, your data visualization might appear too crunched. You can add a sliding window under the data object to enable the user to expand and focus on the periods of interest. From the **Properties** pane, click the **Show overview axis** check box to add the feature.

Figure 5.6 Sliding window to see more data

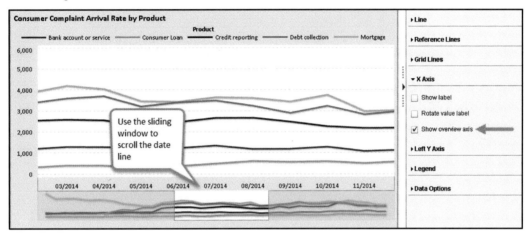

The user can expand the window to see all dates on the chart or focus the timeline on a central period.

Tip 2: Avoiding chart junk

If you read any of the data visualization pioneer Edward Tufte's books, you quickly learn that he is a minimalist. He repeats often that "the data should do the talking," "show only the data," and so on. He provides multiple examples of what he calls chart junk. Tufte uses a data-to-ink ratio to draw out his examples, but it's much simpler to apply his technique than a fancy formula.

Don't add unneeded items, callouts, and decorations to your chart. When you add the data labels to the lines, it quickly changes the flavor of the chart. Notice how hard it is to see the trend when you are focused on reading the values. You make the viewer think the value has more importance than it does.

Figure 5.7 Manage your data

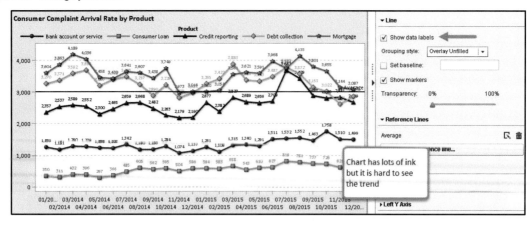

Remember that this is a trend chart. It's not about individual values; it's about how the values changed over time. Use a bar chart or a table if the individual number is important. You might notice that axis labels were added—but do they really assist the reader? It seems clear that the x-axis is a month value item, and the y-axis is a count. The title explains that the chart provides trending for arrival rate. You decide whether it adds detail or ineffective clutter.

Is it information or decoration?

While Tufte discusses minimalization, Alberto Cairo, author of *The Functional Art*, reminds designers that the task is message clarity, not simplification. Too often designers sacrifice content for style and lose their audience. Each visualization is different and this is where your knowledge and discernment enters the design process.

Tip 3: Transparency can be your enemy

SAS Visual Analytics enables you to overlay the lines. So instead of showing the parts to the whole (all complaints broken out by product), you can see how each line contributed over time—as you see in the following figure. The Grouping Style is Overlay Filled, which shows each item with a fill pattern beneath it. You can change the Transparency to 50% to get a nicer look.

Figure 5.8 Colors do not match the Legend

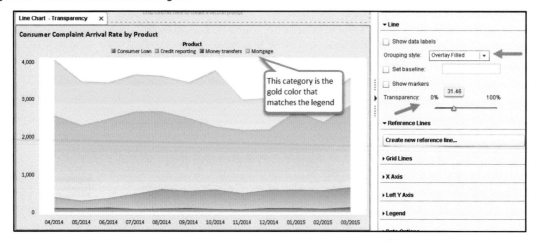

The problem is that the Mortgage is covering the other categories and making everything appear as brown and orange. One remedy for this situation is to stack the numbers so that we can see how each contributed to the total value over time. The grouping style was changed to Stack Filled.

Figure 5.9 Stack the grouped items to clarify your point

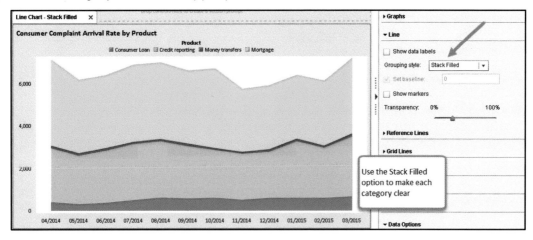

Tip 4: Keeping the date intervals

It is more difficult for the user to understand a timeline when there are missing dates. You might also want to extend the timeline to show the future. You have a few options when you want to include intervals that do not exist in your data.

Changing the data

You can change your data. In the following figure, we want to extend the data to the end of year. Since it is the beginning of the year, we don't have data for the other months yet.

Figure 5.10 Add dates without values

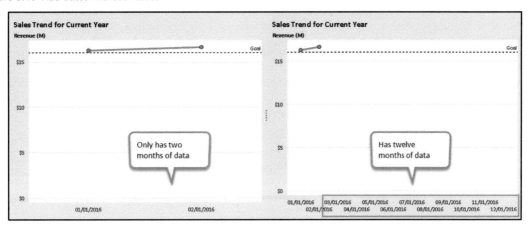

To correct the issue, we can update the date values in the data. In the following example, a helper data set contains only the variable Month and a date for the entire year. This data set was appended to my main data set. SAS Visual Analytics can use the new variable even if the other variables are empty. Notice that the other rows do not have any values, so SAS Visual Analytics has nothing to display. Keep in mind, if you use these rows in calculations, that you might need to work around the missing values or create filters to exclude them.

Figure 5.11 Modifying your data source

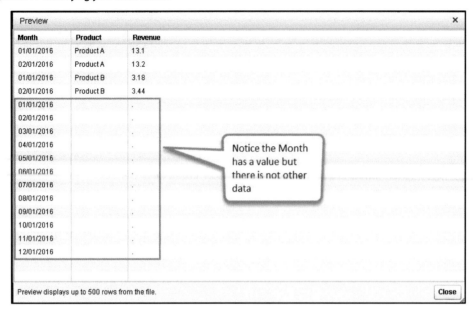

Using a time series chart

There is a time series data object especially for dates and trend charts. The time series object doesn't mind if you only have data for two months. You can use the **Properties** menu to change the fixed minimum and maximum dates. Of course, any report using this method might have to be updated each year, but that seems like a small inconvenience.

Figure 5.12 Time series plot

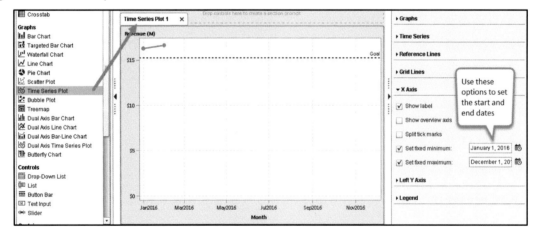

Bar charts

Bar charts provide more detailed information than line charts. This chart type makes it easier to compare exact quantitative categories. There are two types of bar charts: vertical and horizontal. Vertical charts compare categories while horizontal charts work especially well for ranking.

Interpreting the results

In the following figure, you see the count of all consumer complaints received in 2013. The x-axis is categorical data, so no order is necessary. The y-axis is the value that indicates the length of the bar.

Here's what we learn:

- Consumers had as much concern about mortgages as all other categories combined.

- Money transfers and payday loans generated few complaints compared to the other categories.

- Bank account, credit cards, credit reporting, and debt collection had similar complaint counts.

The bar chart makes it easy to compare categories. In this case, you learn that mortgage complaints account for most of the work.

Figure 5.13 Example bar chart

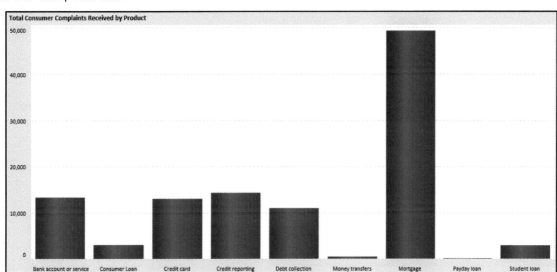

Bar charts: guidelines

When producing these charts, keep the following tips in mind:

- Allow white space between the bars and keep the bars at the same distance.

- Keep bars the same color when the data is a single category. Unless your whole package is using a theme for a particular category, multiple colors usually only distract the viewer.

- Avoid using patterns or anything unusual for the bars. It is distracting.

- Viewers might have a hard time understanding vertical charts when there are more than 10 categories. Add a filter to allow the viewer to determine what is comfortable.

Choosing a line chart or a bar chart

When showing timeline data, you can use a line chart or a bar chart. This is an occasion where you have to determine which is more effective in communicating your point. In the following figure, the same data is plotted both ways. The line chart allows the eye to see the trend while the bar chart highlights specific values better. As discussed at the beginning of the chapter, you have to decide what your message is and what you are trying to show.

Figure 5.14 Bar chart versus a line chart

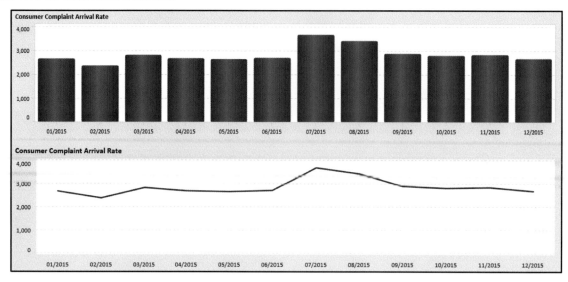

Choosing a grouped chart or a stacked chart

Bar charts really shine when comparing values across groups. There are two ways to compare values with a bar chart: stacked and grouped (or clustered). Determine whether your message is about the whole or the parts. Use a stacked chart to show the part-to-the-whole and the grouped charts to show the contribution by category.

A stacked chart reveals the part-to-the-whole similar to a pie chart. Use this chart when you want the viewer to consider each category as a whole more than the values within the category. In the following figure, you get a sense of how many more complaints are about mortgages than about the other categories.

Figure 5.15 Part to the whole

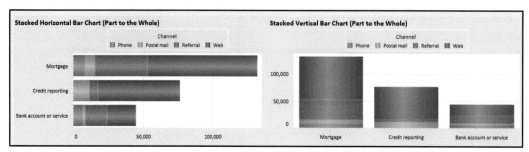

Grouped charts are easier to compare across categories. Notice that the white space is between Product instead of Channel. Your eyes take the visual clue that those items are related within the grouping. This chart does give you a sense of overall counts and it does show the web channel as the most popular contact method. What you also see is that almost no one uses postal mail to complain about his or her bank account, but it is a popular method for the other categories. You most likely didn't notice that, overall, Mortgage had the highest total complaints.

Figure 5.16 Contribution by category

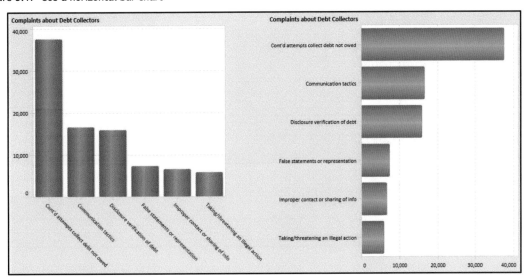

Bar charts: tips and tricks

Here's some tricks for resolving common situations that occur when using bar charts.

Tip 1: Rescue your long labels and your viewer

Horizontal bar charts assist with making comparisons but are also useful if your labels are long. Notice the difference in the labels in this example. The slanted labels are difficult to read mainly because they are too long.

Figure 5.17 Use a horizontal bar chart

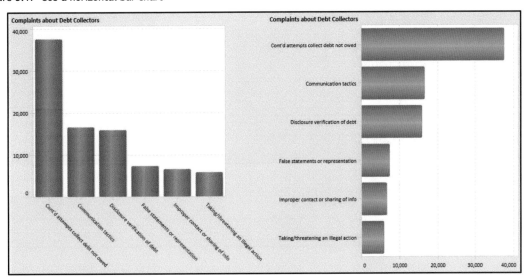

- Use the **Ranks** menu to limit the category to the top 5 or 10 by count or percentage. You can also show the bottom 5 or 10. The **Ranks** menu enables you to select a category and a measure. If you have an item that is tied (for example, two of the items rank as number 3), check the **Ties** check box to display both.

- Use the **All Other** check box to create another item where the remaining items are combined into one. In the following figure, you can see that last bar is called All Other. You want to ensure that this item is a smaller amount than the other bars. Otherwise, the ranking might appear as if you are ignoring a large part of the data.

Figure 5.18 Using the ranks pane

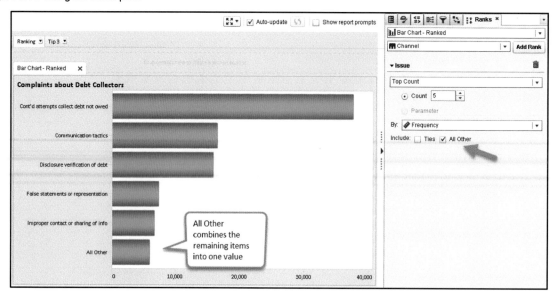

Tip 2: Show the complete percentage

In some instances, you might want to convert a count to a percentage to show the comparison as a whole. If you have a grouped bar chart, you can convert it quickly using the **Properties** tab. Change the grouping scale to **Normalize groups to 100%**. SAS Visual Analytics converts the numbers to percentages and shows the breakout.

Figure 5.19 Change the grouping scale to show 100%

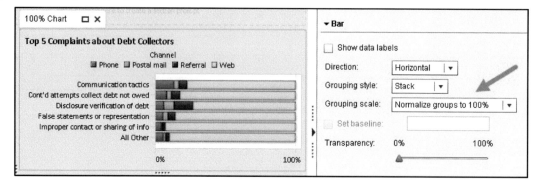

Tip 3: Using a butterfly chart

Butterfly charts are similar to grouped charts but enable the user to focus on two measures. The measures are placed back to back so that they have wings like a butterfly. The following example is from a customer service organization. The butterfly chart compares tickets resolved on first contact to the customer satisfaction rating for the event. Team B resolves more tickets on first contact and has the highest customer satisfaction rating. Likewise, the team with the lower first contact resolution also has the lower satisfaction.

This data object requires that both measures be the same type. In our example, both measures are percentages. If you want to compare measures of different types, you can modify this data object using the Custom Chart Builder feature. The Custom Chart Builder enables you to combine multiple data objects. Refer to the user documentation for more details about the Custom Chart Builder feature.

Figure 5.20 Using a butterfly chart

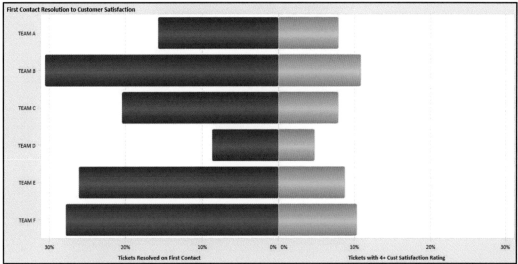

Pie and donut charts

Pie and donut charts show the parts-to-the-whole relationship of data. Many data visualization experts do not advocate using pie charts because as Stephen Few says "they communicate information poorly." If you want to use one of these charts, make sure that you understand the guidelines for doing it correctly. Generally, these charts offer visual relief in a sea of text or boxes. In recent years, donut charts have become popular in infographics.

Starting in release 8.1, SAS Visual Analytics contains donut charts as an option. Although donut charts are not shown in this topic, the same visualization rules apply.

Interpreting the results

A pie chart shows how each slice contributes to the entire pie. Each slice is a category, and a reader should quickly look at the chart and have an answer. Consider the following pie charts from a user survey. These pie charts work because they have few categories and you can quickly read the answers for results. A pie chart is not about precision in value. Does it matter if someone likes pie 72% or 75%? The takeaway remains that people really like pie but might not make them every day.

Figure 5.21 Easy-to-understand pie charts

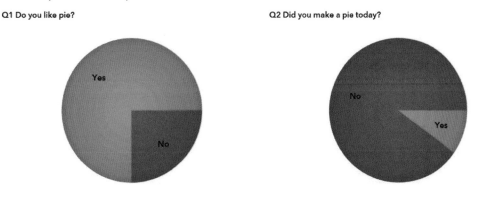

When the same information is presented in a table, the information is more precise and takes up less space. Truthfully, the pie charts revealed the Yes and No answers to the question quicker, but they do use a lot of space. You could argue that a bar chart is equally effective and uses the same space.

Figure 5.22 Table compared to a pie chart

Responses ▲	No	Yes	Total
Survey Questions ▲			
Did you make a pie today?	90	10	100
Do you like pie?	25	75	100

Often, data visualization newbies try to do too much with a pie chart, and it just goes wrong. They do not understand how or when to use a pie chart. Consider the following example. You spend more time correlating labels to slices and comparing the channel details so that you get overwhelmed. It is difficult to know what the author was trying to communicate.

Figure 5.23 Example of why pie charts are ineffective

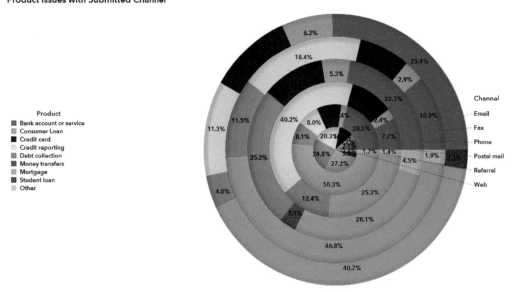

The preceding figure is why many data visualization experts hate pie charts. They argue that pie charts use too much space. Often foregoing a pie chart for a short statement is preferable.

Pie and donut charts: guidelines

Here are the guidelines for how to use a pie chart to display your data.

- Parts to a whole equal 100% – *always*. If your pie chart does not equal 100%, tell the reader in a footnote.

- Limit to 4 or 5 categories, but it's better when one category is significant percentage-wise.

- Legends are superfluous when a pie chart is done correctly.

Removing the legend

You can avoid using a legend if you allow the tool to place the labels. From the **Properties** menu, turn on the **Show category labels** check box. This places the category labels on the pie chart, making it easier to read. Use the **Data label location** to control where the label is placed. You might want the labels on the outside of the chart to keep it consistent. You can choose to have the percentage show by clicking the **Show values as percentage of total** check box. However, a pie chart works best when one category is dominant. This makes the values unnecessary.

Figure 5.24 Good pie charts don't need a legend

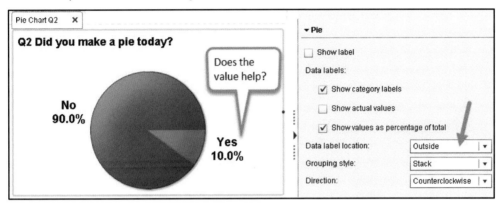

To remove the legend, click the Show Legend check box in the **Properties** panel.

Is the comparison effective?

In the following figure, the data visualization compares complaint arrival by channel. You have 5 seconds to tell me the second most popular channel to receive a complaint. It's hard to do. This is not a bad way to display data, but is it effective? In some cases, it is difficult to tell if Referral and Web generated the same amount. Our eyes are not adept at reading angles and determining which is larger.

It's much easier to understand the complaints by channel when we look at the horizontal bar chart. This is another example where a bar chart makes it easier to understand the data. Using the bars, your eye has an easier time determining the amounts.

Figure 5.25 Too many comparisons

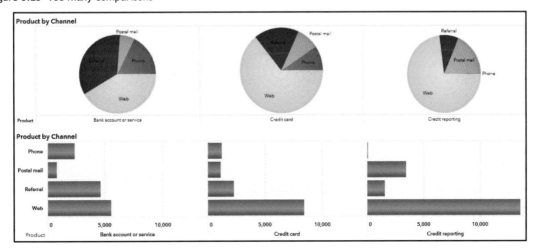

Pie and donut charts: tips and tricks

Use the following tips to overcome common issues.

Tip 1: Limit the categories to focus the reader's attention

When you have too many categorical values in a pie chart, you make the reader's job ten times more difficult. The reader might ask themselves "Is this a ranking?" or "Do these other categories really matter? Why am I being shown this?" Notice how going back and forth between the colors and legend is frustrating. In the following figure, the same data is shown as a pie chart and as a horizontal bar chart. Notice how much easier it is in the horizontal bar chart to determine the products that receive the most complaints.

Figure 5.26 When a bar chart works better

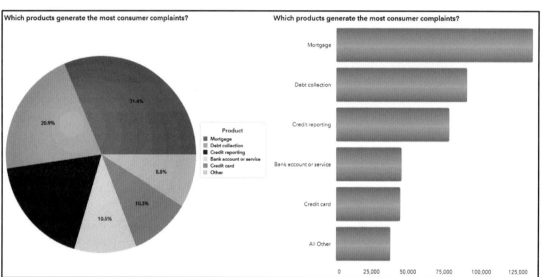

Tip 2: Keep categories a consistent color

If you are presenting survey data, then you have multiple pie charts in a row. In this case, you want the Yes/No category to have a consistent color. You can use a display rule to map the values to a set color.

Click the data object and select **Add Display Rule**. When prompted, select **Color-mapped values**.

Then, create a line for each category and assign the color to it. In the following figure, you can see that Yes has been changed to teal and No changed to orange. You can set as many values as you want.

Figure 5.27 Setting color-mapped values

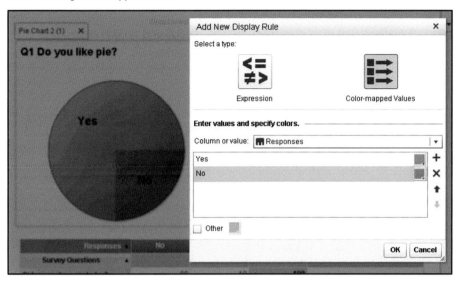

Tip 3: Pie chart as a dashboard gauge

If you are working on a dashboard, sometimes you want to display a single value, similar to the way infographics look. You could use a single cell in a list table, but here's a more clever method. Use an invisible pie chart.

This method retains the value and title but hides the pie itself. Let's build the last one called Unique Customers. For this example, we need a distinct count of the companies that received complaints for the time period and product. This value must be calculated on-the-fly. We can use the Distinct Count feature to count the companies in the data set. When the viewer selects a value from the drop-down list, the value is immediately re-calculated.

Here's the steps for creating a distinct count aggregated measure and creating the infographic look.

1. To create the distinct count value, right-click the Company data item. This data item is a character value that contains the name of each company. The new value appears in the Aggregated Measure area called Company (Distinct Count).

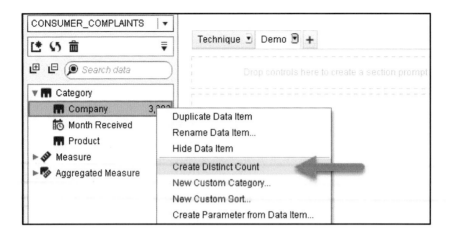

2. Create a new calculated item that is character-based. A pie chart requires the following roles: category and measure. For this example, we need a dummy value that does not cause any filtering to occur.

   a. Select **New Calculated Item** from the **Data** drop-down list.

   b. Type Category Placeholder in the **Name** field.

   c. Change **Result type** to Character.

   d. Type DUMMY in the field. This value never appears anywhere, and later it reminds you why you created it.

   e. Save the calculated item.

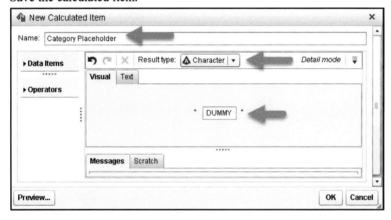

3. Create a new pie chart data item. On the **Roles** tab, add **Category Placeholder** and **Company** (Distinct Count) data items.

4. On the **Properties** tab, do the following:

   a. Uncheck the **Show label** check box.

   b. Click the **Show actual values** check box.

   c. Change the **Data label location** to Inside.

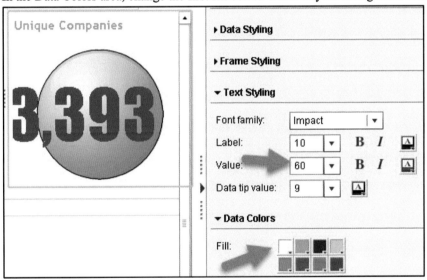

5. On the **Styles** tab, do the following:

    a. In the Data Styling area, change the Data Skin to Gloss. This action causes the HTML5 viewer to display the pie chart as white.

    b. In the Text Styling area, change the Value font size to 60. Adjust the font color and font family if desired.

    c. In the Data Colors area, change the first fill box to White or your background color.

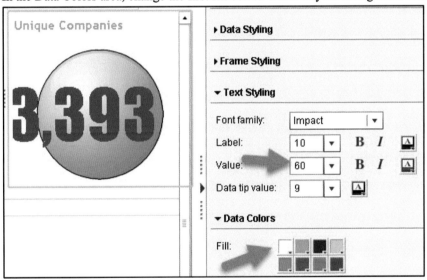

6. Save your report and look it in the Report Viewer application. With the drop-down filters in place, your new value will change as the selections change.

Treemaps

Treemaps enable viewers to see the results from a large number of categories. A treemap is a more efficient use of space than a bar chart. These data objects are especially good for hierarchical data to reveal overall patterns in the data.

Interpreting the results

This object shows the complaints about mortgages for several companies. The box size indicates the number of complaints for 2015. The larger the box, the more complaints the company received. This enables the viewer to understand how many companies are in the category and then the complaint count. The color of the square indicates the percentage change in complaints. If the color is darker, the company received more complaints for 2015 than for 2014. You can filter the results. We might want to remove companies that had few complaints in one year and then no complaints the next year.

Figure 5.28 Treemap example

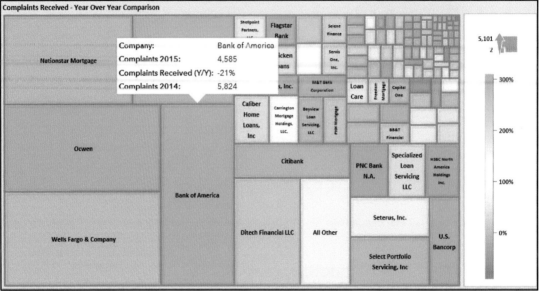

Here's what we learn from this data visualization:

- The larger financial institutions receive more complaints. This is not surprising since they probably hold more mortgages. Notice that it is difficult to judge the exact number of complaints. You just know that it is a similar count.

- You might find that you can group boxes by size and thus understand how the financial institutions are similar. In the lower right of the treemap, there is a second group of institutions that received a similar number of complaints. In the top right, another group received a similar amount.

- We can see that many of the companies shown in teal decreased the complaints or maybe just received a similar number as the year before. By positioning your pointer over Bank of America, we see a 21% decrease in complaints.

The treemap provides an overview of many categories at once in a very small area. By using color, you can add an extra dimension to the analysis.

Treemaps: guidelines

When using a treemap, here are some guidelines.

Add two measures – one for size and one for difference

You can use two or three measures for this chart. The first measure is a sum, count, or average value. The second measure can be a rating, percentage difference, or another value that indicates a change. In Figure 5.27, the size of the box is the sum of complaints, and the color is the year-over-year percentage difference.

You can create the second measure with an aggregated measure or with a derived measure. With a derived measure, you can calculate time-based values to show a percentage change or difference. See the "Tables and Crosstabs" topic in this chapter for a detailed discussion about derived measures.

Add the legend

Like the bubble plot, the legend enables the user to understand what the box size indicates and how the color is judged. You can add the legend by clicking the **Legend** check box on the **Properties** menu. Use the Style pane to control the appearance of the legend, such as background color and font size.

Figure 5.29 Find the right location for your legend

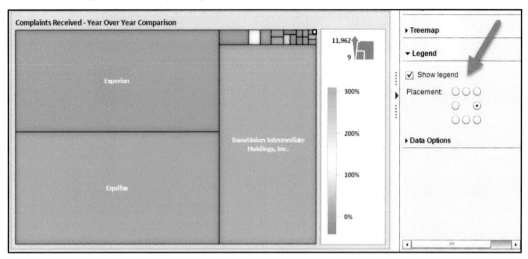

Treemaps: tips and tricks

Use the following tips and tricks when creating treemaps.

Tip 1: Gradient values are easier to interpret

If you do not supply a third measure, all of the boxes are the same color. When you add the third measure, SAS Visual Analytics changes the gradient range from red to green. You can change the color by clicking on the color boxes on the Style menu. If your data is not performance related, you might want the values to be a gradient of a single color.

Figure 5.30 Gradients are easier to understand

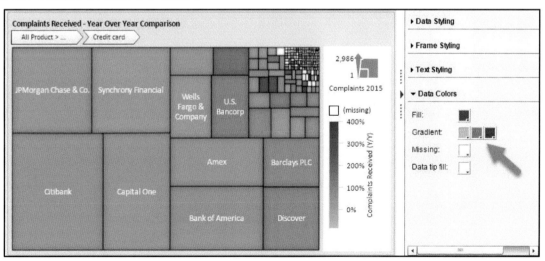

Notice in Figure 5.30 when values are missing, the color is set to white. You can also control that color. If values are missing, it might make more sense to use yellow or gray to highlight the situation.

You can also use the Display Rules to control the colors. This enables you to provide exact color choices. In the preceding example, you might want to highlight companies who decreased their overall complaint count. Refer to the "Tip 1: Using display rules" topic for instructions on creating display rules.

Tip 2: Hierarchies make it easier to navigate the tree

Use a hierarchy to enable the user to drill-down through the boxes. For the preceding treemap, it was showing the company only. We can add a hierarchy that goes from the product to the company at the top and specific issues at the end. In the following figure, you can see that the user has drilled down from Products to a specific vendor. The last level of the hierarchy shows the issues.

Figure 5.31 Users can drill-down with a hierarchy

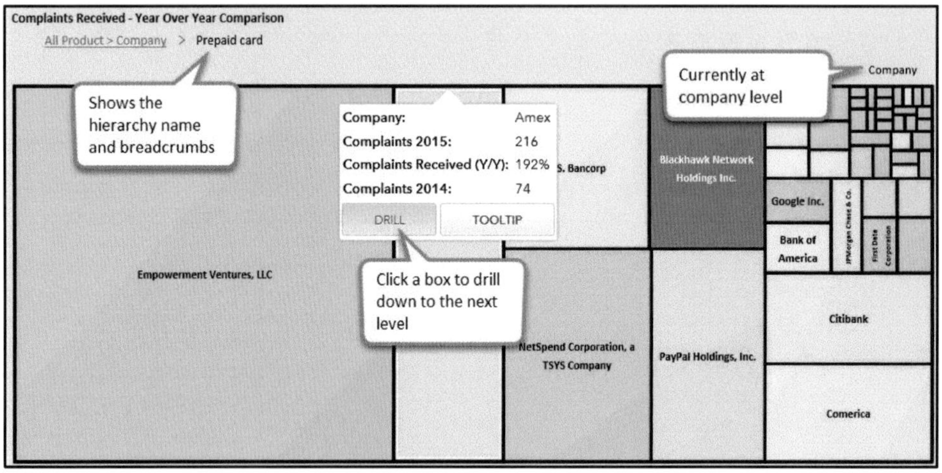

To build a hierarchy:

1. Click the arrow icon and click the **New Hierarchy** choice.
2. Drag the items that you want to the hierarchy. The order in which they are placed is how the hierarchy appears.
3. In this example, the data items are ordered by Product ▶ Sub-product ▶ Company.
4. Provide a name for the hierarchy. Click **OK**.

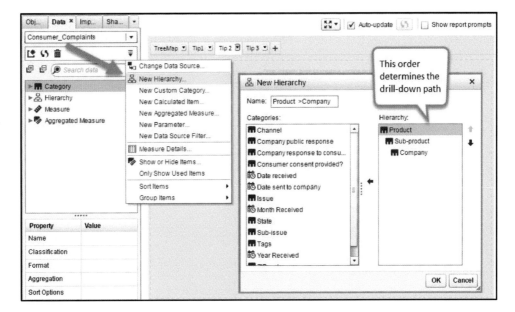

The hierarchy data item is added to the Hierarchy area on the **Data** menu. It is then added to the treemap.

Waterfall charts

Waterfall charts show how a cumulative value increments or decrements. These charts have many names, including *progressive bar chart*, *bridge chart*, and *flying bricks chart*. This chart is another example of understanding the part-to-the-whole values discussed in the "Using Categorical Charts" topic. These charts are commonly used in financial metrics to show a profit-and-loss statement.

This data visualization is considered a good alternative to a pie chart. It is easier for the user to deconstruct what happened to a value, such as revenue.

Interpreting the results

Waterfall charts help the user analyze how a value changed and what contributed to the change. In the following figure, you can see the how the costs change the revenue and the resulting profits. The decreasing value is shown as red, and the increasing value is shown as green. The decreasing values go down, and increasing values rise up. The final amount called Profit After is shown as the blue bar.

Figure 5.32 Example waterfall chart shows revenue change

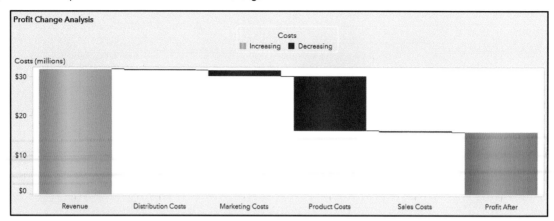

What we learn from this data visualization:

- The largest cost goes toward producing the products. Reducing costs in this area might have a larger overall impact.

- The other costs are minuscule compared to product cost.

Waterfall charts: guidelines for use

Waterfall charts are used to show how a single value changed, such as Revenue. You want to keep this data visualization simple using the similar guidelines used for a pie chart. The exception is that you can have more than five categories since the bars are used.

Add the initial and final values

If your data source only has the values by category, you might want to add the starting and ending value. Select the **Set initial value** and **Show Final (cumulative)** check boxes to add these bars to the chart. You can also change the labels.

Figure 5.33 Adding the initial and final values

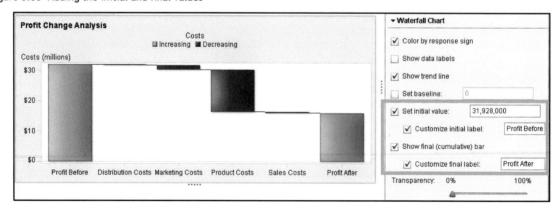

Adding the response sign

You can allow negative values to show as red and positive values to show as green. In the Properties window, select the **Color by response sign** check box. If your data source does not have negative values, then the data object might not be displayed properly.

You can create a negative value using a calculated item. In the following figure, Order Product Cost was multiplied by -1 to create a negative value. Refer to the "Creating Your First Dashboard" chapter for more details about creating a calculated item.

Figure 5.34 Creating a calculated item

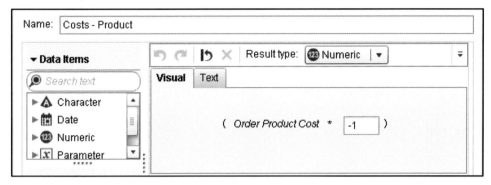

Waterfall charts: tips and tricks

The following tips and tricks can be used with other data objects, but might come in handy when working with these data objects in particular.

Tip 1: Consider a summary data source

If your data is tall and wide, then it might not work with the waterfall chart. Our example data table VA_SAMPLE_SMALLINSIGHTS uses a wide format. This means that the data items are each in their own column and listed as a separate data item.

Figure 5.35 Wide data

Transaction Month ▲	Order Total	Order Distribution Cost	Order Marketing Cost	Order Product Cost	Order Sales Cost
01/2013	$5,460,811	$39,425	$262,387	$2,446,643	$37,960
02/2013	$4,068,557	$31,647	$192,036	$1,800,384	$34,161
03/2013	$3,907,057	$31,745	$181,165	$1,706,472	$37,037
04/2013	$3,712,785	$30,886	$169,285	$1,601,500	$37,414
05/2013	$2,976,536	$27,404	$131,731	$1,260,654	$37,728
06/2013	$2,399,500	$24,489	$106,355	$1,023,600	$33,383
07/2013	$2,635,212	$25,012	$125,297	$1,194,866	$33,779
08/2013	$2,195,139	$20,701	$97,441	$929,524	$28,886
09/2013	$2,163,279	$21,047	$95,805	$918,484	$31,037
10/2013	$2,409,220	$24,211	$106,193	$1,023,345	$38,992
	$31,928,096	$276,567	$1,467,694	$13,905,471	$350,376

The waterfall chart shows how each value contributes to a single category for 2013. The values need to be summarized and transposed as shown in the following figure:

Figure 5.36 Tall data

Year ▲	Item	Costs
2013	Marketing Costs	($1,467,693)
2013	Product Costs	($13,905,471)
2013	Revenue	$31,928,096
2013	Sales Costs	($350,374)
2013	Distribution Costs	($276,565)
		$15,927,993

Since this is a simple conversion, you might find it easier to prepare this chart if you use a summary table that you create outside of SAS Visual Analytics. You can use multiple data sources on the same section. In the following figure, you can see the text file that was created in Notepad and later imported into SAS Visual Analytics to keep this example simple.

Figure 5.37 Creating summary data

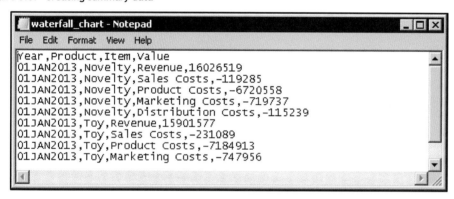

This data contains additional columns, so it can be used with the existing data source that has Year and Product Line as data items. This is a simple way to transpose the data. You could also create this data set in SAS Studio or the Data Builder. Refer to the "Data Builder Name" chapter for more details.

Tip 2: Use a custom sort for the category

With the waterfall chart, you might want the categories to display in a specific order. You can use the custom sort option to change the order. For the data object in Figure 5.37, the categories required a custom sort.

To add a custom sort to a category, right-click the category name and select **New Custom Sort**. Then drag the items from the Category Data column to the Sorted Items column. Place the data items in the desired sort order. Your data object updates automatically.

Figure 5.38 Use a custom sort

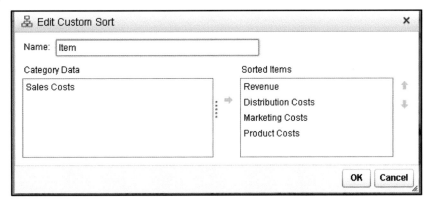

Tip 3: Use section filtering for different data sources

Since the data source needs to work with the other section elements, those were added to the file. For example, this waterfall chart is in the same section as a bar chart. Both of the data elements are controlled by drop-down lists in the section filter. You want the control to work on all of the data objects.

Figure 5.39 Section filtering for different data sources

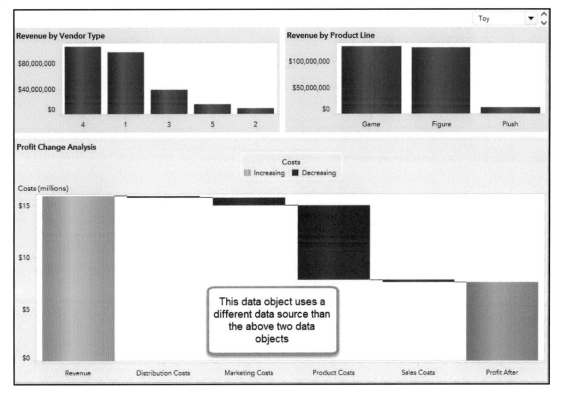

If the data sources have the same values, you can map the data sources. The data items do not need to have the same name. After adding your data objects and control, right-click the control and select **Edit Data Source Mapping**. In the **Source** field, select the data items for the Source and the Target that should be mapped. You can have multiple interactions.

Figure 5.40 Mapping data sources to the controls

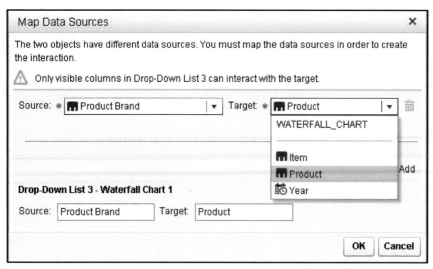

Gauges

Gauges contain a single measurement and communicate a simple message: "Am I doing okay?" If you think about a gas gauge in a vehicle, it tells you how much gas is in the tank. The range is typically 0% to 100% full. You are expected to know how much gas you want in the tank. When translated to a performance dashboard, it uses the same message: *where are you now?*

Interpreting results

The following dashboard gauges measure the organization objectives. The objective or key performance indicator (KPI) is written above the gauge. For each gauge, there is a range of values and a color associated with the value. Take time to review the measures on each of the ranges.

Figure 5.41 Using dashboard gauges

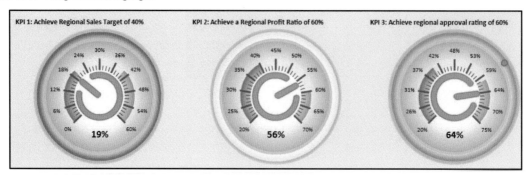

Here's what we can learn from each gauge:

- For KPI 1, the team is failing to meet their target. The value is 19%, which is the lower range and indicated as red. This indicates that the team needs to take action.

- For KPI 2, the team is close to the 60% but not on track.

- For KPI 3, the team is achieving the established goal.

Gauges: Guidelines

Designers talk about gauges with the same disdain usually reserved for pie charts. Gauges have been misused a lot because users do not understand what data to use with them.

Choose the correct gauge

SAS Visual Analytics has five gauges available. The following figure contains examples of the available gauges.

Figure 5.42 Available gauges

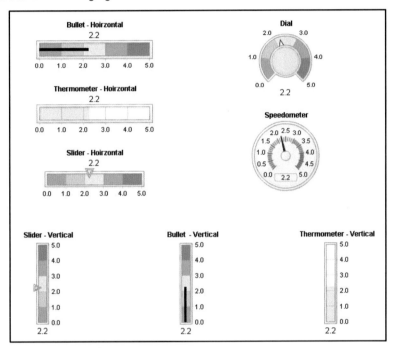

The bullet, thermometer, and slider can be horizontal or vertical, so it appears that there are three additional ones. You can also change the style for each of the gauges to get a different look.

Each gauge is measuring customer satisfaction where the rating can be 1 to 5. The target is 4.5. You can see the target as a notch. The colors use a method called trafficlighting where red indicates poor performance and blue indicates acceptable performance. You can compare how each gauge indicates performance. For example, the thermometer shows only one color. The slider measurement is highlighted.

Is there a best gauge?

In his *Information Dashboard Design* book, Few suggests that the bullet chart is the easiest gauge to read and understand. The user can see where within the range the current performance falls. This gauge also shows each range. Few recommends using blue instead of green for the successful measure. He indicates that color-blind users will have difficulty seeing the difference between green and red and will not be able interpret the chart correctly.

Use data that makes sense

A gauge makes the most sense when using a measurement that has a goal. Many users make the mistake of using a data item that does not fit a gauge. The data item might not be performance-related, so the gauge confuses the user.

In the following figure, the vendor location by average distance in miles is shown for the facility. You want your vendors close to your facility, but do organizations really set a performance goal for the task? This seems more like data that would be shared as part of a presentation when persuading management to open a new facility. Wouldn't it make more sense to show this data as a bar chart or even on a map?

Figure 5.43 Gauges that do not make sense

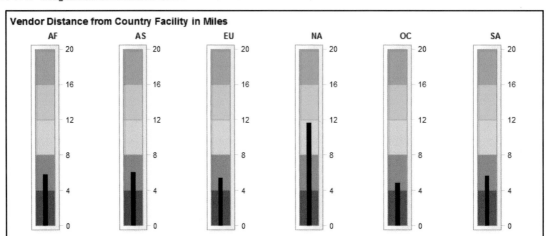

In some cases, you can turn a summed or averaged value into a percentage. This makes it easier to understand. In Figure 5.43, the gauges measured three different data items: sales target, profitability, and approval rating. However, notice that these data items were all converted to a percentage. Each of these data items also had an associated target.

Gauges: tips and tricks

Use the following tips and tricks when working with gauges.

Tip 1: Use display rules

Besides setting the color, the display rules determine the ranges. When creating a display rule, you are adding the intervals and assigning colors to each interval. In the following figure, you can see that there are five intervals that are each 20%.

Figure 5.44 Setting gauge by 20% intervals

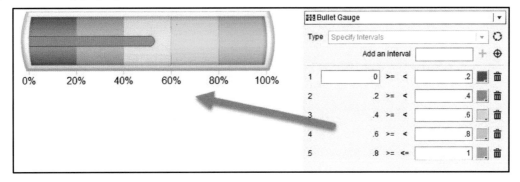

The intervals can be integers and can use a different range of colors. Click the color block to select a new color. The following figure shows intervals as whole numbers with a blue range. This gauge is used to show Customer Satisfaction ratings.

Figure 5.45 Setting gauge by single intervals

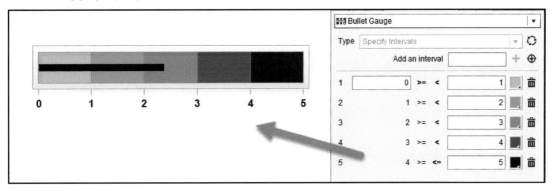

If you need help getting started, click the Auto populate interval icon. In the Populate Intervals window, select the number of intervals. Then enter the minimum or starting number in the Lower Bounds and the maximum number in the Upper Bounds. SAS Visual Analytics suggests the interval ranges that you can then edit.

Figure 5.46 Auto populate intervals

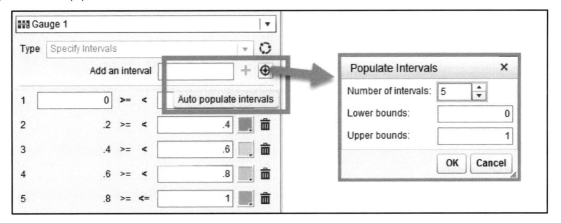

Tip 2: Add a shared rule

If your dashboard has several gauges that all use the same display rules, then create a shared rule. A shared rule enables you to create the display rule once and use it multiple times. You can have as many shared rules as you need.

In this example, each of these gauges uses a 0 to 100% scale where over 90% is the desired goal. To create the shared rule:

1. Create your display rule and click the Shared Rule icon.

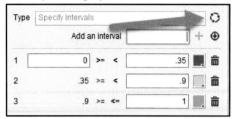

2. When prompted, type the name of the shared rule. Make sure that you are descriptive enough so you will remember later what the display rule measures. The shared rule is applied to the current gauge automatically.

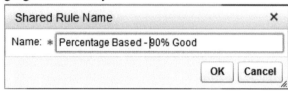

3. To apply the shared rule to a gauge, select **Use a Shared Display Rule** choice from the **Type** field. Then select the desired rule.

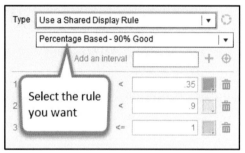

If you later decide that you don't want to use the shared rule, select **Specify Intervals from the Type** field. The gauge then allows you to use the value you want.

Tables and cross tabs

Tables are used when you want to show specific values or detailed information. SAS Visual Analytics has two data objects for listing data: List Table and Crosstab.

Interpreting the results

Tables show detailed information. In the following figure, you can see the approval ratings for sales rep 003R that we created in the "Building Your First Dashboard" chapter. The table has several columns, some with category values and others with measurements. Tables can use display rules, and you can add a total for the last row or last column.

Figure 5.47 Sales rep ratings in a table

Sales Rep Ratings by Region and Month

Business Regions	Transaction Month▲	Sales Rep	Sales Rep Rating (Min)	Sales Rep Rating	Sales Rep Rating (Max)
EMEA	06/2011	0286	100%	100%	100%
EMEA	07/2011	0286	100%	100%	100%
EMEA	08/2011	0286	100%	100%	100%
EMEA	09/2011	0286	62%	99%	100%
EMEA	10/2011	0286	62%	62%	62%
EMEA	11/2011	0286	62%	62%	62%
EMEA	12/2011	0286	62%	62%	62%
			Minimum: 40%	Average: 60%	Maximum: 100%

In a crosstab, the categories are on the right side or top, and the measures are in the cells. The following table contains information similar to the table above, but it's organized differently. Notice that the crosstab can organize the data item into a date hierarchy using month and year. Hierarchies can only be used with crosstabs. The total line is across the top and contains the data across both years in the hierarchy.

Figure 5.48 Using a hierarchy with a crosstab

Sales Rep Ratings by Month and Year

Transaction Year ▲	Transaction Month ▲	Sales Rep Rating (Min)	Sales Rep Rating	Sales Rep Rating (Max)
	Business Regions ▲	EMEA		
Total		40%	60%	100%
2011	06/2011	100%	100%	100%
	07/2011	100%	100%	100%
	08/2011	100%	100%	100%
	09/2011	62%	99%	100%
	10/2011	62%	62%	62%
	11/2011	62%	62%	62%
	12/2011	62%	62%	62%

Tables and crosstabs: guidelines for use

When using tables or crosstabs, readability should be a chief concern. Use the following guidelines when creating tables:

- Use color to ensure that the viewer understands the features of the table. For instance, use a contrasting color for the heading and the total line.

- Lines assist the viewer in following a value across the table.

Tables and crosstabs: tips and tricks

Use the following tips when creating list tables and crosstabs.

Tip 1: Add a sparkline or gauge

In his *Information Dashboard Design* book, Stephen Few presents a simple design based on a table. His example uses a sparkline popularized by Tufte. The following dashboard contains sparklines and gauges—all within a list table.

Consumer Complaints

Submitted via ▲	Lifetime Trend	Y/Y Diff (%)	Complaints 2015
Email	‎〰	-53% ▫	8
Postal mail	〰	-16% ▫	9,489
Referral	〰	-9% ▫	21,550
Web	〰	18% ▪	125,138

The Lifetime Trend column contains a sparkline. A sparkline is just a simple line that shows values over a time period: That is, it's a mini-line chart. In this example, you can see how the Web trend increased while the Email trend became non-existent.

A sparkline requires a date item and a measure. It creates a new column in your table. This list table is based on yearly values, so showing the trend as a monthly or quarterly value makes sense. A daily value would make the sparkline difficult to interpret because it is such a small space, and too many values would appear cluttered. Likewise, a yearly value would not show enough variation.

The bullet gauge in the Y/Y Diff (%) column is one of the gauges available to List Tables. You can also select some of the other horizontal gauges. These gauges use the same methods as the other gauges in the tool. Refer to the "Gauges" topic for assistance in creating and using gauges.

Here's how to create this example dashboard:

1. Add a category to a List Table. The example uses the **Submitted via data** item. Add the Y/Y Diff (%) and Complaints 2015 data items.
2. Add a sparkline to the table.
   a. Right-click the list table and select **Add Sparkline** from the pop-up menu. A sparkline window appears.
   b. Add a column name, a date data item, and the desired measure. Click **OK**.

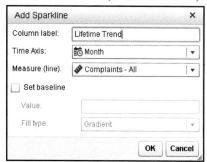

Note: If you need to edit the sparkline, right-click the list table and select **Edit Sparkline** from the menu.

3.   Add a gauge or display rule to the list table.

   a.   Right-click the column that contains the measure you want to use with the gauge and select **Add Display Rule** from the pop-up menu. The New Display Rule window appears.

   b.   Select **Gauge** to add a new gauge.

   c.   Select **Icon** as the gauge type.

   d.   If your measure does not appear in the **Based on** column, you can select it from the drop-down list.

   e.   Decide if you want the icon to appear to the left or right of the column value.

   f.   Set the display rules to determine the colors. This gauge uses reverse logic. For this data, companies want fewer complaints each year, so a negative trend is preferred. Green is used first and red last.

   g.   Click **OK** to continue.

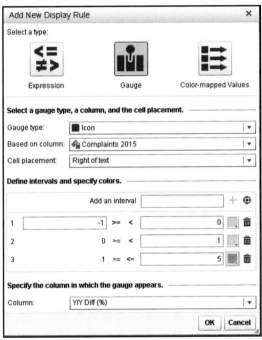

4.   Add more display rules or gauges until your dashboard meets your design intention.

Tip 2: Use a small table for single values

When you want to show a single value, you can use a table. With some creative maneuvering, you can make the font extremely large and then make the table as small as possible. In the following figure, the table was created with a single value. The heading was removed, and options on the **Style** menu were disabled. The font size was changed to 40 points, and a thick font was chosen.

Figure 5.49 Adding a single value

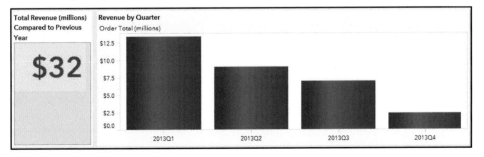

Refer to the "Pie and Donut Chart" topic for an alternate method using an invisible pie chart that works just as well.

Tip 3: Check your aggregations and derived measures

When you create a calculated item, you should test it prior to use. The derived data items can be especially tricky since it's not always obvious what is being calculated. Derived data items are created from a measure.

1. Right-click a measure.

2. Select **Create** and then the derived measure you want.

There are multiple date-based aggregated measures you can instantly create.

Figure 5.50 Adding a derived data items

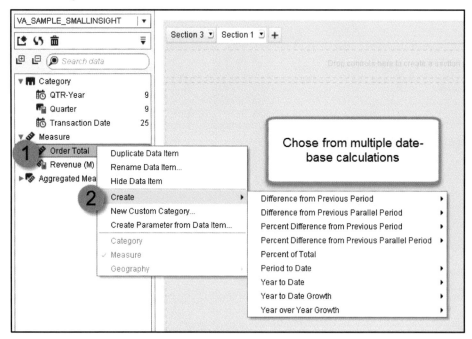

After the measure is created, it is added to the Aggregated Measure list. In the following figure, the four derived items are displayed.

Figure 5.51 Derived measures in a table

QTR-Year	Order Total	Order Total (Year to Date)	Order Total (Difference from Previous Period)	Order Total (Percent Difference from Previous Parallel Period)	Order Total (Year over Year Growth)
4th quarter 2013	$2,409,220	$31,928,096	($4,584,409)	-81.97%	-18.34%
3rd quarter 2013	$6,993,629	$29,518,876	($2,095,192)	5.27%	-18.34%
2nd quarter 2013	$9,088,821	$22,525,247	($4,347,605)	21.33%	-18.34%
1st quarter 2013	$13,436,426	$13,436,426	$75,592	15.79%	-18.34%
4th quarter 2012	$13,360,834	$39,099,900	$6,717,216	-13.30%	153.72%
3rd quarter 2012	$6,643,617	$25,739,066	($847,490)	.	153.72%
2nd quarter 2012	$7,491,107	$19,095,449	($4,113,235)	.	153.72%
1st quarter 2012	$11,604,342	$11,604,342	($3,806,253)	.	153.72%
4th quarter 2011	$15,410,595	$15,410,595	.	.	.
	$86,438,590	.	.	.	.

Here's what each column in the preceding figure contains:

- *QTR-Year* is the date. Derived measures use a date as the basis.

- *Order Total* is the data item used to create the other column. This value helps you see how the result was calculated.

- *Order Total (Year to Date)* shows the cumulative amount for each year. It resets in first quarter.

- *Order Total (Difference from Previous Period)* is the difference in the previous period and this quarter.

- *Order Total (Percent Difference from Previous Parallel Period)* is the percentage difference in the same quarter of the previous year.

- *Order Total (Year over Year Growth)* is the percentage difference in the same quarter of the previous year.

Notice that the total row does not contain any values for the derived measures.

You may have noticed that the last two columns contain the same values. You can edit the derived measure to get a different result. For instance, if you wanted to display the year over year change for the entire year, you would edit the aggregated mesaure to change the Outer Interval to _By Year_ instead of _Inferred_. Refer to the product user documentation for a detailed discussion of derived measures.

Bubble plots

You cannot research bubble plots in the work of any data visualization expert without reading a reference to Hans Rosling's TED Talk, *Let My Dataset Change Your Mindset* (May 2010). It might have been the first time that a bubble plot gained a mainstream appeal, as noted by Stephen Few in his *Show Me the Numbers* book. Rosling provided an intense amount of information in one data visualization. Here's some pointers on using bubble plots to give your data set a sexy new appeal.

The examples in this topic were based on the sample BIRT database provided by the Eclispse Foundation (http://www.eclipse.org/birt/documentation/sample-database.php).

Interpreting the results

Bubble plots enable you to understand the relationship between three values. Two numeric values are plotted by their X and Y coordinates, and the third coordinate is a bubble. In this example, the bubble size is the gross margin. Revenue per Order and Quantity per Order are plotted on the x-axis and y-axis. Each bubble represents a specific product. You can interpret this chart by comparing the bubble size and placement. We are trying to understand our profitability.

Figure 5.52 Bubble plot

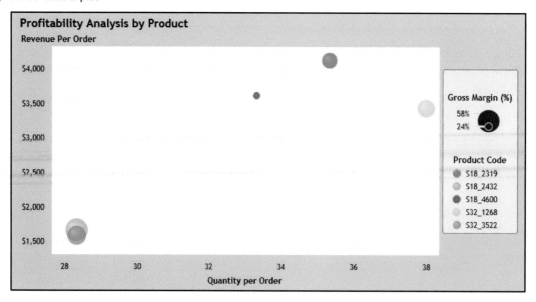

Gross margin means that we had more profit on a product—so the larger the bubble, the more money we earned. What else can we learn?

- The red product has a lower profit margin than the other products despite having double the revenue. What if the product was on sale to lure other customer purchases or if our discount is too much?

- In the bottom corner, the lime green and teal products had identical orders in terms of quantity and revenue. But the lime green one is larger, so it was more profitable. If these are similar products, why is the margin so different? Maybe we switched suppliers and had to pay a higher cost?

- The blue, yellow and teal products had similar margins but at different prices and quantities. How do we sell more of those products?

Bubble plots: guidelines

Many people criticize bubble charts for being difficult to interpret. Don't let that stop you from using it—just be sure to add the supporting information to help the user understand. Most business users can learn to interpret the chart easily when it's properly labeled. This chart is also not suited to precise values because it's meant to provide an overall look and help the audience identify areas of concern. During this analysis process, we were comparing bubble size and not actual profit margins.

Data preparation is key

When preparing data for this demonstration, we used a sample data set from the BIRT_project about a company selling Classic Cars. We joined several tables to get a data set that contains the line items from each customer order.

Here's how the data items were created:

- Gross margin is a calculated measure. Gross margin is Line Item Revenue minus the Line Item COGS over the Line Item COGS. The gross margin was turned into a percentage.

- Quantity per Order was averaged from the raw data value.

- Revenue per Order was averaged from the raw data value.

A legend is a requirement

The legend on the side helps the user understand the bubble size and the color meaning—so it's essential. Otherwise, the user may not understand that the bubble size indicates the gross margin value and the colors are the product codes.

You can turn on the Legend on the **Properties** tab. In the preceding figure, the legend is to the right of the data object. You can place the legend where it makes the most sense in your layout.

Bubble plots: tips and tricks

Here's some tricks to handle common situations.

Tip 1: Use the transparency setting so users see all the data

You can also change the transparency setting so that users can see the overlap when there are more bubbles. The transparency setting is on the Properties pane. For this example, the transparency changed to 70%. This allows the background bubbles to shine through.

Figure 5.53 Use transparency for multiple bubbles

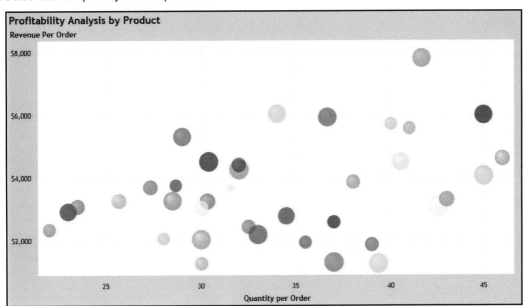

Tip 2: Animating the data

You can add a fifth dimension of time. This data set is based on 2012. It has a value called MONTH.

If you animate the data, this helps the user understand over time what happened to the product.

We can see that we started selling more of the green product, which didn't change the margin that much. What if the product was discounted toward the end of the year or the customer was given a discount for a larger order?

Figure 5.54 Use animation wisely

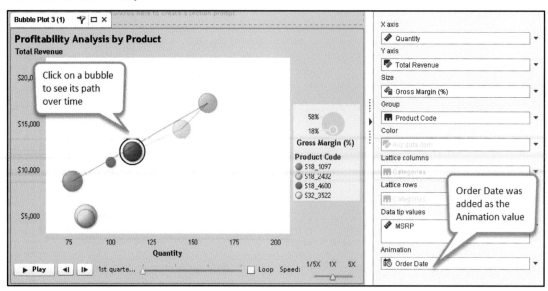

To add animation, use the **Role** tab. You must have a date value because this is showing how something changed over time. Add the date data item to the Animation role. The animation is based on the date value. If your date value is formatted as month, then the animation creates a month-to-month time line. Likewise, if you use a date that is formatted as quarter, then the timeline divides by quarter.

Choose your data value carefully. A timeline that takes too long to display may lose the viewer's interest. Your timeline should emphasize your message quickly or show how the patterns changes over time.

References

Cairo, Alberto. 2013. *The Functional Art: An Introduction to Information Graphics and Visualization.* Berkeley, CA: New Riders.

Cairo, Alberto. 2016. *The Truthful Art: Data, Charts, and Maps for Communication.* San Francisco, CA: New Riders.

Few, Stephen. 2012. *Show Me the Numbers: Designing Tables and Graphs to Enlighten.* 2nd ed. Burlingame, CA: Analytics Press.

Few, Stephen. 2013. *Information Dashboard Design: Displaying Data for At-A-Glance Monitoring.* 2nd ed. Burlingame, CA: Analytics Press.

Kong, Nicholas, Jeffrey Heer, and Maneesh Agrawala. 2010. "Perceptual Guidelines for Creating Rectangular Treemaps." *IEEE Transactions on Visualization and Computer Graphics* 16(6): 990-8. Available at http://vis.stanford.edu/files/2010-Treemaps-InfoVis.pdf.

Parker, Roger C. 2006. *Looking Good in Print, Sixth Edition.* Scottsdale, AZ: Paraglyph Press.

Tufte, Edward R. 2001. *The Visual Display of Quantitative Information.* Cheshire, CT: Graphics Press.

chapter six

the where of data

Traditional business intelligence systems have focused on answering the *who, what*, and *when* questions, but organizations often need to know the *where* of data as well. Businesses want to plan sales territories based on existing customers. School districts want to understand where students live in relation to the school. Companies want to know whether equipment failures are related to specific locations. All of these issues are related to the *where* of the data.

SAS Visual Analytics makes it easy to plot geospatial data, which can add a completely new element to your data visualizations and analysis. In a tabular report, multiple columns might represent customers, competitors, and demographic information. The tabular report might not reveal anything useful. But if you can geocode the data and overlay it on a map, you quickly see where the better customers are, where they are in relation to competitors, and the regions that provide the most market potential based on underlying demographics.

SAS Visual Analytics geo mapping capabilities are based on integration with two mapping technologies: OpenStreetMap and ESRI ArcGIS. The examples in this chapter use OpenStreetMap with SAS Visual Analytics 7.3 unless otherwise noted. In this chapter, you will learn how to create geographic data items and geospatial objects.

Using geospatial data effectively

SAS Visual Analytics makes plotting geospatial data effortless. This is exciting! It is very easy to just use geospatial data objects for everything. Before traveling that path, though, consider if you really have a location-based data story. You want to use geospatial objects thoughtfully. In this topic, we will discuss an ineffective and an effective use of location analysis.

When location is not part of the data story

In her book, *The Wall Street Guide to Information Graphics*, Dona Wong suggests that there are times when geography is not part of the story, so it doesn't make sense to force it to be. In her example, she shows two sales regions where sales were higher in one. In the following figure, the example was re-created using Australian states.

Figure 6.1 Location is not part of this data story

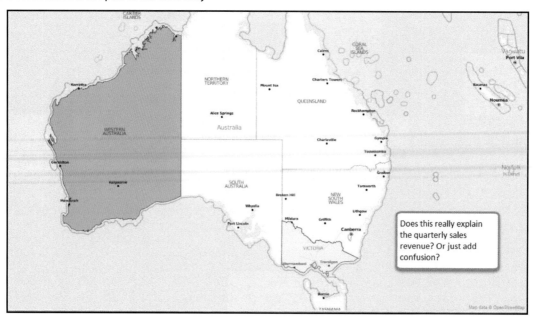

Because the regions are so disproportionate in size, comparing the sales revenue is not helpful. It does not lead to any conclusion except that Western Australia generated more revenue than Victoria. Your viewer does not have any useful takeaway, because the conclusion might be expected. It doesn't seem relevant to a data story in which the focus was really sales revenue. With only two values to display, would a list table or even a pie chart have been a better data visualization choice? The point of this example is to understand that even if you can show a cool geo object, you should ask yourself if it makes sense for your data story.

When location is the data story

Europe is an international business center and a leading tourist destination. If you want to tell a data story about how popular a location it is, you could start by exploring the airport traffic. The Anna Aero website (http://www.anna.aero) contains data that details trends from most of the world's airports. You can use the airport codes and passenger counts to start a data story about the most and least popular cities.

In the following figure, the location of each airport is shown along with the passenger count and the difference from the previous year. In this example, location enhances the story. Instead of fancy calculations, the viewer can simply use their eyes to search for patterns.

Figure 6.2 Location matters in this story

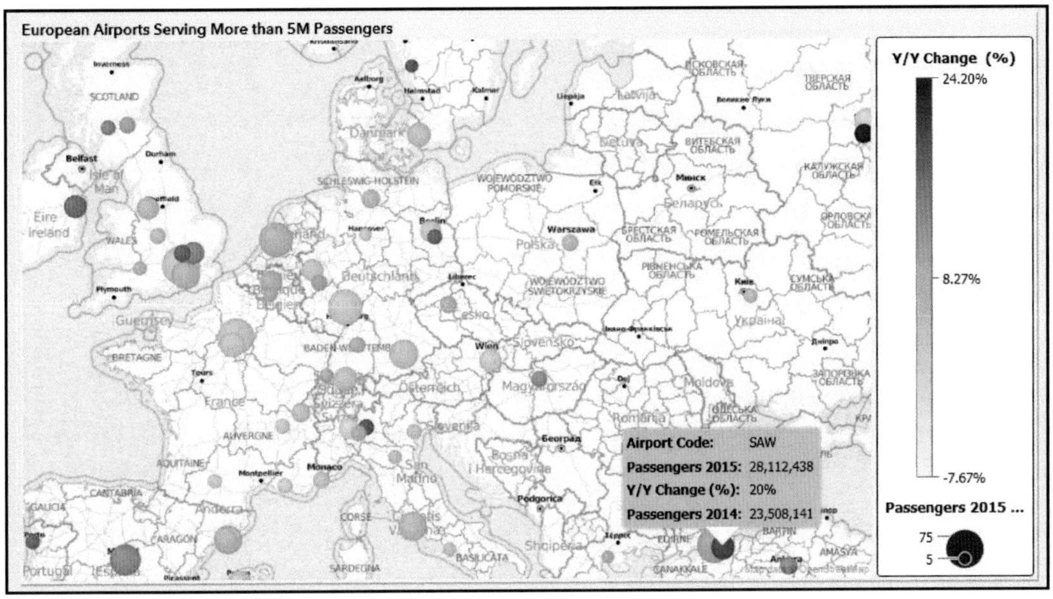

There are multiple observations. You might notice the darker circles that show increased passenger counts. Perhaps you notice where there are multiple airports within a close radius, and you are curious why one has a higher passenger count. When used effectively, geospatial data can reveal previously unknown patterns or assist with confirming suspicions.

Preparing data for geospatial visualizations

Before creating a geospatial visualization, you must have a geographic data item. If a data item contains a location, such as a country or state, then it is considered a geographic data item. Common location examples are customer addresses, store locations, or sales regions. You can use the SAS predefined geographic data elements or create custom geographic data items. This topic describes how to create each type.

Creating a predefined geographic data item

To keep things easy, SAS Visual Analytics has predefined geographic data elements ranging from general values such as country names, to specific values such as ISO country codes. If your geographic data item contains a country name, then it can be matched to an internal table so that the location can be plotted on a map. Starting with SAS Visual Analytics 7.1, geographic data items can be country name, ISO 2-Letter codes, ISO Numeric Codes, or SAS Map ID values. You select the predefined method when you create the geographic data item.

These geographic data elements represent the center of the area. If you are showing France, it can be shown with a country outline or at the center of the country. The following table contains the available predefined geographical data elements provided by default and examples of how the incoming data items are expected to appear. The table shows the data values expected from three countries.

Geographic data element	Examples from Australia	Examples from the Netherlands	Examples from the United States
Country or Region Name	Australia	Netherlands	United States
Country or Region ISO 2-Letter Codes	AU	NL	US
Country or Region ISO Numeric Codes	036	528	840
Country or Region SAS Map ID Values	AU	NL	US
Subdivision (State, Province Names)	Queensland	Noord-Nederland	North Carolina
Subdivision (State, Province) SAS Map ID Values	AU-3	NL-01	US-37
US State Names	—	—	North Carolina
US State Abbreviations	—	—	NC
US ZIP Codes	—	—	27513

On the SAS Support site, there is a Geographic Lookup Values for SAS Visual Analytics (at http://support.sas.com/rnd/datavisualization/vageo/71/VA71LookupValues.html). This page contains a list of these values to help you understand your specific location. The tables at this site list the countries and the associated ISO numeric codes.

SAS Visual Analytics uses internal tables in the MAPSGFK library that is shipped with the product. You can review the tables in this library to ensure that your data matches the expected name by using an application such as SAS Studio. For additional assistance in creating geo data, you can use the GEOCODE procedure that is available with the SAS/GRAPH software.

What is an ISO code?

There is an international standard called ISO 3166 published by the International Organization for Standardization. This standard applies numeric values to countries and regions that everyone can use. There are several advantages to using numeric references, particularly in the data world.

If a programmer is using a non-Latin based language, such as Chinese or Hebrew, the number makes it easy to look up values. Also, when new countries form, a new number can be assigned while maintaining the older number for historical purposes.

Creating a predefined geographic data item

After importing data into SAS Visual Analytics, you must assign the data item to a Geography role before it can be used with any of the geo objects. You can create a geographic data item from an existing character or numeric data item. To create a geographic data item:

① Right-click the data item that contains the geographic element that matches the predefined role. In this example, the Country data item contains the country names, such as Australia or Brazil.

Note: Some users prefer to duplicate the data item before assigning it to this role.

2 Select Geography ▶ Country or Region Names. Your data item is moved under the Geography section. You can use it with geographic roles.

3 Choose a geographic role.

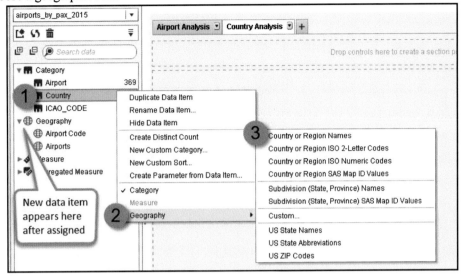

Dealing with location accuracy

If SAS Visual Analytics cannot plot your country data item, you might need to convert a country's common name to its official name. For example, Russia, United States of America, and Great Britain could be in your data set, but SAS Visual Analytics cannot plot them. When you search the country names in the MAPSGFK.WORLD data set, you learn that these countries use a different IDNAME. Often it is easier to convert the values to the ISO numeric code rather than using names.

Figure 6.3 MAPSGFK world data set values

	ID	IDNAME	ISO
1	AE	United Arab Emirates	784
2	GB	United Kingdom	826
3	RU	Russian Federation	643
4	TZ	Tanzania, United Republic of	834
5	US	United States	840

Creating a custom geospatial data item

All geospatial data items represent a location on the planet Earth. A specific point or address has a set of coordinates, which are called latitude and longitude. You might recall from elementary school when you studied the globe and learned how it was divided by imaginary parallel lines that circle the globe from and east to west (called latitude) and from north to south (called longitude).

When you provide a location's latitude and longitude, you are referencing these lines. If you think about the world's airports, it's possible to describe the geospatial location with just latitude and longitude coordinates. In the following figure, the airports are highlighted on the map, and the table on the left shows the airport name with its coordinates. Notice that the latitude numbers are similar because these airports are in a similar eastern European location. There is some variation in the longitude numbers as the airport is further south. Compare the Charles De Gaulle (Paris, France) coordinates to the Dublin (Dublin, Ireland) coordinates to better understand the values.

Figure 6.4 Airports with latitude and longitude

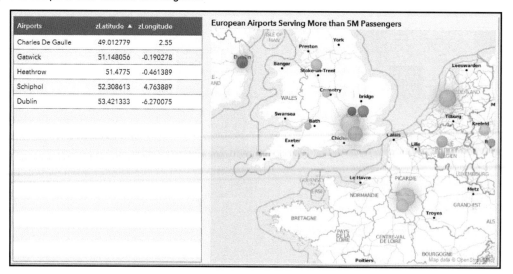

Creating a custom geographic data item

To create a custom geographic item, you must have the latitude and longitude coordinates available in the data set. The coordinates can be based on the World Geodetic System (WGS84), Web Mercator, and the British National Grid (OSGB36). The default is the World Geodetic System (WGS84).

What is a coordinate system?

There are three coordinate systems available for custom data points. These standards were developed for diverse purposes but are now commonly used.

- WGS84 was developed by the United States military for satellite-positioning systems.

- Web Mercator is a web standard. It was first used with Google Maps.

- OSGB36 is a British-developed system that is heavily used in British-based maps.

You should choose the system that works best for your specific location or geo data. In most cases the WGS84 system works.

Let's use the airport coordinates as the basis for the new geographic item. We use the airport name to create this data item, but other data items such as Airport Code would also work.

To create a custom geography data item:

1. Duplicate the Airport data item and name the new item Airport Name.

2. Right-click the new data item, and then select **Geography ▶ Custom**. A Geography window appears.

3. Select your data items for latitude and longitude in the appropriate fields. Your new data item appears in the Geography area.

Figure 6.5 Adding a custom data point

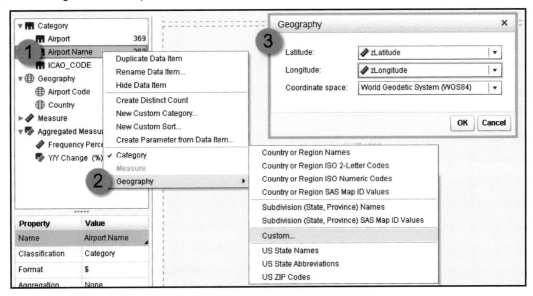

Finding geo coordinates

If your data set does not have the geo coordinates available, you can get them through several sources.

- The SAS MAPSGFK library contains multiple countries and regions.

- There are open-source databases available that you can find with a web search.

- Google has an API that you can query through code. The free service has a daily access limit, but you can subscribe to their service or other commercial services.

Displaying geospatial objects

There are three ways to display geo data in SAS Visual Analytics:

- Coordinate – Pinpoints an exact location on the map using a custom geographical item

- Regional – Outlines a regional area

- Bubble – Combines a bubble plot to show a value at the location

These objects enable you to highlight your geospatial data in different ways and for different stories. Let's explore the different ways that these data objects are used.

For the remaining topics in this chapter, the examples are created using the storm events data set from the United States National Climatic Data Center website. This database contains US storm events (such as tornadoes and thunderstorms) since 1950. The data set contains other facts such as the number of deaths or injuries and the estimated property damage. The tornadoes are rated by their intensity on the Fujita scale from F0 to F5 with F5 being the most destructive. In 2007, the Enhanced Fujita scale was introduced and tornadoes were categorized as EF0-EF5.

Get to the point with geo coordinate data objects

Perhaps you've heard people talk about tornado alley—it's an area down the middle of the United States where tornadoes occur more frequently. Tornadoes are powerful and scary storms that produce wind speeds capable of sending a wood board through a metal car door. These storm events are responsible for massive property damage and loss of lives. Geo coordinate maps are excellent at showing exactly where an event occurred. In the following figure, the teal markers indicate where tornadoes with EF5/F5 strength of 230 mph+ (370 kph) winds arose in the past 50 years.

Figure 6.6 F5/EF5 tornado locations

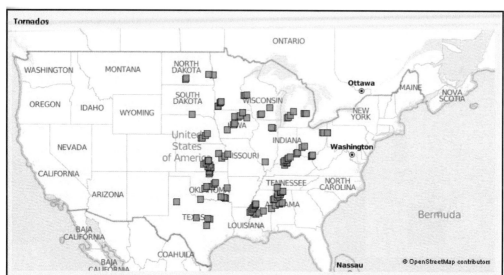

To make this geo coordinate object a little more interesting, let's add the EF4/F4 tornado touchdown points for the same time period. By contrasting the teal and gold markers, the viewer sees that an EF5/F5 tornado is less common.

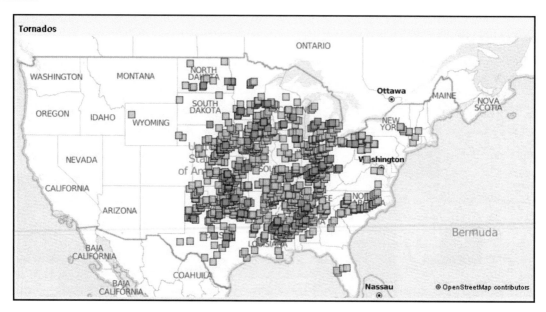

While the data points are chaotic, it's clear where severe tornados occurred. This data would not have had the same impression if we had plotted it as a line chart or even a pie chart. The touchdown points help you realize why those particular states have a higher disaster recovery budget.

Tip 1: Dealing with odd locations

This data object uses a custom geography data item that is based on supplied latitude and longitude values. If the coordinates are incorrect, then the map might show your data in the middle of the ocean. In our sample data, some of the coordinates were entered incorrectly. This resulted in tornados appearing in the Atlantic Ocean. To correct this situation, the latitude and longitude values in the data set would have to be edited or filtered.

Figure 6.7 Tornados in the ocean

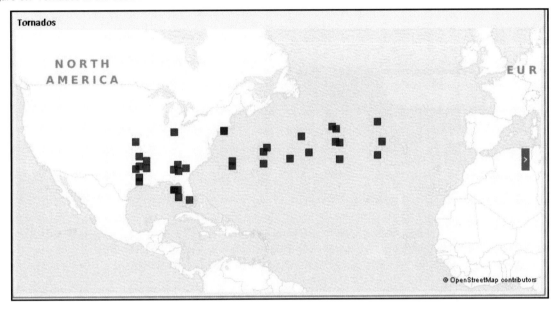

Tip 2: Controlling the data

When you have too much data to display, SAS Visual Analytics issues a yellow icon and warns you to add some filters to your data. With custom geographic data items, it is more likely to happen. The solution is to control how much data appears at once by setting filters.

Figure 6.8 There is too much data at one time!

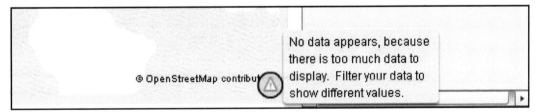

Here are a few suggested filters:

- Add a date range slider to compare events along a time scale. Adding Event Year to the slider enables the user to compare which years might have had more active storm seasons.

- Split the data item categories. Use the display rules to assign the tornado scale to a different color so that each level is clearer. Then add a List filter and assign the Tornado F/EF Scale to the list. Users can select which tornado scale they want to compare.

Figure 6.9 Add filters to keep data visualization manageable

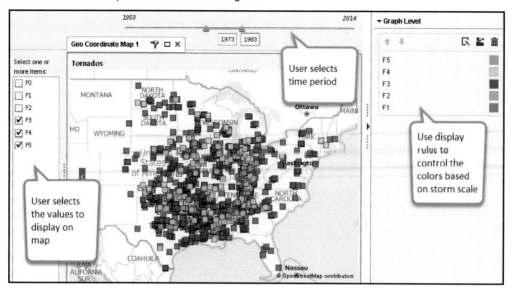

Compare area with geo regional data objects

Use the geo regional data object when you need to introduce a subject about location. This geospatial object helps a viewer understand where to focus their attention or understand how much variation occurs for a value. These objects are also called *choropleth* maps, which is Greek for multitude of areas.

When you start thinking about dangerous storm events, you can imagine that these events cause considerable property damage. States more prone to severe tornados will plan larger disaster recovery budgets. It would be interesting to compare the damage costs by state. Using a geo regional map, you can place a value over an entire region, such as a country or a state. Color is then applied over the regions to indicate the intensity of the value.

Figure 6.10 Understanding regional events

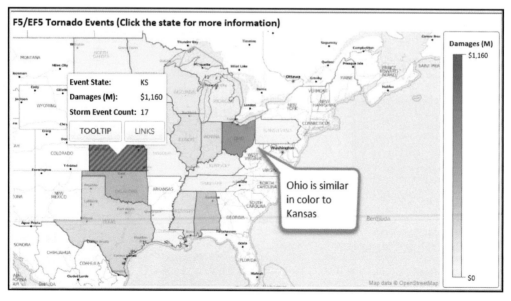

In the preceding figure, you can see the associated property damage cost for the tornadoes across the areas. The darker the color, the costlier the storm damage. Use an average or percentage to make the values comparable or normalized. By exploring the visualization, you can easily see the areas of most damage, but it's harder to understand where there is the least damage. Be sure to use a legend so that the user understands the color range.

When you position your pointer over each state, a data tip appears that contains the assigned data items values. Since Ohio and Kansas are similar in color, viewers might be interested to learn more. Most of Kansas is farm land and rural areas, while Ohio is more densely populated and industrial. Being in tornado alley, Kansas probably experiences more tornados and thus more crop damage. With the larger population, it might be costlier for Ohio when there is an extreme storm event.

Tip 1: Improving your geo regional map

There are a few settings that can make a geo regional data object a nicer user experience.

- Add data tips to provide more information when the user positions the pointer over content.

    You can add as many as you like, but make sure that the data items enhance instead of confuse the viewer. For the preceding example, we added the Storm Event Count as a data tip.

- Adjust the color transparency for the overlay so that the user can see the underlying values.

    If the underlying values are masked, it might cause confusion. For this visualization, the transparency was adjusted to 25%. It was just enough to maintain the color while still allowing the underlying value to peek though.

- Adjust the gradient color to ensure enough contrast.

    The ocean is a light blue, so a contrasting color that does not appear too similar to the landscape features is required. In Figure 6.9, a single color for the Gradient value is used. It is easier to decode a value when the color intensity increases as the value increases.

Choose lighter colors

In *Envisioning Information*, Edward Tufte has a fascinating discussion of color with maps. His suggestion is to use colors that are found in nature. He encourages using a color palette on the lighter side and provides several examples used across several centuries.

Tip 2: Adding rich details for exploration

The geo region data object is excellent for getting the user to focus on specific areas. It leads to more questions about the storm events, so it might be convenient to use an info window to provide more details. This info window shows the storms by duration with estimated damage. A quick storm can result in as much damage as a longer one, although this probably depends on where the tornado touches down.

Figure 6.11 Use a pop-up window to provide more details

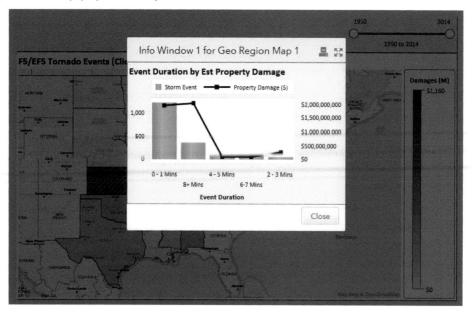

When the user clicks on the state, the info window appears with additional information. This example uses a bar-line chart, but it can be anything you can create in a section. This map is a good way to start a story. It provides an overview and helps the viewer understand where to focus their attention. In this case, it was Kansas and Ohio.

The only pitfall to an info window is that the viewer might not recall the values from the previous pop-up. Use this technique for data discovery or as a way to entice someone into your story. This data story is completely about the location and comparing how the events affected the states.

Adding an info window to your map

Info windows are pages that you can link to from another page. Use the following steps to add an information window to your map.

1. Create a tab. In this example, the geo regional map was created.
2. Create another tab with the data objects of your choice. For this example, a bar-line data object was used to show the event duration and estimated property damage.
3. Select the down arrow next to the title and select **Display as Info Window**.

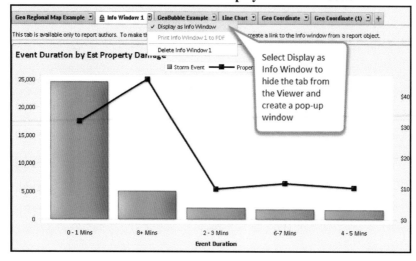

4. Return to the page that you created in step 1. Right-click on the map, and then select Add Link > Info Window Link. In the window that appears, select which info window you want.

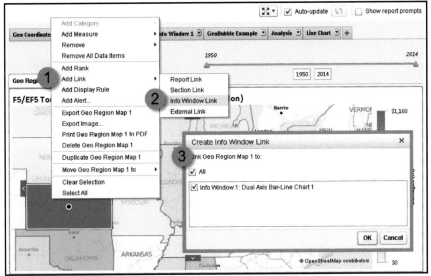

Once you turn the tab into an info window, it does not appear to the viewer. You can use an info window in other situations to provide information about the tab.

Show overall trends with bubble plots data objects

Bubble plots receive a lot criticism for being difficult to understand. These charts can pack a lot of data into a few variables. A layperson might spend more time trying to understand a bubble plot, but this doesn't seem true for the geo bubble maps. Possibly it's because the user sees the map and understands that it is related to location.

In the previous topic, we created a geo regional map to show the average damage cost from F5 tornadoes for each state. One issue with the method was that users had to position the pointer over each state to see how many storm events were associated with each event. If a user wants details, it is a little awkward. A geo bubble map resolves this issue..

A geo bubble plot places a bubble on the geographic location and enables you to control two aspects of the bubble: its size and color. In the following example, the bubble size is the event count (the number of tornadoes) while the color shows the estimated property damages (shown with the scale). Now it is more apparent that Kansas endured a similar number of events as Mississippi, but the price tag was a little larger. However, it also shows that Ohio had a similar cost but fewer events than Kansas.

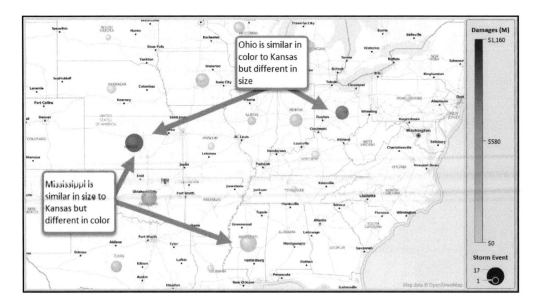

Tip 1: Ensure that the legend is visible

When you use bubbles to encode data, you are asking the user to compare the bubble size and the bubble color. The legend ensures that the user has some visual cues to assist with understanding. You can place the legend anywhere around the object. In the preceding example, the legend is placed on the right.

Tip 2: Watch the default colors

By default, the geo bubble object uses a gradient scale of red to blue. This scale is acceptable when working with performance data and is commonly referred to as trafficlighting. The color mimics the traffic signals where red means stop and green means go. However, we have a logic problem in this instance. The red indicates the least amount of damage and the blue indicates the most. Technically, any property damage is bad. (After all, we are not measuring how well the tornado was at damaging property!)

The gradient scale was changed to teal in our chart. The bubbles are not as close to the ocean and provide enough contrast with the circle. However, notice that the bubble over Tennessee is barely visible. The bubbles were set to 30% transparency to make the state names visible. Perhaps another color would be more suitable? You can experiment with your data object and decide.

Expanding location intelligence

Starting with SAS Visual Analytics 8.1, users have unlimited access to the ESRI base maps from within SAS Visual Analytics. This provides geo search functionality and ad hoc selection of data points on a map. Here's an example of a geo search where the user was looking for how close Los Angeles, CA customers were to the retail chain Sports Authority.

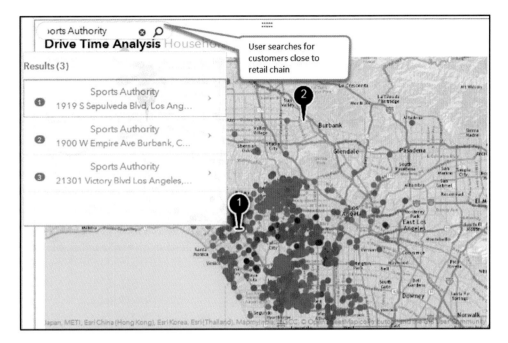

For users who want additional functionality, they can subscribe to the ESRI premium features. The premium service offers drive-time analysis, drive-by-distance analysis, and the ability to create custom shapes. In this example, the user was looking for customers within a 5- to 10-minute driving distance of the store location. The darker inner area is the 5-minute drive, while the lighter inner band in the 10-minute drive.

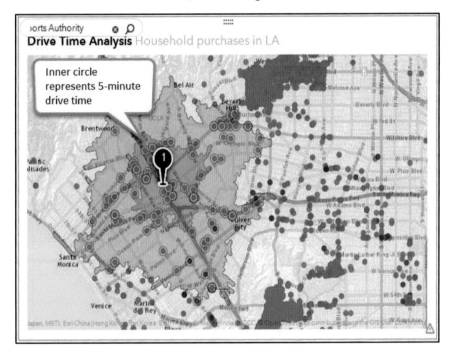

Understanding details about mapping technologies

SAS Visual Analytics geo mapping capabilities are based on integration with two mapping technologies: OpenStreetMap and ESRI ArcGIS. SAS Visual Analytics enables its users to view their enterprise data mapped across the various locations on the map.

OpenStreetMap This is an open-source project, where a worldwide user community maintains the data about roads, boundaries, trails, and much more.

ESRI ArcGIS Maps This advanced mapping platform uses highly interactive and informative geographical maps. The maps are maintained by ESRI, a SAS partner.

The SAS Visual Analytics environment must be configured to point to one of these mapping technologies. An OpenStreetMap server is hosted by SAS and is available as part of the default configuration. Organizations might want to host and maintain their own OpenStreetMap server. Organizations can also use the ESRI server (ArcGIS for Server, version 10.1 or higher) for access to maps. Refer to the *SAS Visual Analytics: Administration Guide* for your release for more configuration details.

Many SAS Visual Analytics users are concerned about what information from their data must be shared in order to retrieve map tiles from OpenStreetMap or ESRI ArcGIS Maps. After all, if the data is confidential to their enterprise, it needs to be kept secure. Fortunately, none of your actual data is leaked outside of the environment. SAS Visual Analytics simply requests the specific map tiles necessary to render the selected geographic area. The highlighted regions, bubble plots, and all are created within the SAS Visual Analytics application.

References

Aanderud, Tricia. 2016. "Where in the World is SAS Visual Analytics?" Available at https://www.zencos.com/blog/review-geoplot-in-sas-visual-analytics/.

Massengill, Darrell. 2016. "The GEOCODE Procedure and SAS Visual Analytics." *Proceedings of the SAS Global Forum 2016 Conference.* Paper SAS3480-2016. Cary, NC: SAS Institute Inc. Available at http://support.sas.com/resources/papers/proceedings16/SAS3480-2016.pdf.

Nori, Murali, and Himesh Patel. 2016. "Location, Location, Location—Analytics with SAS Visual Analytics and ESRI." *Proceedings of the SAS Global Forum 2016 Conference.* Paper SAS4060-2016. Cary, NC: SAS Institute Inc. Available at http://support.sas.com/resources/papers/proceedings16/SAS4060-2016.pdf.

Schulz, Falko, and Anand Chitale. 2014. "More Than a Map: Location Intelligence with SAS Visual Analytics." *Proceedings of the SAS Global Forum 2014 Conference.* Paper SAS021-2014. Cary, NC: SAS Institute Inc. Available at http://support.sas.com/resources/papers/proceedings14/SAS021-2014.pdf.

Tufte, Edward R. 1990. *Envisioning Information.* Cheshire, CT: Graphics Press.

US NOAA Data. Storm Events Database. Accessed 2016. See https://www.ncdc.noaa.gov/stormevents/.

Wong, Dona M. 2013. *The Wall Street Journal Guide to Information Graphics: the Dos and Don'ts of Presenting Data, Facts, and Figures.* New York, NY: W. W. Norton & Company, Inc.

chapter seven

approachable analytics

In Chapters 5 and 6, we introduced you to many of the objects available in the Designer application of SAS Visual Analytics. These objects let you create visualizations to display your data so that you can communicate a message to a viewer. This works well for reporting and dashboards, but sometimes your data needs additional investigation to see what is going on underneath the covers. SAS Visual Analytics has a very similar application to the Designer called the Explorer that gives you access to additional objects and data analysis features. At first glance, you might not be able to see the difference between the Explorer and Designer, since they are laid out similarly.

Compared to the Designer, which focuses more on displaying your data, the Explorer section enables you to learn more about your data. Organizations are always searching for that piece of information to give them a competitive advantage, but you can only find that if you are getting deep into analyzing your data. In the Explorer application, you are given all of the designer objects as well as more advanced ones that let you see your data in different views. Some of the objects also have analysis features that run calculations behind the scenes to give you even more information about your data.

In this chapter, we walk through the Explorer and show how it is set up differently than the Designer. Then we go over some of the advanced objects that you can use in the Explorer as well as the additional data analysis features that are built into the objects.

Note: The Explorer application is for SAS Visual Analytics 7.3 and all other previous versions. In the 8.1 version, the Explorer and Designer are merged into the same section along with all of the objects. That version is covered in Chapter 13.

About the Explorer

In the Explorer application, you create explorations, which are metadata objects that contain visualizations and other data settings. Explorations can be saved and shared with other users. Visualizations are where the objects are used within an exploration. Each exploration can have multiple visualizations but each visualization can only have one object.

At first glance, you might not be able to see the difference between the Explorer and Designer since they are laid out similarly.

Figure 7.1 Explorer layout

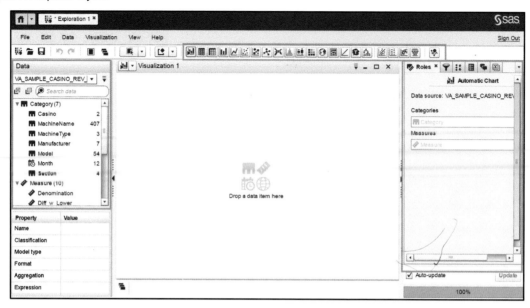

The Explorer is set up with a panel on the left side for your data. This is where you can add data and see all of the data items once they have been added. The drop-down list at the top of the panel gives you the options to manipulate data such as adding a new hierarchy, calculated item, data source filter, and so on.

All of the objects can be found as icons in the toolbar near the top of the window. Clicking on any of them places that object into the visualization. You can also select an object by clicking on the drop-down list that sits to the left of the visualization name. The objects can be controlled with the right panel. This contains tabs where you can add data items, set up filtering, and change other properties.

Figure 7.2 Creating visualizations

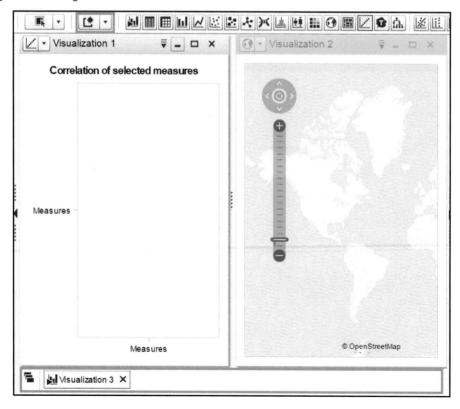

Visualizations are added to the canvas area by clicking on the icon to the left of the objects. This icon also has a drop-down menu that contains all of the objects so that you can do everything with one step. When you add a new visualization, the canvas splits and gives you a window for each one as shown above with Visualization 2. These can also be minimized by click on the minimize icon in the top right corner of each window. The visualizations are then placed in the bar at the bottom of the canvas shown at the bottom of Figure 7.2 with Visualization 3.

Automatic chart feature

A feature that is unique to the Explorer is the first object called Automatic Chart. This object is different from others in that it changes based on the data items that you provide it. Depending on the mixture of categories, measures, geography items, and date fields, SAS chooses the chart that works the best for that combination.

SAS has a built in algorithm to determine which chart you get.	
One measure	Histogram
One category	Bar chart
One aggregate measure	Crosstab
One datetime category and any number of other categories or measures	Line chart
One geography and up to two measures	Geo map
One geography and three or more measures	Bar chart
One document collection	Word cloud
Two measures	Scatter plot or heat map
Three or more measures	Scatter plot matrix or correlation matrix
One or more categories and any number of measures and geographies	Bar chart

Figure 7.3 Using the automatic chart feature

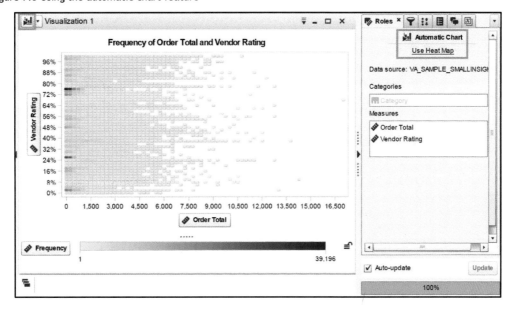

In the example above, you can see that we are using the Automatic Chart by the top left corner of the visualization and by the information contained in the **Roles** tab. We took the VA_SAMPLE_SMALLINSIGHT data set and added Order Total and Vendor Rating as measures to the chart. The chart generated a Heat Map from that information and that is what is shown above. We could click the **Use Heat Map** to switch over to a Heat Map permanently or we can continue to change the data items.

Figure 7.4 Removing roles in an automatic chart

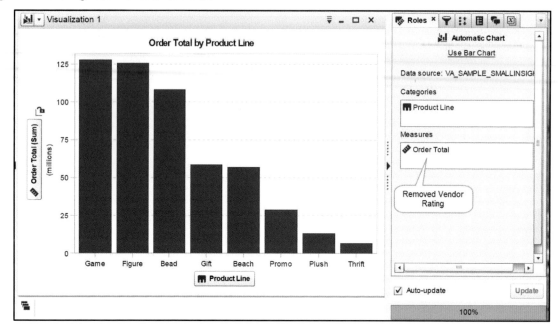

In this example, we removed Vendor Rating and added Product Line, you can see that the Autochart has now generated a bar chart for us.

The Autochart feature in the Explorer is a good way to start learning more about a data set, especially if it is one that you are just looking at for the first time. By adding and removing data items, you get a better sense of what your data contains as well as different views of it through all of the charts.

Box plots

In getting familiar with statistics, mean and median as well as maximum and minimum are some of the first concepts taught. This is because these statistical values explain a lot about your data and you can get a better sense of the values that you are working with from them. By using any measure in your data, the Box Plot object in the Explorer automatically distributes the data for you and displays a visualization of those statistics in a box-and-whisker format. For this example we are going to use the CARS data set in the SASHELP library.

Interpreting the results

The Box Plot object requires just a single measure for the visualization but a category and additional measures can be incorporated. In the following figure, we added the MPG (Highway) data item as a measure in the Box plot.

Figure 7.5 Box plot example

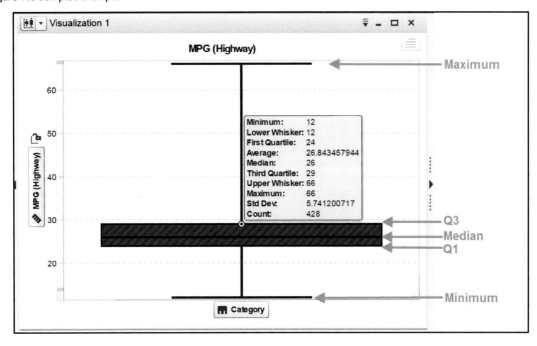

The dark blue shaded area in the middle is our box and the lines below and above it are our whiskers. The whiskers represent the minimum and maximum values of the range of data where the boxes represent the middle 50% of data points. The means that Q1 is the start of the 25% range and Q3 is end of the 75% range. The range from end of Q1 to end of Q3 is considered the interquartile range. The median is middle bar between the two where half of the data points are below it and half are above it. If you position the pointer over the box plot in the middle, you get the context box that gives you all of the exact values for the statistics.

The example above is the default setting for the Box Plot, but there are some changes that you can make in the **Properties** tab to better visualize the distribution of your data.

Figure 7.6 Box plot example with outliers

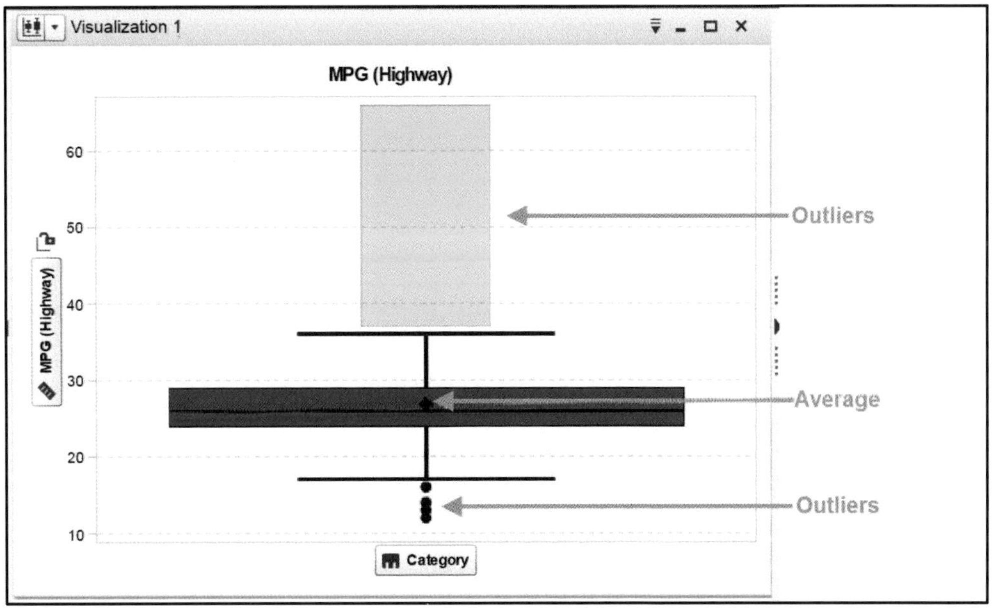

In the above figure, we checked the **Show averages** box and changed the Outliers drop-down list from **Hide Outliers** to **Show Outliers** in the **Properties** tab. The average shows up as a diamond in the box plot and the outliers show outside of the whiskers as either a light blue shaded box or black dots. There are always dots unless there are too many points to plot, which then they are shown as the light shaded box.

The Box Plot identifies an outlier as any data point that is farther than 1.5 times the size of the interquartile range away from it. So if our interquartile range is 24-29, that would be a distance of 5. After multiplying that by the 1.5 and adding it to our initial range, we end up with a range of 16.5-36.5. Anything outside of that range is now considered an outlier in the object.

Should you exclude outliers?

Before you can determine what to do with an outlier, you need to understand the cause. If the outlier is a measurement error, then it makes sense to exclude it. For example, if the MPG was listed as 288, it is likely that someone made a data entry error. The outlier can be excluded. There might be other cases where your model or underlying assumptions are incorrect. Study the outliers to ensure you understand their causes.

Depending on which one you choose, each of the Outliers options changes the way your data looks and can change the underlying statistics. With the default **Hide Outliers**, the outliers are not shown in the Visualization and the data points that would be outliers are incorporated into the whiskers. **Show Outliers** displays the outliers in the visualization and updates the whiskers to not include the outlier. Outliers are still considered for all of the other statistics. The **Ignore Outliers** option takes all of the outliers out of the visualization and the statistics are updated without them. That option is shown here below, you can see how the values in our box-and-whisker plot have changed.

Figure 7.7 Box plot ignoring outliers

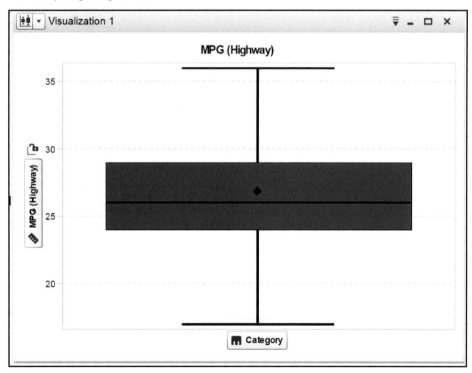

Adding more data items

The Box Plot can go beyond a single measure and handle a category and/or multiple measures. From our previous example, we added the Type data field as a Category in the **Roles** tab. This displays a separate box-and-whisker plot for each category.

Figure 7.8 Box plots with a category

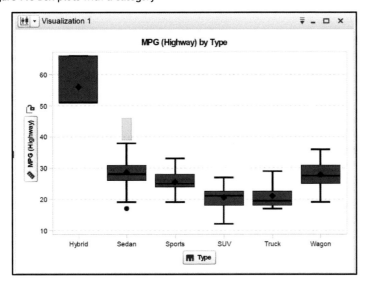

The distribution across categories allows for better analysis now that you can see how each one is broken out. The Hybrid box-and-whisker plot only has three data points, which is why it does not have any whiskers. Also notice how all of the box-and-whisker plots vary in size and shape. For the Truck, the minimum value is very close to the Q1 and Median values. This shows how that category has a lot more data points on the lower end compared to higher end of the range where the top whisker is.

Now we're going to add MPG (City) to the Measures in the **Roles** tab.

Figure 7.9 Box plot with a category and multiple measures

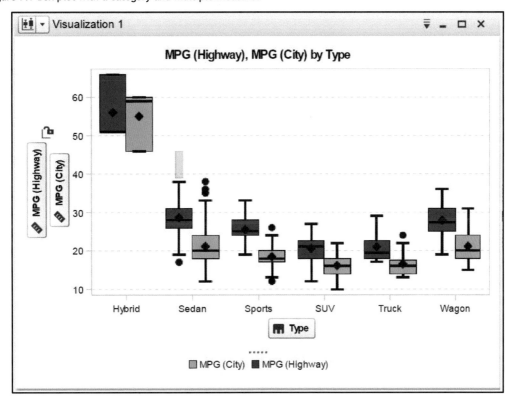

By adding another measure, our box-and-whisker plots now doubled since there is one of the new measures for each category. Its interesting how Truck and Hybrid categories do not have much of a change from Highway to

City, but the Sedan, Sports, and Wagon have a difference. Also, the Sedan is the only category that has multiple outliers for both the City and Highway measures.

When to use Box Plots

As you can see from the above example, Box Plots are a good way to see into the measures and look at the distribution of values. Here's a few situations to consider using a box plot:

• Exploration – Box plots can be a good place to start looking at your data since you can see how each of the measures are distributed and how they look with different categories.

• Outliers – Depending on the data set, you might want to find out if you have outliers that you would like to exclude from your analysis. The Box Plot provides a way to easily calculate and visualize them.

Histograms

As with Box Plots, Histograms are another way for you to see a frequency distribution of your data. Only one measure can be used with them, but histograms can be an effective way to see how your data is spread out as counts or percent of frequency. For this example, we are going to use the SASHELP.CARS data set that we used in the Box Plot example and switch over to a histogram.

Changing objects in a visualization

Within a Visualization, there are multiple ways that you can change the object to get a different look at your data.

Figure 7.10 Where to change an object

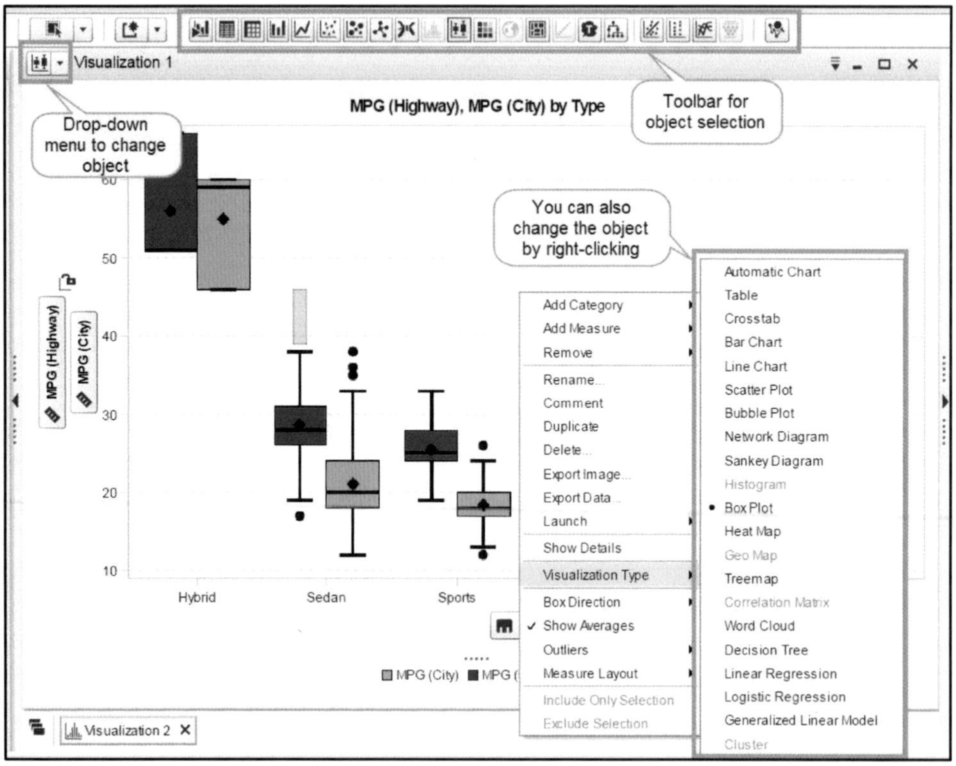

Now you'll notice with this example that the Histogram is not available. That's because at the end of the Box Plot section we had data items Type, MPG (Highway), and MPG (City) selected in the **Roles** Tab. When changing objects, the visualization uses the data items that are being used in the **Roles** tab. Some objects have restrictions on number and type of date items that they can handle. In the histogram's case, it only uses a single measure so that is grayed out until there is only one measure in the **Roles** tab.

After taking out the category Type and measure MPG (City), we then select the histogram and the visualization is updated.

Figure 7.11 Change visualization to histogram

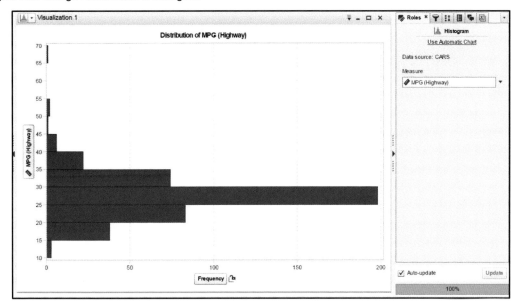

Histogram options

In the **Properties** tab there are a few options that you can apply to the Histogram. Similar to a bar chart, you can change the bar direction to horizontal. Also, you can change how the frequency is displayed by selecting Count or Percent. The default is Count, but by changing it to Percent your one axis updates to show how much of a percent each bin has out of all the points of data. Finally, you can also choose your own Bin count. The number of values in your measure determines the default bin count that is automatically applied.

Figure 7.12 Histogram example

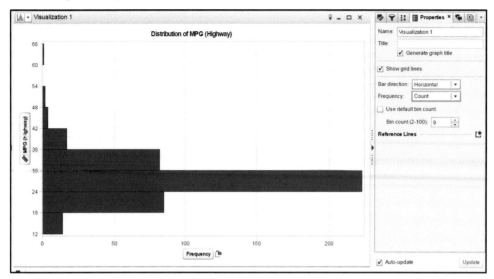

As shown above, when you use your own bin count, the object takes the maximum and minimum values and then evenly spread out the bins for that range.

When exploring data, histograms can be a good way to get an understanding of how measures are distributed. The box plot shows you plenty of statistics about a measure, but it can't show the variance of how packed your data can be in one area like the histogram can.

Using a correlation matrix

Finding pieces of information within your data that can lead to a competitive advantage or help improve an organization is what data analysis is all about. Finding relationships between data items is one way that can lead you to those bits of insight. Using the Correlation Matrix is one way to measure relationships between measures in the Explorer. The object takes in different measures, compares them against each other, and then determines whether and how strong a relationship is between them. For this example we are going to use the VA_SAMPLE_K12_STUDENT data set that is shipped with SAS Visual Analytics.

Calculating a correlation

Correlations in SAS Visual Analytics are calculated using Pearson's product-moment correlation coefficient calculation. This calculation takes in two measures and all of their values and generates a coefficient value that describes their relationship.

The range of the coefficient value can be anywhere from -1 to 1. Anything from -1 to 0 indicates a negative relationship, which means that as one of the measures increases the other decreases and vice versa. A correlation of 0 shows no relationship at all. Positive numbers from 0 to 1 indicate a positive relationship, which means that as one measure increases or decreases the other follows. SAS identifies these ranges of ratings for correlations as being Weak, Moderate, or Strong.

Figure 7.13 How SAS categorizes correlation values

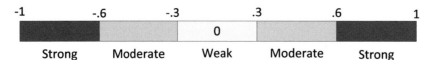

Understanding the matrix

In this example, we look at a combination of comprehension levels, scores, attendance days, and discipline days for students in a school district. You can get a matrix of correlations of all the measures against one another by using the **Within one set of measures** option in the **Roles** tab.

Figure 7.14 Correlation matrix example

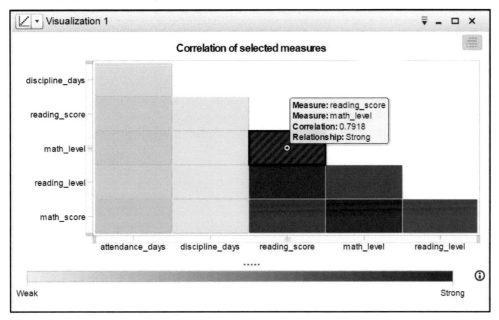

Here's what we learn from the above figure:

- There's a strong relationship between math and reading scores.

- Attendance days are not related to test scores or comprehension levels.

- Discipline days are not related to test scores or comprehension levels.

The strength of the correlation determines the color of the box. If you position the pointer over any of the boxes, then you get to see the actual numbers as well as how SAS has classified the correlation.

What's interesting in this example is how attendance days and discipline days are not related to scores at all. One might think that the less that students are in school or disciplined for school would mean less learning, but that might not be the case.

Now if you do not want the full matrix and instead just want to compare a single measure against others or two different sets against each other, then you can use the **Between two sets of measures** option in the roles tab under **Show correlations**. This breaks the chart out into an X and Y axis that you can control which measures you want to see against each other. Below, we wanted to see which measure had the highest correlation value with Math score, so we put it on its own in the Y axis.

Figure 7.15 Correlation example between two sets of measures

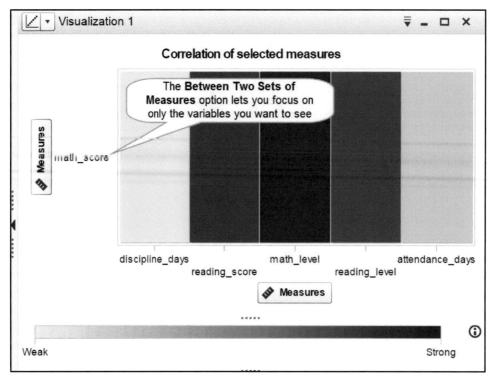

Interpreting a correlation value

With a lot of data and a strong correlation between the values of two measures, you might assume that the correlation between the values indicates a relationship between the concepts that the values are measuring. Sometimes that is not always the case. The phrase *correlation does not equal causation* is common in the field of statistics and means that just because two measures have values that are related—which is measured by correlation—it does not mean that the concepts behind the measures have a direct relationship. There are many different forms of an apparent relationship between data items. In Steven Few's book *Now You See It*, he breaks down correlations to meaning one of four possibilities:

- One measure causes the others behavior

- Neither causes the other's behavior, both are caused by other variables

- Neither causes the other's behavior, another variable connects them

- Correlation is erroneous due to insufficient or bad data

In our previous example, the math and reading score had a strong positive correlation with each other. This indicates that as one goes up, the other should follow. Because we also saw minimal relationships between the math and reading scores and the attendance days and discipline days, we might conclude that some other factor, such as the intelligence of each student, is causing the high correlation between the math and reading scores.

Shark Attacks and Ice Cream Sales

If you looked at the amount of ice cream that is sold compared to the number of shark attacks by month or season, those two measures would have a strong correlation value. Both occur more often in the summer months compared to the winter. Obviously, they do not have anything related to each other except that they change as the season's turn. This would be an example of neither measure causing the other's behavior because there is another variable that connects them—which is seasonality.

Forecasting

Forecasting is not an object by itself and is rather an extension of the Line Chart object. It is included here as its own section since it is one way to do predictive analysis in the application and has a lot of options for you to forecast data.

Using data that contains a time frame, you can use the Forecasting option in the Explorer Line Chart object that predicts how the data trends to some upcoming time frame. In this section, you learn how the forecasting is done and how to use the Scenario Analysis option that comes with it. For our example, we are going to use the VA_SAMPLE_SMALLINSIGHT data set.

Working with the forecasting option

In the **Roles** tab of the line chart is where you can find the option for forecasting. The option is grayed out until a date item is added in the Category section. Once that is populated, you can select the Forecasting option. When selected, a vertical line appears in the line chart dividing the ending date of the user's data and the beginning of the forecasting results.

Figure 7.16 Forecasting example

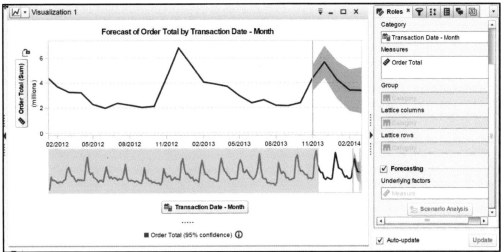

As long as you have a date field and a measure, anything can be forecasted. Popular examples include sales, weather, and company performance. For this example, we are going to stick with the Small Insight company data. Below is an example turning the forecasting option on for the Order Total measure and Transaction Date - Month (duplicate Transaction Date with MMYYYY format)

The data ends in October 2013, so the forecast starts in November 2013 which where the gray vertical line is placed. The dark blue line in the forecast shows the most likely trajectory of the stock price and the blue shaded area is the confidence interval. By looking at the legend at the bottom, you can see that we are working with a 95% confidence interval. This means that the model projects a 95% chance that the future Order Total falls somewhere in the blue shaded area.

Figure 7.17 Forecasting options

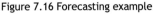

For this example, the forecast is only going out to the next six quarters. This is called the forecast duration and can be changed with the confidence interval by going to the **Properties** tab. At the bottom of the tab, there is an option to change those values, shown in Figure 7.17 above.

As you increase the forecast duration the confidence band typically expands since the further into the future you go, the more uncertainty there is. It's important to note here that models like these work better with as much data as you can give them. If you only have a few points, then the model is going to have a hard time coming up with accurate results.

Building better forecasts

A good indicator of future performance is past performance. When creating a forecast the more historical data you can provide, the more likely your forecast is to produce a better result.

How is the data modeled?

The forecast runs your data through six different models and selects the one with the best fit. Here is a list of the different exponential smoothing models available:

- Damped-trend
- Linear
- Seasonal
- Simple
- Winters method (additive)
- Winters method (multiplicative)

As the data is modeled, the Root-Mean-Square-Error (RMSE) is calculated for each model behind the scenes. The RMSE is a measure of how close the predicted values are to the real data. The lower the RMSE, the more accurate the model is. SAS Visual Analytics then selects the model with the lowest RMSE to use in the forecast.

Figure 7.18 Forecast analysis tab

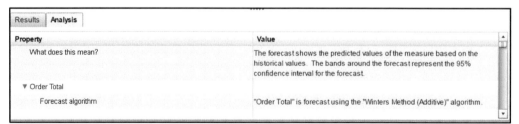

After selecting the forecasting option, you can see which model was used as well as a table of the results by clicking on the ⓘ at the bottom of the line chart. Shown in Figure 7.18, the Winters Method (Additive) algorithm was selected for the forecast used in the first example.

Look for underlying factors

In order to improve our analysis, we don't just want to look at one historical measure and base the forecast on those values. There could also be other data points that might have an influence on the modeling of that measure, and if they are brought in then our model can become even stronger since it has multiple variables incorporated.

The models that the application runs to build our forecast are able to include other measures into the analysis. By going to the Underlying factors section in the **Roles** tab and clicking the drop-down list, you can add one or more measures from your data set into the analysis. As with the original forecasting, SAS runs the data through the models, adding autoregressive integrated moving average models (ARIMA) to go with the original six, to determine the best fit. If the added measure does not have an influence on the model, then it is grayed out. When the new measure does influence the model, the chart is updated with the results. In the below figure, we added in the Sales Rep Rating as a possible underlying factor.

Figure 7.19 Forecasting with underlying factors

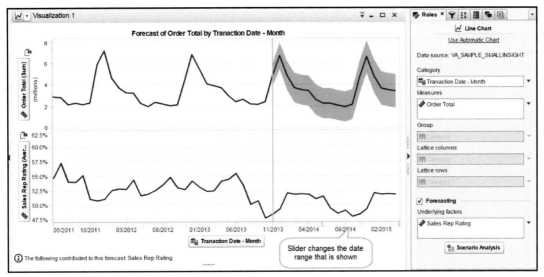

Note: The data goes all the way back to December 1997 but the slider has been moved to just show the past three years.

Continuing our forecast example, adding Sales Rep Rating as a possible underlying factor, the forecasting has been updated with the results. The top chart is similar to our original forecast of Small Insight's monthly sales except now the forecasted section has improved. In our first run, the projection for 6 months out had a 95% confident predicted monthly sales range of $1.19-$5.16 (millions). When using Sales Rep Rating as a factor, that confidence band is now narrowed to $2.01-4.82 (millions), which is a notable reduction in the range.

Using the scenario analysis

Once you have found an underlying factor that influences the forecast, the Scenario Analysis button at the bottom of the **Roles** tab becomes available to use. After clicking on it, a window shows the forecasted data field and the underlying factor. There are two options for users to change, Goal Seeking and Scenario Analysis.

With Scenario Analysis, you can go in and manipulate the underlying factors and see how the forecast would change based on those new values. In our example, we are trying to get our average Sales Rep Rating around 60% and want to investigate how that could affect our monthly sales. We set this expectation by clicking on the Sales Rep Rating button on the left side of the screen and selecting "Set Series Values". A pop-up window appears and this is where the values are set with a fixed number, a numeric increment, or a percentage increase.

Figure 7.20 Forecasting with scenario analysis

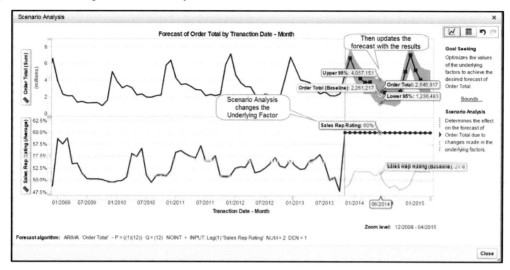

After you click **OK**, the forecasted numbers for the Sales Rep Rating are updated with the 60% set increase. There is a gray line in the underlying factor's forecast section that indicates the original data points. Since the underlying factor has been altered, only Scenario Analysis is available to use and is the only option available in the right menu. When Apply is selected, the forecast is then updated with the new results.

In Figure 7.20, the data points and the confidence band have now started to trend higher. The gap is not that far off from the original with the first forecasted quarter, but if you position the pointer over the month interval, the original baseline data is shown along with the updated forecast points. The forecasted monthly sales for April 2016 have risen from a baseline of $2.26 million to $2.65 million. You could take away from this model that improving the Sales Rep Rating over time might have a significant influence on the monthly sales.

Figure 7.21 Forecasting with goal seeking

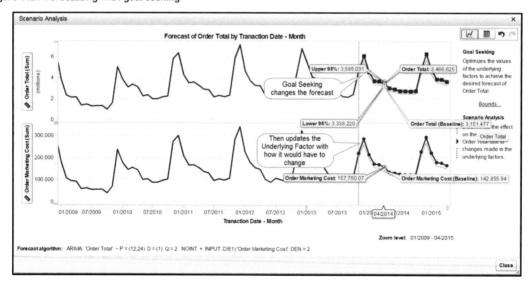

Goal seeking works in a similar way except that you are changing the forecasted values and then seeing how the underlying factors would have to change to get those results. Since the underlying factors can have just a small influence on the forecast and they also do not have a confidence range, you only get an accurate result with something that is highly correlated. So for this example, we're going to keep the Order Totals by month, but instead use the Order Marketing Costs as an underlying factor.

For the analysis in this example, we increased the forecasted Order Total by 10% by clicking on the data item's button on the left side. Once you do that, an Apply button appears on the right side underneath Goal Seeking.

When that is clicked the graph updates with the results. You can see that the two line graphs are very similar and we know that since the more you market your products the more likely they are to get sold. At the six-month mark, the Order Marketing Cost has gone from $142,856 to $157,750 for an increase of 10.42%. This goal seeking analysis shows that if we ignore other factors, the marketing costs would have to rise by 10.42% in order to hit the 10% increase in Order Total.

Word clouds

All of the objects that we looked at so far have been focused on analyzing measures with some being able to add categories for an added layer of investigation. Switching things up, word clouds are objects that explore categorical data items. Each word cloud object takes a category field that contains text and can analyze it for words of importance, frequency of words, or add a measure to place a value on certain words. For this example, we are going to not use a data set already in SAS and instead use the option to import data from twitter.

Loading social media data

At the Add Data Source window in Explorer, you have option to load from any of the tables already loaded into LASR or you can import data from your local machine, a server, Hadoop (if installed), or SAS can go out and grab public data on the Internet. In the Other section of the Import Data window, there are options to get data from Facebook, Google Analytics, and Twitter.

Figure 7.22 How to load social media data

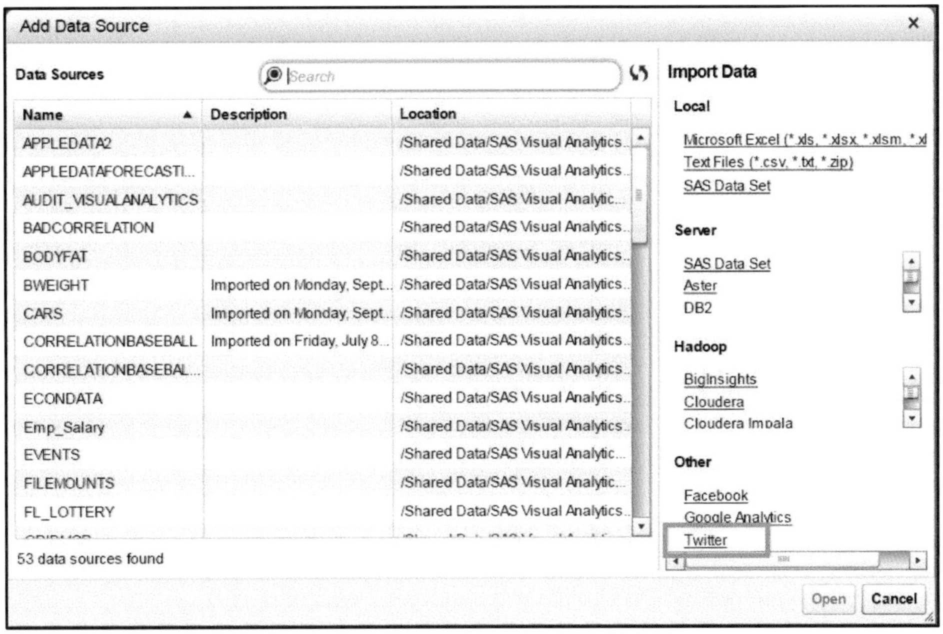

When you click the Twitter link, it first asks you to log in to an account. Once you do that, you are able to click the link again and get to the Import Twitter Data screen. For this example, we signed in as the Twitter account @zencos which you can see in the bottom left corner of the window. In this window, you can also enter in what you would like to search for, the number of tweets to pull, and the output table name for LASR.

Figure 7.23 Import twitter data window

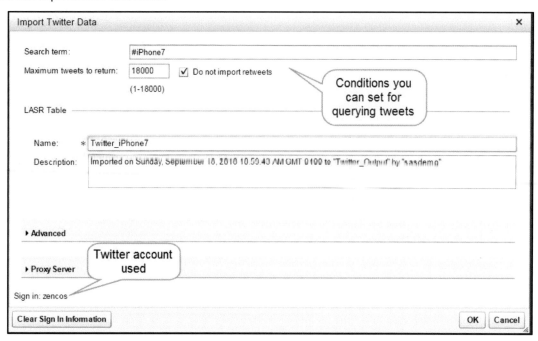

In our example, this is data set was created two days after Apple released the iPhone7. We want to gauge how people react and feel about the product. With that being said, we enter #iPhone7, which is the most popular hashtag used for the product on twitter. 18,000 is entered for the number of tweets since that is the maximum allowed and we want to view as much data as possible for our analysis. We also check the **Do not import retweets** box so that we are only grabbing original tweets and not duplicate ones. After clicking OK, the data pull begins and takes a little more than a few seconds since it is scraping all publicly available tweets that contain the hashtag and twitter handle that we are searching for.

Setting up the word cloud

The Word Cloud object has two different ways to visualize the category data item that is being analyzed. One is to use category values, which takes the category data item as a whole string and use frequency or another measure to determine how to display those values. The other is to use text analytics, which takes the category data item and examines each word in the string. Each word is then displayed based on frequency or importance within the text.

Using category values

Under **Show word cloud** in the **Roles** Tab there is the options where we can select category values. With the category values, we want to look at location to see where people are tweeting from, so we add authorlocation to the Words role in the **Roles** Tab.

Figure 7.24 Word cloud example

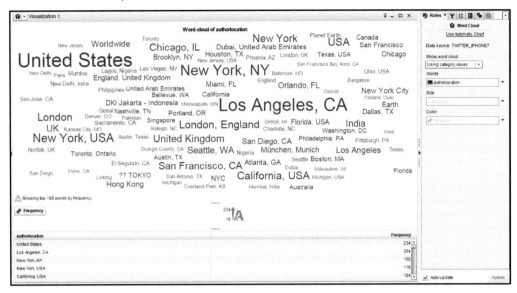

It turns out that there were quite a few people from the United States and its major cities that were tweeting about the product. Apple is headquartered in the United States and many of its customers live in the United States so that would make sense that a lot of people from these areas would be tweeting about the new phone. It was also released in 24 other countries throughout the weekend, which is why you see other countries and cities in the world scattered across the word cloud.

Note: Twitter gives users the option put in their own locations, which is why the data is not standardized.

Also, notice at the warning sign in the bottom left corner. The word cloud limits the number of words allowed so that it can properly display the disparity in size for each of the words and so that they are also readable.

The **Roles** tab also lets you change what determines the size and color of the word, which is similar to the Treemap object that was covered in Chapter 5. We are going to leave the Frequency in the size but put the measure retweetcount into the Color field. This aggregates that measure for each of the location words displayed in the object. You can change the color gradient by going to the **Properties** tab.

Figure 7.25 Word cloud with a measure

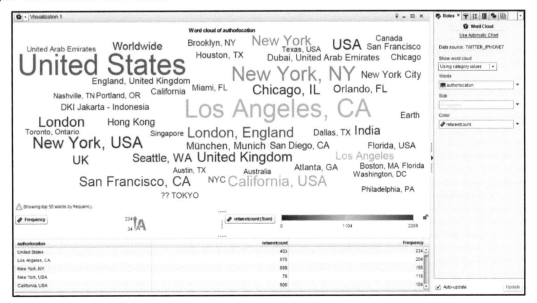

San Francisco, CA had an overwhelming amount of retweets among their tweets as well. Because Apple is headquartered near San Francisco and because many other companies in the industry are also located near San Francisco, there were probably a lot of employees, journalists and consumers tweeting about the iPhone 7.

Was the product release a positive or negative experience for everyone? Let's jump into the text analytics option to find out.

Using text analytics

On the **Roles** tab you can select **Using text analytics** to switch to how the word cloud handles the data. This option needs a Document collection instead of a category so that it can analyze individual terms inside the category data field. You can create a Document Collection by right clicking on the category data item and selecting Document Collection. For this example, we do that with the body data item. This is the actual text from the tweet that is in each row of data. The body data item is then available in the Document collection drop-down list on the **Roles** tab.

Figure 7.26 Using text analytics

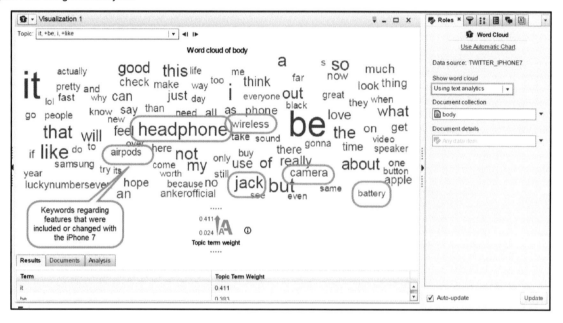

After selecting a document collection, the word cloud is then updated with the results. Each term is given a Topic term weight that analyzes the frequency of the term as well as the importance of it. The value given then determines how large the term appears in the word cloud. You can see that there are a lot of common words but others that are important to what we are looking for. There were many hardware updates to the new iPhone that included a better camera, improved battery, new home button, and removal of the headphone jack. These are all popular terms from the tweets that were analyzed.

Now we want to look more into if these people that were tweeting about the new features were happy with the change. In the **Properties** tab, there is a Text Analytics Settings section where you can choose to check Analyze document sentiment. By clicking on this option it brings up a window where you can also check an Identify term roles box, which groups like nouns together, and specify how many topics you want created. After clicking **OK**, the word cloud is updated with the sentiment analysis. Similar terms are also grouped into topics that can be found in the top left corner or as a tab in the bottom analysis section. So we want to find a grouping that is similar to our new features. By clicking on that drop-down list, you can find terms that are commonly found together.

Figure 7.27 Text analytics with sentiment analysis

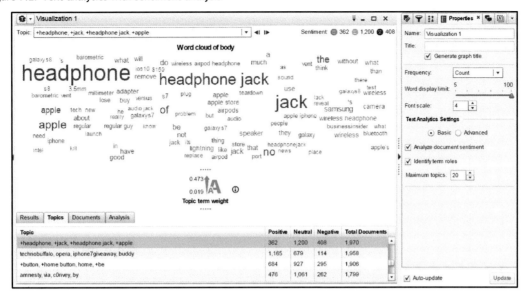

The sentiment analysis looks at everything in the document collection field and determines the nature of the text. Each item gets categorized as positive (green), neutral (yellow), or negative (red). The results can be found in the upper right corner of the word cloud as well as in the **Topics** tab. With mostly neutral and a few more negative than positive tweets, there is definitely a mixed reaction regarding the decision to remove the headphone jack. However, when switching to topics that included iPhone7 or home button, the reactions were about three to one in favor of the positive ones. It appears that people are publicly enjoying the new product, but they are still on the fence about having to deal without a place to plug in their headphones.

Word clouds with unstructured data

In a 2014 SAS Global Forum paper "SAS Admins need a Dashboard, Too", they use a word cloud example that looks at SAS procedures and DATA steps executed on a server. In the word cloud, you were able to see which ones were taking up the most memory and how much CPU time they were taking up on the server. This data was pulled from APM artifact tables, which are similar to logs. This is a useful visualization so that administrators can see what executions could be slowing down a server just by picking up the most common words in an unstructured log field. Thinking about this makes you wonder what sources of unstructured data you might have around that could be easily analyzed with a word cloud.

Scatter plot

A scatter plot is a graph that plots individual points for each row of data based on where they land according to the X-axis and Y-axis variables. Similar to the Correlation Matrix, the Scatter Plot object is used to show relationships between two measures. However, this object also adds in a visual aspect to it in that you can see all of your data points and where they fall between the two measures. Using each measure as an axis, the scatter plot displays each point in the chart which then gives you a two dimensional view of how the data is distributed across both of the measures. This can give you an idea of how the measures are related to one another. For this example, we use the bodyfat and cars data sets that are located in sashelp library.

Data analysis

The setup for the Scatter Plot is straightforward, you just need to add your two measures into the visualization or into the **Roles** tab.

Figure 7.28 Scatter plot example

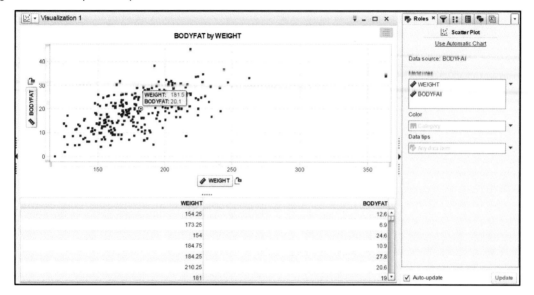

In this example, we added WEIGHT and BODYFAT as our measures. For each row of data, a point is plotted on the graph based on the values of the two measures. If you position the pointer over any of the data points, their values show in the details box.

The graph gives us a good indication on how the data varies between the two measures. Most of it is concentrated between 150-200 for WEIGHT and 10-30 for BODYFAT. Other than that, the data fluctuates a lot where even someone at a weight of 150 can be anywhere between 5-30 bodyfat. That being said, we are interested in whether there is a possible relationship between the two measures. So if BODYFAT goes up or down, can we expect a change with WEIGHT as well? For that type of analysis, we can add lines of best fit to the scatter plot to help us out.

Lines of best fit are a way to model the relationship between variables. This is done in the scatter plot object by going to the **Properties** tab and clicking on the Fit Line drop-down list. The fit line is formed between the two measures by taking in all of the data points and calculating the line that best represents the relationship for the data by maximizing the R-square value. R-squared can range from zero to one, the closer the value is to one signals a more significant possible relationship between the two measures. In this example, we have selected a Linear line of best fit.

Figure 7.29 Scatter plot with a fit line

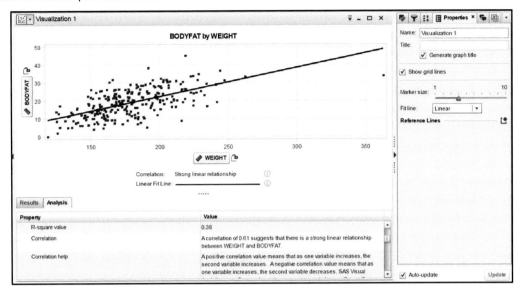

After the selection is made, all possible Linear lines are calculated and the one with the highest R-square value according to the data is displayed. You can see that it goes straight through the data points and has an upward trajectory. In the **Analysis** tab at the bottom is where you can find the R-square value (0.38) and also the correlation value. Just like the calculation in the correlation matrix, linear fit lines display the correlation calculation as well. You can see here that with a correlation value of 0.61, SAS tells us that there is a possible strong relationship between these two measures.

In the Fit Line drop-down list, there are also other options that include Best Fit, Cubic, Quadratic, and PSpline. Quadratic and Cubic can be used if your data is varied or might have multiple points of change where a trend takes the data in a new direction. Quadratic lines have one curve where Cubic lines have two, similar to an S shape. The PSpline line fits the line in pieces, which can have multiple curves and breaks across the data. The Best Fit option calculates the R-square value of the Linear, Cubic, and Quadratic lines and then displays the one with the highest R-square value. In the following figure, we switch our selection to the Best Fit option.

Figure 7.30 Scatter plot with best fit option

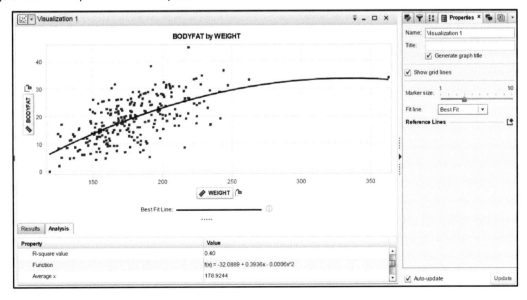

For our two measures, the Quadratic line of best fit had the highest R-square value and fit our data the best. You can tell that it is a Quadratic line by the single curve. There is a property in the **Analysis** tab that tells you which line was selected. The R-square value in the **Analysis** tab is 0.40 compared to 0.38 that we had with the Linear line.

Interpreting lines of best fit

In Stephen Few's book *Now you see it*, he goes over four patterns to look for when analyzing relationships in data.

- **Direction** - Does the slope go up or down? If the slope is going up, then you have a positive relationship, which means as one measure increases, so does the other. When the slope is going down then you have a negative relationship and as one measure increases, the other decreases.

- **Strength** - How condensed are the data points to the line? If most of the data points follow the line, then the relationship is going to be stronger. However, if they are scattered all over or they are all compressed into one small area, then a relationship might not be as obvious.

- **Shape** - Is it a straight line or curved? A straight line signifies a simple relationship, when one measure goes one way, the other measure goes follows suite. A curve means that there could be a changing point. This means that as your data is following the line, there comes a point where the relationship changes. These points of curvature can be very important to understand more about your data.

- **Outliers** - Are there any outliers? Outliers can be good to find examples of what doesn't follow the relationship.

For our bodyfat to weight example, our best fit line is a positive curved line with a clustered area of values and a few possible outliers. The positive relationship was not that apparent at first, but with the addition of the line it's easier to visualize how the data does trend in an upward manner. This indicates a possible correlation that as bodyfat or weight increases, so does the other. Now the curved shape is a bit vague. We have an outlier on the far right side that is not close to any of the data points. With that point's bodyfat being low compared to the upward trajectory of the line where the points are condensed, it could have thrown off our model. We finish this analysis in the Heat map section, which is another way to visualize data in a manner like the scatter plot.

Adding categories

Stepping away from the data analysis portion of the scatter plot, there is also a way to add categories to your chart, which can make for great visualizations. In the **Roles** tab under Color, you can add a category into the chart that splits the data markers into different shapes and colors. In the figure below, we are looking at the CARS data set with measures of HorsePower and Weight. The Type category was added in as a color.

Figure 7.31 Scatter plot with categories

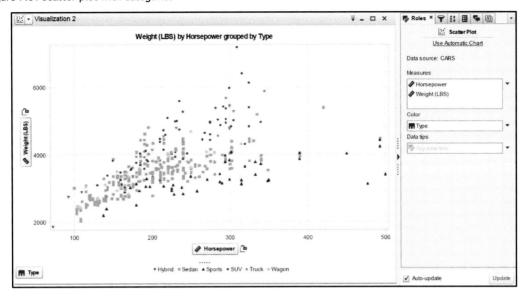

In the legend at the bottom, all of the types of cars are separated into different colors as well as shapes. When you look into the graph, it becomes very easy to see the variance between all of the types. The sports cars have relatively low weight and their horsepower differs throughout the graph, the trajectory is only slightly upward. The SUVs and trucks are the opposite having a steep upward trajectory with weight to horsepower but never reaching over 350 horsepower.

Adding a category can give you good insight into how the individual data points are spread out and how the values in the category compare. When you add a category, this does take away the option to add a fit line.

Heat map

The Heat Map is a unique object that provides an alternative to a scatter plot that is more capable of visualizing relationships when using categorical data. For the data types that it uses, there is an X-axis and a Y-axis that can contain both measures and categories. For the measures, they are binned in to cells that cover a certain range. With categories, each unique value has its own cell. There is also an option for color that is defaulted to Frequency, but any measure can be used here. This role changes the color of the cell depending on where the value of the measure falls according to the range of colors. For the example with two measures, we continue our analysis with the bodyfat data set from the Scatter Plot. Then we use the Insight Toy Company data set to look at how a measure changes the object and what you can look at.

Data analysis

In the previous section on Scatter Plots, we looked at the BODYFAT data set and how the data was spread out according to the weight and bodyfat measures. In the figure below, we have added them into the axes of the heat map except this time we have removed an outlier from the data set.

Figure 7.32 Heat map example

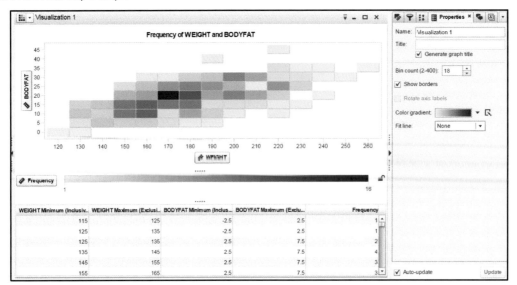

This is the exact same graph that we saw with the scatter plot except now we can tell how concentrated the data is by the color of the bins. The Bin count in the **Properties** tab lets you change the sizes of the bins and you can add more, making the ranges smaller, or subtract some, making the ranges larger, by changing the number in the box. The color gradient determines the color range of the measure that you have in the color role. For this chart we have just left it as the defaulted white to blue. You can see in the chart how the middle sections that are much more concentrated with data points become darker shades of blue.

Figure 7.33 Heat map with fit line

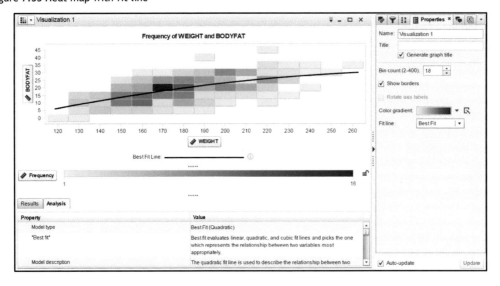

In the **Properties** tab there is also an option for the Fit line as there was with the scatter plot. This is only available when you have two measures as the axes. As we did with the scatter plot example, we select the Best Fit option and it is shown in the figure below.

Now back when we were analyzing our fit line from the scatter plot, we got a Quadratic line as our best fit but were unsure about the outlier having an effect on our model. In this instance, we have removed that from the data that we are working with in the filters tab and get the same result. This Quadratic line begins to flatten when we get to the higher range in bodyfat and weight. When that happens, it starts to indicate a non-linear relationship compared to the other parts of the graph. This means that in those higher ranges, with an increase in weight, we can't expect the same or possibly any increase in bodyfat.

Using a category

Even though using two measures works similarly between the heat map and scatter plot, adding in a category is much different. In a scatter plot, you added a category as the third data item (which was color), and the object split out the marks for the data points according to that category. With a heat map, the category goes into an axis. This enables you to view all of the values of the category according to where they fall in the range of the measure on the other axis. Then the color of each cell, which represents the collective value for the measure of all data points that fall into that cell, gives you another visual to analyze. In the below figure, we look at Facility Country and Product Quality data fields in the Insight Toy Company data set with Frequency in the color role.

Figure 7.34 Heat map with a category

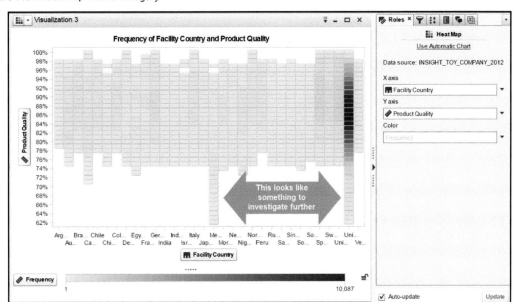

There's a lot to interpret in this visualization. This data set is based on orders. What sticks out right away is how concentrated those orders are in the United States facilities. This could just be from most customer orders being within the United States and having more facilities there than any other country. More interesting though, is how the United States and Mexico are the only countries with orders that have a Product Quality lower than 70%. That's not just a few orders either; this includes orders in every bin from 70% down to 62%. There are 30 other countries and all of them are in fairly similar ranges. It's probably worth investigating further into the facilities producing those low product qualities.

Similar to the bubble plot and treemap from the Data Visualization chapter, the heat map analyzes three different data items, which gives a unique look at the data. This can be overwhelming to analyze, but there is information to be discovered this way. If you were to only look at the product quality averages for all of the countries in Figure 7.34, the United States and Mexico would trend lower but you would not see how drastic it is compared to the other countries like it is shown in the heat map.

Other tips when using the Explorer

The Explorer and Designer applications look similar, but do have differences in functionality. Here are a few additional features to be aware of with the Explorer.

Include and exclude

Sometimes there could be a cluster of data or category value that you want to look more into. By using the include and exclude option, you can easily apply a filter to your data in the object and get to what you want to look at. Using this method can be much quicker than finding the exact requirements for filters if you are just exploring your data. Here's how you can access these options:

1. Select or highlight the data that you want to keep or exclude from the analysis. Then right-click the area.

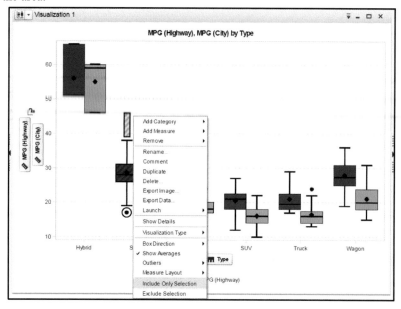

2. At the bottom of the options are the Include and Exclude choices. Select the one that you want to use.

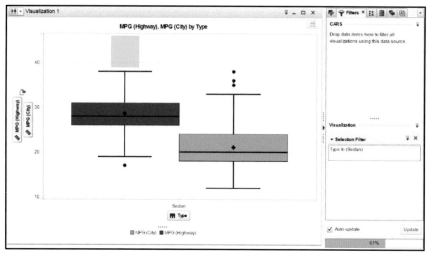

After your selection is made, the visualization is updated. In the filters tab on the right panel, you notice that the selection filter has been updated with what was selected. You can always delete this filter to go back to the original visualization.

3. These filters even stay with you as you change objects. In this example, we right-clicked the object and selected a scatter plot.

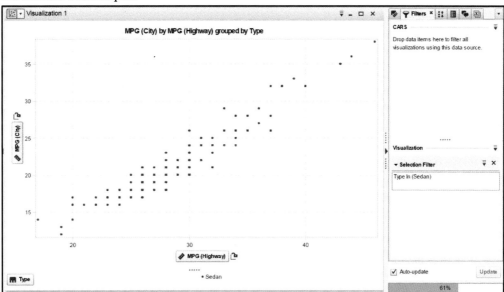

Moving visualizations to the Designer

As you have seen, the Explorer offers a few more objects and data analysis features than the Designer does. That's good since the Explorer is meant more for diving into your data, but sometimes you might want to use those visualizations in a report so that you can share it with other users. However, if you try to open an exploration in the Designer you won't be able to find it.

When opening in the Designer, the application is looking for report objects. Explorations and reports are saved as different objects, which is why you do not see any of your explorations in the folders. You can get around this problem by exporting a visualization as a report object. Then you can Import it into a report. Here are the steps:

1. Open the Exploration that has the Visualization that you want to move into the Designer. Then, select **File ▶ Export ▶ Export as a Report**.

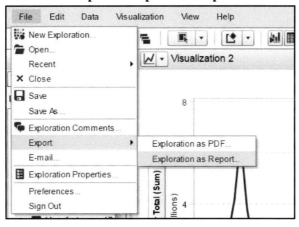

2. Select the visualizations that you want to export as a report. You can select more than one. Click **OK** and then save the Report.

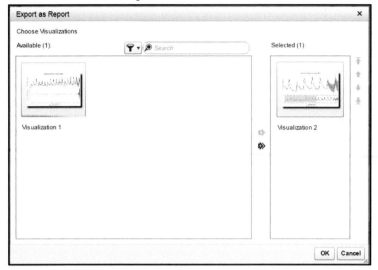

3. Go to the Designer and open a report. Then click the **Import** tab in the left panel. Choose **Select a report to import** in the drop-down list and then **Import a report**. Find your visualizations that you saved as a report.

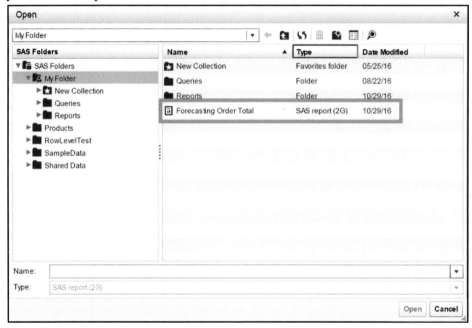

4. Open the report object and you can see your exploration with all your visualizations and their objects listed in a folder structure in the **Import** tab. Drag the objects into the canvas.

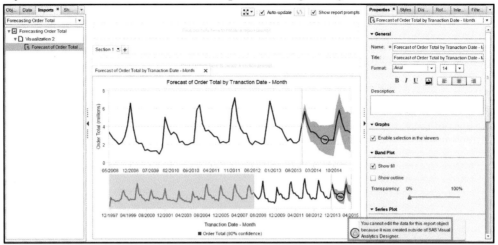

Proceed with caution!

In the preceding figure, we brought in a visualization where the data analysis feature was not available in the Designer. There is a warning sign in the bottom right corner of the object that lets us know we cannot edit the data. Since these features are not available in the Designer, anything involving the data cannot be changed, so there are no options for the Roles, Display Rules, Filters, and so on. You can change how object looks with some options in the Properties and Styles tabs. So before moving a visualization object over it's a good idea to make sure your data is finalized.

References

The following sources were used in the chapter or provide more information about the topics discussed:

Aanderud, Tricia, and Michelle Homes. 2014. "SAS Admins Need a Dashboard, Too." *Proceedings of the SAS Global Forum 2014 Conference.* Paper 1247-2014. Cary, NC: SAS Institute Inc.

Few, Stephen. 2009. *Now you see it: Simple visualization techniques for quantitative analysis.* Oakland, CA: Analytics Press.

Gonick, Larry, and Woollcott. Smith. 1993. *The Cartoon Guide to Statistics.* New York, NY: HarperCollins Publishers Inc.

Huff, Darrell. 1954. *How to Lie with Statistics.* New York, NY: W.W. Norton & Company, Inc.

Milton, Michael. 2009. *Head First Data Analysis.* Sebastopol, CA: O'Reilly Media Inc.

SAS Institute Inc. 2015. *SAS Visual Analytics 7.3: User's Guide.* Cary, NC: SAS Institute Inc.

part three

administration and data loading

The SAS Visual Analytics solution provides a remarkably powerful and dynamic set of software tools with which you can accomplish astounding feats of large-scale digital data manipulation and analysis. It's important to understand how those software tools function and interoperate so that you can get the best and most efficient operations out of them.

In this part you will learn additional methods for loading data, how to administer the LASR Analytic Server, and tips for tuning your system.

- Chapter 8 Loading Data

  The SAS LASR Analytic Server supports a wide-range of data sources. This chapter briefly explains what types of sources are supported as well as the considerations of serial versus parallel loading.

- Chapter 9 LASR Administration

  To successfully maintain the SAS LASR Analytic Server, the SAS administrator should be familiar with the SAS Business Intelligence architecture, Hadoop architecture, and how their respective software services inter-operate.

- Chapter 10 Performance Considerations

  SAS software offers the enterprise an extremely flexible deployment and operational architecture. Optimizing the software for your data and users for best utilization is a necessary step. This chapter discusses the considerations for scalability, availability, and efficiency.

loading data

SAS Visual Analytics 7.3 relies exclusively on the SAS LASR Analytic Server as both data repository and analytic engine. For this section of the book, we want to look at how data gets into LASR. As it turns out, data can be loaded from several sources directly into the LASR Analytic Server. Each source has different potential options, dependencies, and features.

In this chapter we will do the following:

- look at how the SAS LASR Analytic Server is optimized to work with large volumes of data

- explore the SASHDAT file format, which is specifically designed to work with high-performance distributed data

- illustrate other techniques for parallel loading of data.

- investigate the automatic loading of data into the LASR Analytic server, which is available to SAS Visual Analytics

In-memory is different

The LASR Analytic Server is the key component that makes SAS Visual Analytics unique. The LASR Analytic Server is an in-memory data storage area that lets users quickly access and combine data. Before the LASR Analytic Server, each time that you queried data or performed a calculation, the computer would have to retrieve data off disk. This would take up a lot of time for large volumes of data, especially if multiple users were on the server at once. With the LASR Analytic Server, all tables are pre-loaded into RAM, so the data is easily accessible for various analyses. And if you want to increase the amount of data or otherwise improve performance, additional servers can be added to the system, enabling the LASR Analytic Server to distribute the workload across more machines.

It's about speed

There are now two different ways that data can be loaded into the LASR Analytic Server, serial or parallel. Remember that the LASR Analytic Server is in-memory, so when it goes down or gets restarted, all tables in the server need to be reloaded. In the serial loading process, data is loaded from a source system, passing through a single I/O connection that can act as a bottleneck, not allowing data to flow into the system as fast as possible. By using a parallel loading process, data is transferred from source over to LASR across multiple I/O channels simultaneously, which is far more time effective.

Understanding the non-distributed deployment

When the SAS LASR Analytic Server software is running on a single host machine, SAS Visual Analytics is operating as a non-distributed deployment. This means that all of the data loaded in memory for LASR is kept to a single physical machine—not distributed across the memory of multiple hosts. Other software components of the SAS system can be deployed together on just one host alongside LASR or could split across different hosts themselves as licensed for your site.

Figure 8.1 SAS Visual Analytics non-distributed deployment

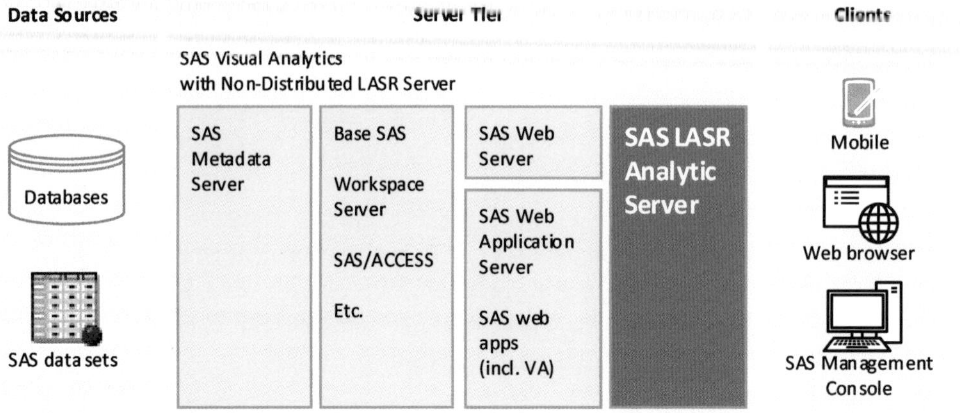

In the illustration above, users access the SAS Visual Analytics web application from the web browser on their PCs or from the SAS Mobile BI app on their mobile devices. The SAS Visual Analytics web application coordinates user access and authorization with the SAS Metadata Server. User requests for report content and other data-driven displays are sent from SAS Visual Analytics to the LASR Analytic Server, where it acts upon data in memory to perform the necessary analytic tasks. Administration of the LASR Analytic Server—namely loading and unloading tables as well as stopping and starting the LASR service—requires use of the SAS Workspace Server by an authorized user. Data from any source that is accessible to Base SAS (with an optional SAS/ACCESS engine) can be loaded into the non-distributed LASR Analytic Server.

When working with a non-distributed LASR Analytic Server, data is always loaded serially because the data flows through a single point in two places:

- The LASR Analytic Server itself is a single entity.

- The Workspace server is also a single entity that acts as a bridge for transferring data into the LASR Analytic Server.

Understanding the distributed deployment

Instead of running on one server host, a distributed LASR Analytic Server is deployed in pieces across multiple machines. All of the in-memory analytics features offered by LASR in a distributed deployment are the same as the features offered in a non-distributed deployment. The only difference now is that the data is spread across the memory of the LASR Worker nodes—effectively breaking a large problem into several smaller ones that can be processed simultaneously. This is why the distributed LASR Analytic Server is so fast. The following figure shows how the distributed environment is set up.

Figure 8.2 SAS Visual Analytics distributed deployment

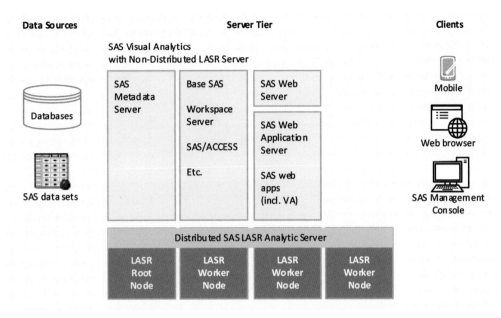

Just like the non-distributed deployment of SAS Visual Analytics, many of the SAS software components can reside on a single server or be split across multiple machines. The difference is that the LASR Analytic Server is now hosted on at least four machines, across a root node and multiple worker nodes. The LASR root node controls the actions of the LASR workers. The LASR workers store the data, which is loaded in RAM, and each performs operations on its own share of data.

When working with a distributed LASR Analytic Server, data can be loaded either serially or in parallel. We can use the same technique to serially load data into a distributed LASR Analytic Server as shown above for the non-distributed LASR Analytic Server by using the SAS Workspace Server. When loading serially, data is sent only to the LASR root node, which then distributes the data individually to each of the LASR workers.

But a distributed LASR Analytic Server can also load data in parallel from a supported set of data sources. Data loaded in parallel is sent to each LASR worker directly from the source, while the LASR root node coordinates and tracks the activity. The actual distribution of the data at load time is handled by the data source.

Loading data to LASR from HDFS

The Distributed SAS LASR Analytic Server can load data directly from a Hadoop Distributed File System (HDFS). This only works with specific data types and in an environment where LASR services are deployed symmetrically alongside HDFS.

Figure 8.3 LASR deployed symmetrically alongside HDFS

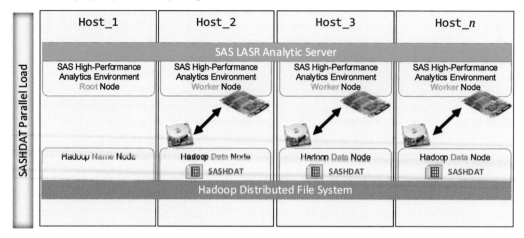

When the LASR Analytic Server is deployed with this type of configuration, it can be directed to load data that is hosted in HDFS directly into RAM. The data must be stored either as plain-text files in CSV (comma-separated values) format or, preferably, from SASHDAT files.

SASHDAT is unique

SASHDAT is the fastest and most efficient technique to (re-)load data into LASR.

Enabling support for SASHDAT files

SASHDAT is where things get really interesting. So let's look at some facts about this file format:

- The "H" is less about Hadoop and more about High-performance–it's optimized for analytics and concurrent processing.

- The metadata for SASHDAT (labels, encoding, formats, partitioning, and so on) are carefully managed for each HDFS file block.

- SASHDAT explicitly avoids fractional rows (which is a common challenge with other HDFS-stored data).

- The SASHDAT file format is binary, compressible (in SAS 9.4 M2), encryptable (in SAS 9.4 M3), and backward-compatible with older software releases.

- Because the SASHDAT file format was developed for working in massively parallel processing (MPP) environments like Hadoop, it provides the fastest and most efficient way to load large amounts of data into the LASR Analytic Server.

To make SASHDAT work, there are some architectural requirements to attend to:

- We must have a LASR Analytic Server running in Distributed mode. That is, the LASR Analytic Server software is deployed to run simultaneously across multiple machines at the same time. We call this massively parallel processing (MPP) because it provides a way to scale up the processing power of LASR substantially.

- Distributed mode LASR is provided by the SAS High-Performance Analytics Environment software—the same software that also enables the SAS High-Performance Analytics Procedures (assuming that software is licensed as well).

- We need to use the Hadoop Distributed File System (HDFS). HDFS is the primary underpinning technology on which most Hadoop technologies are based. Like Distributed LASR, HDFS is also deployed to run simultaneously across multiple machines at the same time. HDFS is able to leverage this type of environment for massive scalability as well as for improving availability.

- Finally, distributed LASR must be symmetrically co-located with HDFS. "Co-located" means that both software solutions must be deployed alongside each other on the same set of machines. "Symmetrically" means that the LASR root node (which acts as the "boss" of LASR) must reside on the same host machine as the HDFS name node (which acts as the HDFS boss) and further that LASR worker nodes must be placed one-for-one alongside the HDFS data nodes.

If these requirements are not all met, then we cannot use the SASHDAT file format. Notably, this means that SASHDAT is not available to us if we're using single-machine (SMP) LASR, or if HDFS resides on a different collection of hosts in our environment, or if we simply don't have HDFS at all.

The exception to the rule

One exception to the requirements of SASHDAT is the MapR Distribution of Hadoop. MapR is shipped with its own closed-source file system known as MapR-FS.

Figure 8.4 A remote (or asymmetric) MapR Hadoop cluster can also host SASHDAT files

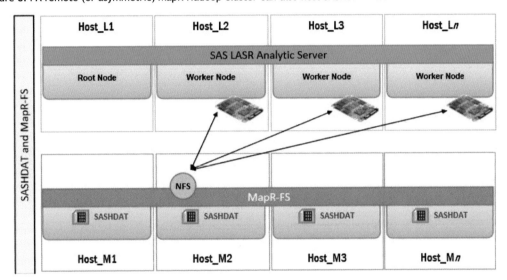

When it comes to SASHDAT, the SAS R&D team devised a way to leverage MapR NFS to place SASHDAT files into MapR-FS. Ultimately, this means that LASR can read and write SASHDAT files from MapR-FS over NFS, so co-location of services is not required. (Foreshadowing: Look for similar functionality when you are using any distributed file system that appears locally mounted on the in-memory workers of CAS on the SAS Viya platform.)

SASHDAT does not require SAS/ACCESS

Let's briefly clarify what we do not need to have in order to use SASHDAT: SAS/ACCESS Interface to Hadoop software. SAS/ACCESS does not provide any of the SASHDAT capabilities. Distributed LASR is fully baked with the ability to implement SASHDAT tables in HDFS without using SAS/ACCESS at all.

The SAS/ACCESS Interface to Hadoop software is, of course, powerful and flexible software that enables a wide range of possibilities in working with the native strengths of a Hadoop cluster. So while it's not directly responsible for creating SASHDAT tables, it definitely comes in handy for working with Hive tables, Pig and Map Reduce jobs, and much more that might be on the ETL path to creating SASHDAT tables.

Loading data to LASR from Base SAS

We can use Base SAS—and services built on top of it like the SAS Workspace Server and SAS Stored Process Server—to transfer data over to LASR (or into SASHDAT tables in HDFS). Pretty much any data source that Base SAS has access to can be used to feed LASR as part of your enterprise's data management processing.

Examples of data sources which Base SAS can load over into LASR include:

- Base SAS data sets
- SAS Scalable Performance Data Engine (SPD Engine) tables
- Raw text files

And more

Any data source that is accessible to Base SAS (with optional SAS/ACCESS engine) can be loaded into LASR.

Figure 8.5 Some of the default data sources available to Base SAS

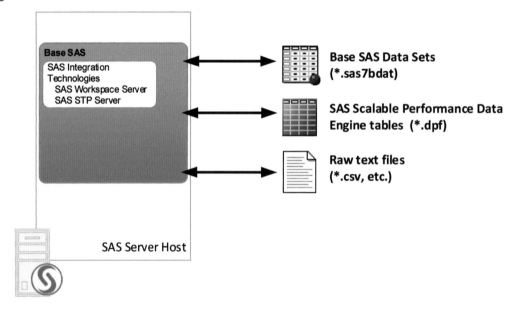

If additional SAS software has been licensed at your site, then those products can be used as well, such as the following:

- SAS/ACCESS software: provides the ability for SAS to communicate directly with third-party data providers. Specific offerings are available for providers such as Oracle, DB2, Aster, Hadoop, and many more.

- SAS Scalable Performance Data Server (SPD Server) tables

Figure 8.6 Some of the additional data sources available when optional SAS software is installed

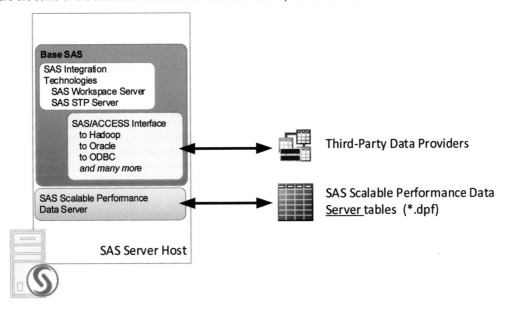

Either PROC LASR or the SASIOLA LIBNAME engine can be used to load data from supported sources directly into LASR memory. Once the data is in the LASR memory, either it can be dropped from RAM (to be reloaded from source later), or LASR can save it out to disk in CSV format or in SASHDAT format.

SAS also provides the SASHDAT LIBNAME engine to simplify the process of saving data straight to SASHDAT format. There are a couple of important things to remember about the SASHDAT LIBNAME engine:

1. LASR, not SAS, is responsible for actually reading and writing the SASHDAT content to HDFS.

2. The SASHDAT LIBNAME engine is unidirectional. Data can be written from SAS (through LASR) into SASHDAT files, but it's not possible to read that data back to SAS directly through the same libref. The intent of SASHDAT is to act as a high-performance repository for loading large volumes of data into LASR, not SAS.

Of course, saying "it can't be done" is not something that usually applies to SAS. So if you really want to read data from SASHDAT (through LASR) back to SAS, there is a way to do it: Use the HPDS2 Procedure.

Figure 8.7 Using SAS PROCs or LIBNAME engines to load data into or out of LASR

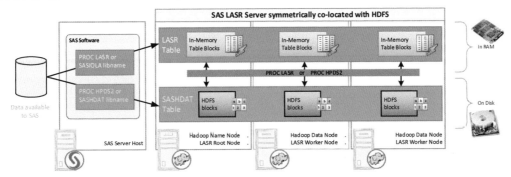

Loading data to LASR with SAS In-Database technology

We've talked a lot about SASHDAT and its speed and efficiency in support of parallel loading of data out of HDFS into a Distributed LASR Analytic Server. But it's not the only parallel loading technique available to us. SAS offers In-Database technology that works with a number of third-party data providers which can also provide a mechanism for parallel loading of data into LASR.

The key component of SAS In-Database technology is the SAS Embedded Process (EP). The EP is also based on MPP architecture and is deployed across all of the host nodes of a supported data provider.

Figure 8.8 The SAS Embedded Process is often deployed to a separate cluster of machines apart from LASR

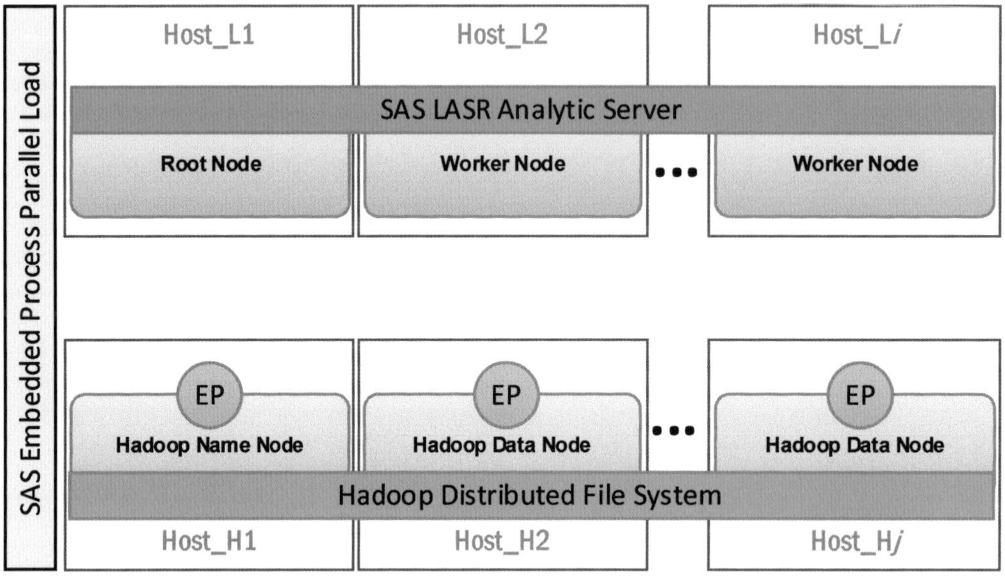

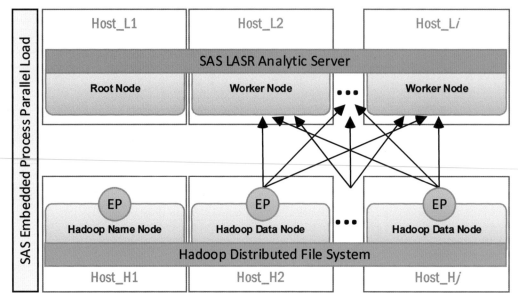

The idea with the EP is that it can take data as directed from its host data provider, and the individual nodes of the EP can each stream their respective portions of the data equally to each of the LASR Workers.

Figure 8.9 Each EP node will distribute its data evenly to each of the LASR Workers

To be clear, parallel loading of data to LASR is not the sole reason why the EP exists—it's just a really nice side benefit that we can use when we need it. The primary goal of SAS In-Database technology is to bring the statistics to the data as a more efficient approach for working with data in very large volumes. In particular, the SAS Embedded Process is deployed into the remote data provider to work directly where the data resides, so it can perform the requested analysis and return only the results. This approach minimizes large-scale data movement. SAS In-Database technology provides SQL pass-through; code, data quality, and scoring acceleration capabilities; as well as support for SAS High-Performance procedures.

Even with the EP's significant set of features, there are still many occasions where we will want to use the SAS Visual Analytics software for analysis, discovery, and reporting. This means transferring the data that we need from the remote data provider using the EP's ability to stream that data efficiently over parallel channels to the LASR Workers.

Loading data to LASR from a different LASR Analytic Server

Often, sites will use more than one LASR Analytic Server at a time. In those situations, it is sometimes necessary to copy in-memory tables from one LASR Analytic Server to another LASR Analytic Server using the IMXFER procedure.

Figure 8.10 Use PROC IMXFER to copy data from one LASR Analytic Server to another

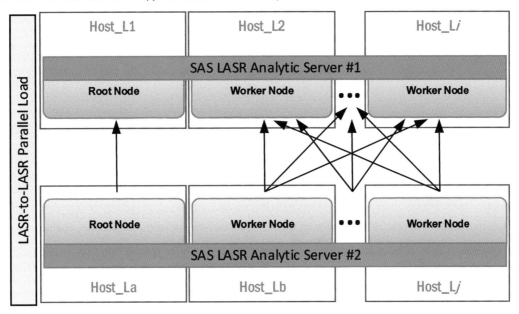

The LASR servers can reside in the same collection of host machines alongside each other, or they can be physically separate, running on different machines. Other than having enough physical RAM available to complete the transfer, there's no requirement for both LASR servers to span the same number of hosts.

By default, LASR will attempt a parallel transfer of data, equally distributing the data from each source node to each of the destination worker nodes (see the arrows between worker nodes in Figure 8.10 above). However, if there are network limitations such that the workers in one LASR server cannot "see" the other LASR server's workers, then use the HOSTONLY argument to force a serial transfer of the data between the root nodes of the two LASR Servers (illustrated by the single arrow between root nodes in Figure 8.10).

Loading data into LASR automatically

It's often helpful when data is automatically loaded or updated in the LASR Analytic Server. SAS Visual Analytics offers two techniques to accomplish this goal. Which one you'll use primarily depends on the type of data source you're working with.

SAS Autoload to LASR facility

SAS offers an Autoload facility for loading data into LASR. The Autoload facility does not run on the LASR Analytic Server host machines—it is deployed to a host where the SAS Workspace Server for SAS Visual Analytics resides. Each LASR library in your environment will need its own Autoload implementation.

The Autoload facility is scheduled in the host operating system to run at repeated intervals (usually every 15 minutes). It offers the ability to automatically start the associated LASR Analytic Server (if it is not running already) and then load, append, or unload tables in that LASR Analytic Server as directed.

In its current incarnation, the Autoload facility can work only with data files that reside locally on the SAS Workspace Server host machine in the following formats:

- Base SAS data sets
- Microsoft Excel spreadsheets (XLS, XLSX, XLSB, and XLSM formats)
- CSV (text-delimited file format)

Figure 8.11 The SAS Autoload Facility works with SAS data sets, Excel documents, and CSV files

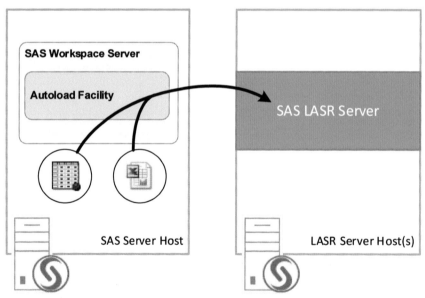

To be clear, the Autoload facility is not suitable for use with data stored in any other medium. It does not work with third-party DBMS tables, SASHDAT tables, nor SAS Scalable Performance Data Engine or SAS Scalable Performance Data Server tables. It also does not integrate in any way with the SAS In-Database Embedded Process.

The SAS Autoload to LASR facility is very useful within the constraints of its operation. Use it to enable the following:

- Automatic (re-)start of the associated LASR Analytic Server

- Automatic (re-)load of data to the associated LASR Analytic Server

- Configurable scheduling to minimize downtime

Keep the following in mind when you're using those capabilities:

- Data must be copied to the Autoload drop zone in a supported format.

- Data is loaded serially to LASR.

Keep data fresh

Use the SAS Autoload Facility to ensure that a LASR Analytic Server is automatically started and loaded with data that is frequently used.

LASR Reload-on-Start feature

LASR also offers a feature known as Reload-on-Start, which will automatically reload previous data back into LASR when it's started. When enabled, it makes a copy of participating tables and places them in the designated backing store. The backing store keeps copies in only one format: Base SAS data sets. Reload-on-Start is enabled on a per-library basis and supports the option to exclude individual tables as needed.

Reload-on-Start only works with select data sources:

- Imports of local files from users

- Imports of Google Analytics, Facebook, or Twitter data

Figure 8.12 Reload-on-Start relies on SAS data sets as a backing store for data loaded from user-imported data, Google Analytics, Facebook, and Twitter

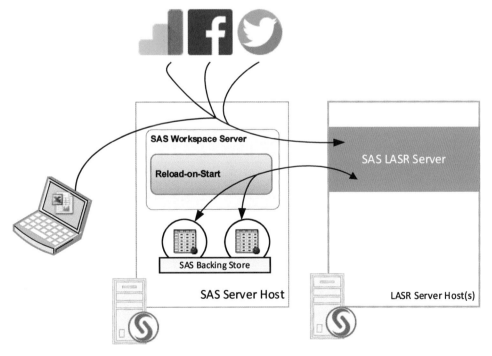

Like the Autoload facility, Reload-on-Start also does not work with third-party DBMS tables, SASHDAT tables, nor SPD Engine or SPD Server tables. Nor does it integrate with the SAS In-Database Embedded Process.

This feature is intended for relatively smaller size tables. The data that is reloaded to LASR comes only from Base SAS data sets over a single, serial network connection to LASR. As table size increases, watch out for increased disk consumption on the SAS server as well as longer loading times from SAS to LASR.

Within these constraints, the Reload-on-Start feature can be very helpful to ensure that the supported tables from the backing store (not from the original upload source) which users expect are indeed available when LASR is (re-)started.

References

The ability to quickly and efficiently load tables into the LASR Analytic Server is important to ensure that SAS Visual Analytics has the data necessary for users to get their jobs done. To get the specific details that you need to be successful working with various data sources and LASR, refer to the following SAS documentation online at support.sas.com:

SAS Institute Inc. 2016. *SAS Visual Analytics 7.3: Administration Guide.* Cary, NC: SAS Institute Inc.

SAS Institute Inc. 2016. *SAS LASR Analytic Server 2.7: Reference Guide.* Cary, NC: SAS Institute Inc.

SAS Institute Inc. 2016. *SAS High-Performance Analytics Infrastructure 3.5: Installation and Configuration Guide.* Cary, NC: SAS Institute Inc.

SAS Institute Inc. 2016. *SAS/ACCESS 9.4 for Relational Databases: Reference, Ninth Edition.* Cary, NC: SAS Institute Inc.

SAS Institute Inc. 2016. *SAS Scalable Performance Data Server 5.3: Administrator's Guide.* Cary, NC: SAS Institute Inc.

SAS Institute Inc. 2016. *SAS Scalable Performance Data Server 5.3: User's Guide.* Cary, NC: SAS Institute Inc.

chapter nine

LASR administration

The LASR Analytic Server is critical to the operation of SAS Visual Analytics. Therefore, it is important to become familiar with the administration tasks that are necessary to care for the LASR Analytic Server. This is because the LASR Analytic Server is incredibly powerful and flexible, and there are many considerations for its administration.

In most circumstances, SAS Visual Analytics is only one part of a larger solution. Other SAS offerings as well as third-party software can play an important role in the daily operations of the environment. Each of these bring their own administration tasks and utilities to the table.

This chapter will focus on many of the administration tools and tasks for the LASR Analytic Server. There's a lot to cover–let's get to it!

Administration overview

The person responsible for administration of SAS Visual Analytics has a lot of ground to cover. She must manage users and resources; maintain security and system integrity; and then monitor operations and audit activities.

Specific to the LASR Analytic Server, the administrator will handle the following:

- Starting and stopping LASR Analytic Servers
- Loading tables into and dropping tables from LASR Analytic Servers
- Defining data libraries and access controls
- Monitoring resource utilization

Administration tools

SAS provides several tools for administering the SAS Visual Analytics environment. Depending on the task at hand, the administrator of SAS Visual Analytics will need to access the correct tools and to complete the full set of actions necessary to achieve her goals.

SAS Management Console

The SAS Management Console is an application (based on Java) for administration of critical SAS Enterprise Business Intelligence environment components—including many items used by SAS Visual Analytics. The SAS Management Console effectively acts as a point-and-click graphical interface to the SAS Metadata Server. So wherever metadata describing the SAS Visual Analytics environment comes into play, we will need to familiarize ourselves with using the SAS Management Console to manage it.

Figure 9.1 Logged on to SAS Management Console as the Unrestricted User with full control over all items

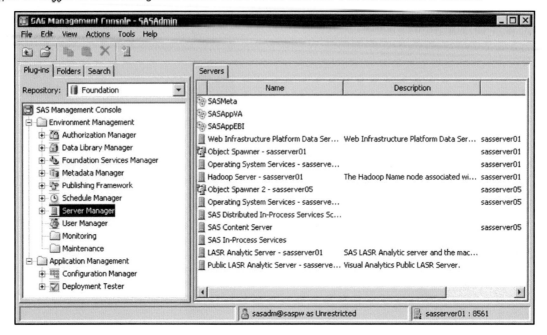

Use the SAS Management Console to define and manage the existence of LASR Analytic Servers, LASR libraries, and LASR tables in metadata. Security access controls to the data in LASR is also maintained with the SAS Management Console.

SAS Visual Analytics Administrator

The SAS Visual Analytics Administrator is a web application that is accessed from your web browser. Log on using your credentials that have been granted the Visual Analytics Administrator role privileges in the SAS Metadata Server.

Figure 9.2 Using VA Administrator to monitor system resource use

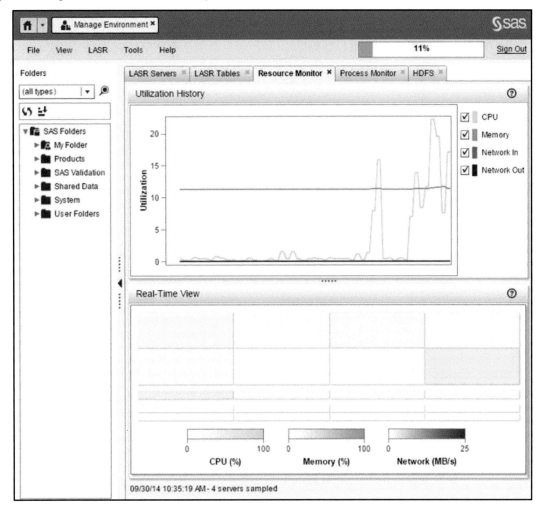

With SAS Visual Analytics Administrator, the administrator can perform these tasks specific to LASR:

- Start and stop LASR Analytic Servers.

- Load and unload LASR tables.

- Check on the status of LASR Analytic Servers (running or not) and LASR tables (loaded or not).

- Apply row-level security to tables in LASR.

- Monitor system resource utilization in real time (CPU, RAM, I/O).

SAS Visual Analytics Administrator provides "live" monitoring of the environment. It does not have the ability to show any historical information–only what is currently happening.

SAS Environment Manager

SAS Environment Manager was first introduced with SAS 9.4. It's based on open-source technologies from the VMware Hyperic to provide a modular, extensible administration and monitoring framework. The SAS Environment Manager is built from several disparate components that work together to provide a single service, including agents on each host managed in the environment and a server that consolidates all of the agent data, stores it, and provides a web-based user interface. Log on to the SAS Environment Manager using your credentials that have been granted the appropriate level of administrative role privileges in metadata.

Figure 9.3 A dashboard shown in SAS Environment Manager for monitoring the metrics captured for our environment

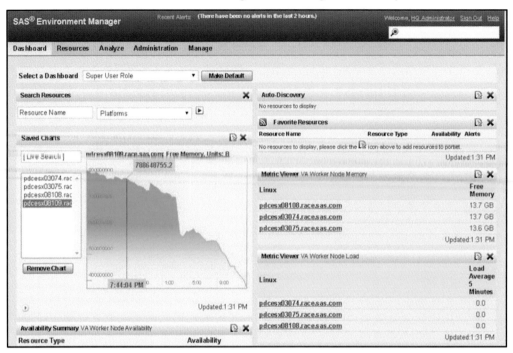

SAS Environment Manager can be used for "live" monitoring of the environment. But more importantly, it constantly captures, tracks, and records system activity so that you have access to historical information as well. Because SAS Environment Manager is effectively watching the environment whether you are looking at it or not, it can also provide alerts (over email, text message, and so on) to notify you if critical conditions are encountered.

Use SAS Environment Manager to do the following:

- monitor all system services and resources (including items related to the LASR Analytic Server)

- set alerts based on conditions that you choose

- view and report on current and historical performance

- perform administrative control actions for most SAS services and web applications

SAS Program Code

With programmatic interfaces accessible from Base SAS, SAS Enterprise Guide, SAS Studio, SAS Data Integration Studio, the administrator of SAS Visual Analytics can create new interactive or batch programs that can ultimately be used to administer almost any aspect of the data lifecycle in support of in-memory tables in LASR. SAS programming experts can craft SAS code that can start and stop LASR Analytic Servers, load data from any source supported by the environment into LASR and beyond, even to programmatically creating and modifying objects stored in the SAS Metadata Server.

Figure 9.4 Using the SAS Studio web app to submit SAS program code to work with LASR

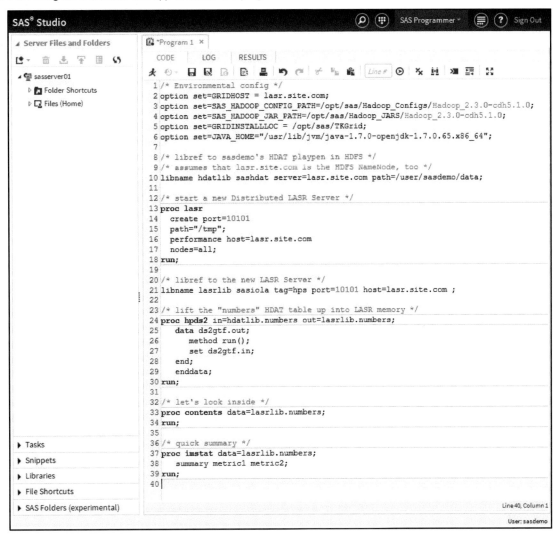

The visual administration tools are handy and powerful. Having a graphical user interface helps make the work of tasks appear more logical and intuitive. Mature site operations, however, will require some level of scripting, programming, and scheduling to ensure that table updates can occur automatically. So creating and maintaining your own SAS program code will be a useful skill.

Other tools

A SAS Visual Analytics solution deployment relies on the tools shown here, but also on many others. While we've been focused on SAS utilities for administering the environment, there are other software products which you might need to consider.

Other tools that can be useful for management of your SAS solution environment:

- SAS High-Performance Computing Management Console

  - Can be used at sites that prefer it

  - Not related to the SAS Management Console

  - Primarily for creating and maintaining large numbers of user accounts

- Operating system utilities

    ○ Linux: netstat, top, iftop, ps, mpstat, and many more

    ○ Windows: Task Manager, Perfmon, the System Event Viewer, and so on

- Hadoop utilities

    ○ Deployment management: Cloudera Manager, Ambari

    ○ Hadoop web applications: DFS Health, YARN Manager

    ○ Hadoop Command-line: Hadoop, hdfs

While we won't discuss details of those other utilities in this book, they are still important contributors to your administration toolbox in support of the SAS Visual Analytics solution deployment.

Interesting LASR Administration Tasks

LASR Analytic Server administration, especially as it ties into the greater SAS ecosystem, is a big topic. We want to get you started by introducing you to some interesting tasks which you're likely to encounter when administering a SAS Visual Analytics solution at your site.

The role of SAS metadata

SAS Visual Analytics relies exclusively on LASR Analytic Servers and LASR tables, which are defined in the SAS Metadata Server. If you are a SAS programmer, you can easily write your own program code to start a new LASR Analytic Server, load data into it, run actions, and get results back. However, unless you take the additional step to register that new LASR Analytic Server instance and any new tables in metadata then SAS Visual Analytics won't see them and cannot work with them.

SAS metadata also defines access controls to manage the content available for users to view, interact with, and possibly administer as well.

Generally speaking, objects in metadata describe things that should already (or will soon) exist. In some cases, the metadata is referenced by the described item so that it knows about specific start-up or operational parameters. The point here is that metadata is meant to describe something that exists independently of the metadata itself. If you move or delete an item in the real world, the metadata will not automatically reflect that change. SAS Enterprise Business Intelligence software will coordinate its internal use of metadata with physical items. However, if you manually (or programmatically) create your own metadata objects, then you will be responsible for ongoing maintenance of those objects to ensure that they reflect the correct state of the real-world items going forward.

Defining new LASR Analytic Servers

SAS Visual Analytics relies exclusively on the SAS LASR Analytic Server to provide data and analytics for reporting and exploration. The LASR Analytic Server provides a secure, multi-user environment for access to data that is stored in memory. The LASR Analytic Server was originally built to handle the largest data volumes, but can also work with smaller tables as well.

SAS Visual Analytics needs at least one LASR Analytic Server with data in memory in order to provide reports to users. But if circumstances warrant, you can define multiple LASR Analytic Servers, which can co-exist on the same machines or be deployed to their own set of hosts.

By default, two LASR Analytic Servers are created during the deployment of SAS Visual Analytics software:

- LASR Analytic Server on port 10010

- Public LASR Analytic Server on port 10031

SAS Visual Analytics needs LASR

SAS Visual Analytics relies exclusively on the SAS LASR Analytic Server to provide data and analytics for reporting and exploration.

Depending on the needs of your site, there are several reasons that you might choose to create additional LASR Analytic Servers.

- Resource usage separation – direct groups of users to different LASR Analytic Servers on separate hosts, which might be owned by different responsible parties

- Security – direct groups of users to different LASR Analytic Servers to protect access to data

- Dev, Test, Prod – separate environments to ensure smooth testing and transition of updates

- Resource availability – if your original host machines are fully used, then deploy another LASR to new hosts

First of all, defining a new LASR Analytic Server in your environment assumes that the necessary software exists on all host machines. With that in place, then we can define a new LASR Analytic Server using the SAS Management Console:

Figure 9.5 Using the SAS Management Console to create a new LASR Analytic Server

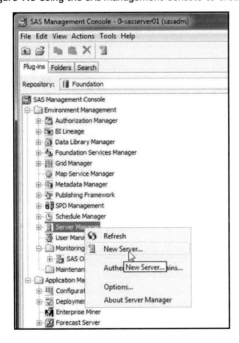

In SAS Management Console, connect to the SAS Metadata Server with a user account that has appropriate administrative privileges. Then right-click the Server Manager item and select **New Server**. The New Server Wizard will appear and provide a list of different server types. Select **SAS Servers ▶ SAS LASR Analytic Server**. Click **Next** and give your new LASR Analytic Server a name and optional description. Then we get to the interesting part.

Figure 9.6 The New Server Wizard for creating a new metadata definition of a SAS LASR Analytic Server

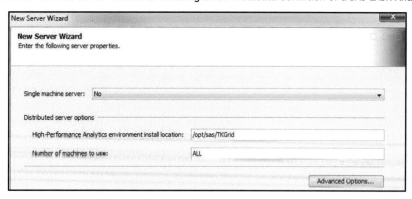

On the third screen of the New Server Wizard, you can choose whether to define a "single machine server," which refers to the Non-Distributed (SMP) LASR Server. By default, the answer is **No**, which will create a metadata object that describes a Distributed (MPP) LASR Server.

LASR runs on different hardware architectures

The Non-Distributed SAS LASR Analytic Server is hosted on a single machine. But the Distributed SAS LASR Analytic Server runs on a minimum of four machines – one for the LASR root node and at least three LASR worker nodes.

For an MPP LASR Server, you must also provide the answer to two more questions:

- High-Performance Analytics Environment installation location

  The HPAE software is deployed separately from the rest of VA. It provides the underlying software used to launch an MPP LASR Server on multiple host machines. The value of this prompt is usually something like /opt/sas/TKGrid_3.1/TKGrid. But it might vary at your site.

  Keep in mind that if you intend to use the SAS In-Database Embedded Process with a supported remote data provider to perform parallel data loads to MPP LASR, then you must provide the path to the associated TKGrid_REP directory instead.

- Number of machines to use:

  The HPAE is installed on at least four machines as the minimum requirement for an MPP LASR Server, and often to many more. You can choose to run LASR on ALL of them (the default) or some subset number. You cannot specify *which* subset of machines to use in metadata. If less than ALL, then LASR is started on the number of machines you specify in the order listed in the tkgrid.hosts file in the HPAE configuration on disk.

Open the Advanced Options in metadata of the new LASR Analytic Server, and you can control key memory usage criteria.

Figure 9.7 Specifying memory limits of the LASR Analytic Server

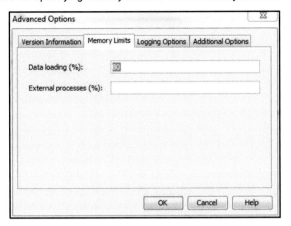

Careless use of LASR can easily overrun the system resources in your environment. RAM is a key resource that is critical not just to LASR but to the operating system and any other software running on the same host machines. To help ensure that LASR behaves well, we can specify values for the following options:

- Data loading (%) – default is 80% - If the LASR Analytic Server is currently holding tables that consume 80% or more of RAM, then new tables cannot be loaded.

- External processes (%) – If specified, then processes external to LASR cannot retrieve data from or run actions in LASR if this number is exceeded.

New LASR Analytic Servers can also be defined for use by SAS Visual Analytics in the SAS Environment Manager application. As with SAS Management Console, you'll need to sign on to SAS Environment Manager with a user account that has the appropriate level of administrative privileges and navigate into the Administration section (available from the sidebar menu in the upper-left corner of the web page). Once there, you can bring up the New Server wizard and enter the information needed for LASR:

Figure 9.8 Creating a new LASR Analytic Server for SAS Visual Analytics using the SAS Environment Manager administration tool

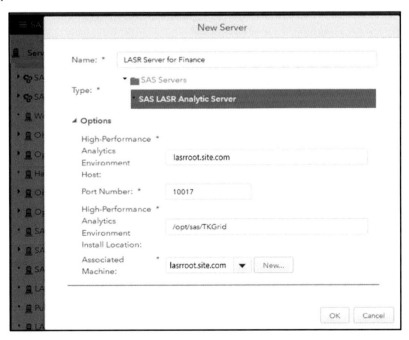

As an administrator, your ability to proactively manage the LASR Server's memory usage is helpful in maintaining a smooth operating environment.

Once your new LASR Server is defined, chances are that SAS Visual Analytics can work with it. There are some considerations to keep in mind, which are not addressed directly in metadata:

- SAS Visual Analytics users who wish to administer LASR services (starting, stopping, and loading data) must have their own OS user accounts (or using SAS token authentication) with the ability to launch a SAS Workspace Server.

- For MPP LASR, the OS user account that launches the SAS Workspace Server must also exist on all hosts of the MPP LASR cluster and also have non-password SSH configured for that account.

- For SAS Visual Analytics users who only need read-access to the data which is already loaded into LASR, then OS user accounts are not necessary.

SAS Visual Analytics, the SAS LASR Analytic Server, and other SAS solutions must often interact with third-party software systems, often even co-existing with them on the same hardware. For example, it's a common practice to symmetrically co-locate a Hadoop environment alongside MPP LASR to enable the ability to work with SASHDAT tables in HDFS. If those Hadoop services – especially memory intensive software like Spark and Impala – are busily used, then there could be significant contention for the limited amount of RAM which LASR relies on. So proper planning and execution of LASR administration ensures that this powerful tool behaves well at your site.

> ### Requirements to administer LASR
>
> SAS Visual Analytics users who wish to load or unload data as well as start or stop LASR Servers must have operating system accounts sufficient to launch a SAS Workspace Server and also perform passwordless SSH to each of the LASR host machines.

Defining new LASR libraries

A LASR Server isn't good for much if it doesn't have any data loaded in-memory to perform actions on and generate analytical results. For SAS Visual Analytics to work with data, we need a library reference defined in metadata so that SAS Visual Analytics knows which LASR Analytic Server to connect to. Furthermore, the SAS Metadata Server maintains access controls on objects like LASR Analytic Servers definitions, librefs, and tables to ensure that users can only see the things in the environment that they're supposed to see.

SAS library references (librefs) describe the connection details for SAS to communicate with a given data source. LASR libraries are used to connect SAS with LASR Analytic Servers. In order for SAS Visual Analytics to work with LASR data, the LASR libref must also be defined in the SAS Metadata Server.

Librefs provide a way for SAS to separate user access to various data sources. And so the reasons for creating new LASR libraries closely parallel those for creating new LASR Analytic Servers, including:

- Security – restricting access to in-memory data based on access controls defined per libref

- Data organization – data sourced from different locations will each require their own libref

Managing LASR Analytic Servers with code

Besides using point-and-click user interfaces like the SAS Visual Analytics Administrator to manage LASR operations such as starting, stopping, loading data, and establishing limits, you can also write SAS program code which is convenient for automated scripting. For example, with a well-designed set of programs, you can start up multiple LASR Analytic Servers and load them with data from disparate sources all at once.

As always, SAS offers more than one programmatic technique by which you can manage your LASR Servers and their associated data.

Distributed Mode LASR

For LASR Servers operating in distributed mode (MPP), we can use the LASR procedure. PROC LASR provides the following major functionality:

- Start and stop the specified SAS LASR Analytic Server.

- Load and unload tables from LASR memory.

- Save LASR's in-memory tables to disk in HDFS.

For example, the following code can be used to start an MPP LASR Server:

```
1  proc lasr create port=10011
2
3    path="/opt/sas/config/Lev1/Applications/
            SASVisualAnalytics/LASR/Signatures"
4
5    signer="webserver.site.com:7980/SASLASRAuthorization";
6
7    performance host="lasrroot.site.com"
8    install="/opt/sas/TKGrid"
9    nodes=all;
10
11 run;
```

Notes

- Line 3 is formatted to fit on this page in readable fashion – make sure that your actual **path** does not have any spaces.

- The **create** parameter will direct SAS to start up a LASR Server with the specified attributes.

- Ensure that the **port** value that you specify – it doesn't have to be 10011 – is actually available. Otherwise, this LASR Server will not start if another service (LASR or otherwise) is already listening at that port number.

- The **signer** functionality is accessed through an HTTP RESTful interface provided by the SASLASRAuthorization web application. This application is often, but not always, a different host machine than the Distributed LASR Server's Root Node host.

- The **install** parameter specifies the physical path to the SAS High-Performance Analytics Environment software (TKGrid). If you expect to perform parallel loading of data from the SAS Embedded Process in a remote data provider, then this path should point to the associated **TKGrid_REP** directory instead.

Stopping an MPP LASR Server is even simpler:

```
1  proc lasr stop port=10011
2
3    performance host="lasrroot.site.com"
4
5  run;
```

Notes

- The **port** attribute in combination with the **host** provides the key criteria for stopping the intended LASR Server.

- The **stop** parameter directs the LASR Server to not accept any new client connections, to not allow any current actions to finish executions, and then to terminate the server processes.

If this LASR Server is already defined in metadata (with matching attributes like port number, signer, and installed codebase location), then its status in SAS Visual Analytics Administrator or SAS Environment

Manager will change to reflect the results of your successful code execution – and you can further control the LASR Server there in those interfaces as well.

Non-Distributed Mode LASR

We programmatically manage operations of Non-Distributed (SMP) LASR Servers with two SAS program concepts: the SASIOLA libref and the VASMP procedure.

For SMP LASR, we can use the SASIOLA LIBNAME engine to do the following:

- Start and stop the specified SAS LASR Analytic Server.
- Load and unload tables from LASR memory.

And use PROC VASMP to do the following:

- Stop (only!) the specified SAS LASR Analytic Server.
- List the tables currently available in-memory for SMP LASR Server.
- Provide administrative information and control over the SMP LASR Server.

The following code starts a new LASR Server and directs it to continue running:

```
1  libname lasrlib sasiola
2          startserver host="smplasr.site.com" port=10011
3          signer="webserver.site.com:7980/SASLASRAuthorization";
4
5  proc vasmp;
6          serverwait port=10011;
7  quit;
```

Note:

- Conceptually, a SAS libref – defined by the **libname** statement – is only available during the lifetime of the SAS System execution. But LASR is more than a libref. It can persist and work with multiple instances of SAS.
- The SASIOLA library engine and the VASMP procedure only work with Non-Distributed (SMP) LASR Analytic Servers
- The **serverwait** parameter in PROC VASMP directs the LASR Analytic Server to persist operations until it receives a direct termination directive.
- Without the **serverwait**, when the SAS instance that executes this code terminates, the new LASR Server would also terminate at the same time (when the SASIOLA libref is cleared).

The VASMP procedure can also show more information about the specified LASR Server:

```
1  proc vasmp;
2
3          serverinfo / host="smplasr.site.com"
4                       port=10011;
5
6          serverterm;
7
8  quit;
```

Note:

- The **serverinfo** parameter will direct SAS to return descriptive details about the specified LASR Analytic Server
- The **serverterm** parameter directs SAS to send a termination command to LASR so that it will shut down after finishing any ongoing actions.

- Other parameters available from PROC VASMP include the following:

  o **SERVERPARM**: used to specify an override of the global LASR Server settings that were defined in the SAS Metadata Server.

  o **TABLEINFO**: returns information about the in-memory tables available in the specified LASR Server.

As an alternative to using PROC VASMP to stop SMP LASR, we could also submit a simple SAS libname statement such as the following:

```
libname lasrlib clear;
```

Note:

- The **clear** parameter will de-assign the libref in SAS and also send the termination command to the LASR Server

- LASR will stop accepting new client connection, complete the current set of ongoing actions (if any), and then shut down.

Working with the Autoloader Facility

SAS Visual Analytics provides an Autoloader Facility to enable users of the system to stage their SAS data sets (or delimited text files, like CSV) on the SAS Workspace Server host machine for automatic upload to the associated SAS LASR Server. By default, the deployment of the SAS Visual solution software will define an autoload site for use with the default Public SAS LASR Analytic Server.

What is a public user?

In SAS terminology, the term "public" usually refers to the SASUSERS group of users – that is, users who have successfully authenticated with a known metadata identity. This is more selective than the term "anonymous," which refers to any non-authenticated user.

The Autoload Facility is provided as a convenience, but is not required for operation of SAS Visual Analytics. After the deployment of your SAS software, manual steps to direct an operating system scheduler to invoke the Autoloader on a regular basis (for example, every 15 minutes) will be needed to fully activate the Autoloader functionality.

Figure 9.9 The SAS Visual Analytics Autoloader Facility will ensure that the provided data is available in the LASR Server

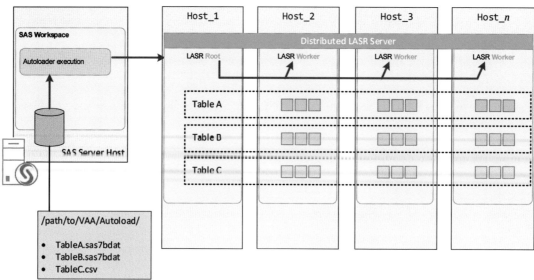

The Autoloader Facility works with either SMP LASR or MPP LASR. If MPP LASR is the target, then data is only loaded serially. There is no option available to enable the Autoloader Facility to work with parallel-loading data sources.

With the Autoload Facility configured and running, then the following occurs:

- The data from new tables placed in the Autoloader staging area directory will automatically upload to the LASR Server.

- If the associated LASR Server is not running, the Autoload Facility will start it.

- Tables can be removed from LASR using the other Autoload directory for that purpose.

Users of the Autoload Facility must have the ability to create and save files in the physical directories on the host(s) for the SAS Workspace Server(s). To ensure that users do not clobber each other's files, consider enabling the "sticky bit" on the Autoloader's staging directories.

Besides the default provided Autoload for the Public LASR Analytic Server, you have the ability to create additional sources (directories with data on the SAS Workspace Server) and targets (LASR Servers, public or not).

Monitoring resources used by LASR

The SAS LASR Analytic Server is a high-performance *in-memory* analytics engine. To do its job, data tables are loaded into RAM on the machine(s) where LASR is running where they remain until they are unloaded or until the LASR Server itself is shut down. All of the software on your LASR hosts—the operating system, any co-located data providers, and so on—rely on RAM to function. LASR expands on that to use RAM as a persistent data storage for its in-memory tables.

When dealing with many users who are relying on SAS Visual Analytics to provide them with access to reporting and analytics, ensuring that resource consumption is in line with expectations is important. Also remember that the LASR Server can be deployed to function in two ways:

- **Distributed LASR (MPP)** – where multiple LASR Workers, each on its own host, perform in-memory analytics as coordinated by the LASR Worker, which is also on its own host machine.

- **Non-Distributed LASR (SMP)** – where LASR runs on a single machine only. It gives us the speed of in-memory processing but without the additional gains provided by breaking the task up into smaller chunks and distributing those to multiple workers for parallel processing.

The SAS Visual Analytics Administrator web application can provide useful insights into what resources LASR is working with.

Figure 9.10 Monitoring the memory that is used in LASR Servers

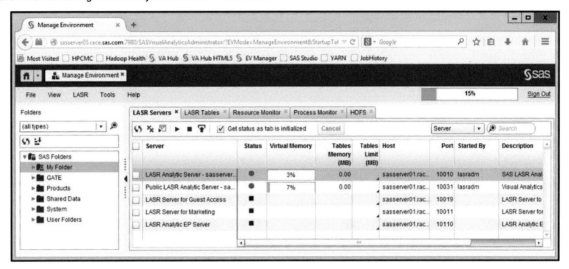

In the screen capture above, SAS Visual Analytics Administrator provides us with a quick glance at our environment with the following:

- Five defined LASR Servers

- The host each is running on (either SMP or the LASR Root Node for MPP)

- Their current execution state

- RAM consumed by each (only instances of MPP LASR that are currently active)

LASR Server status

Let's take a closer look at the server status:

Figure 9.11 The execution state of each LASR Server

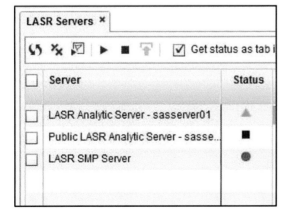

There are three status modes that can describe the current execution state of a LASR Server:

Status Icon	Description
●	Green Circle: The LASR Server is running and online.
■	Red Square: The LASR Server is not running.
▲	Yellow Triangle: The LASR Server is running and online, but the amount of data that it has in memory exceeds the tables limit value defined for it (default is 80%)

First, in order for SAS Visual Analytics Administrator to show a LASR Server in the list, that LASR Server must first be defined in SAS metadata. So regardless of the status shown, the list itself is an indicator that the LASR Servers have been defined in metadata such that SAS Visual Analytics Administrator is aware of them.

These status icons only show whether the server is running. A green circle does not necessarily mean that any data has been loaded into the LASR Server yet. You'll need to check the **LASR Tables** tab to get that information.

The yellow triangle is a helpful indicator in reference to the LASR tables limit value. When the data loaded into memory meets or exceeds that value, the LASR Server will not allow more data to be loaded. You're probably wondering how that value could be exceeded. It's because that value is ascertained only *after* a table has been loaded into RAM. A good example is if the limit is set at 80% of total system RAM and your tables in LASR currently only consume 79%, then the next table load – regardless of its size! – will be allowed to proceed.

LASR memory usage

The **LASR Servers** tab of SAS Visual Analytics Administrator shows the RAM consumed in support of hosting LASR tables in memory.

Figure 9.12 SAS Visual Analytics Administrator reports on LASR memory usage

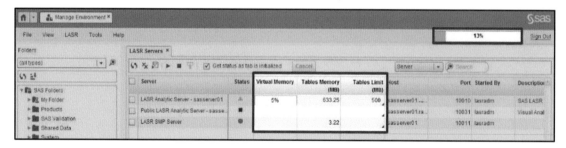

SAS Visual Analytics Administrator reports on memory differently for LASR running in distributed (MPP) mode than it does for non-distributed (SMP) LASR.

The columns shown here display the following:

- Virtual Memory – MPP LASR only – a percentage of the amount of RAM consumed by the Distributed LASR processes across the entire cluster.

- Tables Memory (MB) - the amount of RAM consumed by data in LASR tables which currently reside in memory

- Tables Limit (MB) – an optional, pre-defined limit on the amount of RAM beyond which no additional tables can be loaded into that LASR Server

The green bar in the upper right corner is a gauge of showing a percentage of the amount of total RAM utilization of all LASR hosts in aggregation in a distributed (MPP) environment. It does not appear for SMP-only deployments of LASR. If you position the mouse pointer over that gauge, a tooltip will appear with more information.

Figure 9.13 RAM utilization gauge for the LASR cluster with details in the tooltip.

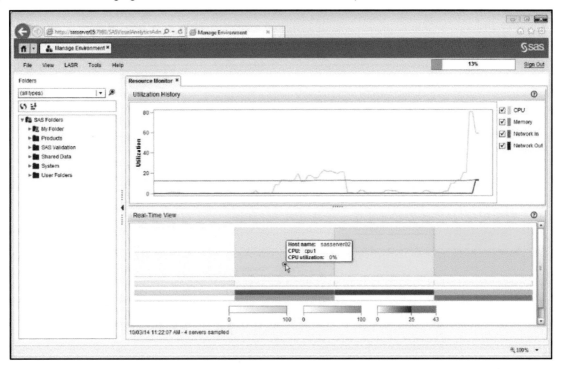

Altogether, this item is explaining several things to us:

- 13% of all RAM is currently in use in the cluster. This counts not just LASR usage, but also the operating system and any other third-party RAM utilization as well.

- The tooltip shows 7.93GB of RAM currently used by the LASR Server(s) out of a total 62.31 GB available in aggregate across all hosts

Resource Monitoring

SAS Visual Analytics Administrator also offers an interactive and dynamic client that shows activity updates known as the Resource Monitor. The Resource Monitor provides graphical displays of data to provide information about current utilization of system resources.

Figure 9.14 The Resource Monitor in SAS Visual Analytics Administrator tracking CPU, RAM, and I/O across all nodes of the LASR cluster

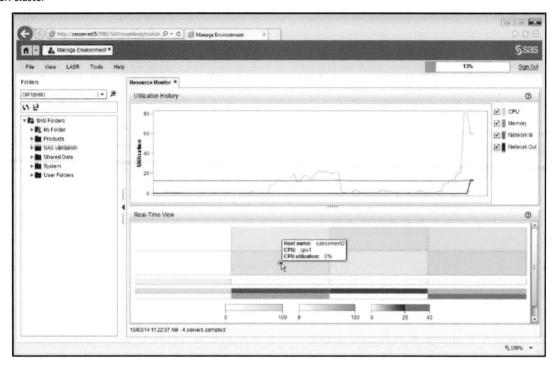

From top to bottom, the Resource Monitor shows:

- Utilization History – color-coded lines in a histogram tracking utilization of CPU, RAM, inbound network I/O, and outbound network I/O

- Real-Time View – a collection of three heat maps that display the current state of the following:

  ○ Utilization of each CPU core on all hosts of the cluster – notice the green-shaded rectangles above, representing 8 CPU cores for our 4-machine LASR cluster

  ○ Total RAM utilization on each host – look for the light-blue shaded set of rectangles, 1 each for the 4 machines of our LASR cluster
    – Network I/O on each host – the red-shaded set of 8 rectangles where inbound traffic per host is shown on top and outbound traffic is shown on the bottom.

For the Real-Time View, notice that the color-coding of these heat maps is increasingly darker as the utilization increases. If the value of a particular metric exceeds the expected norm, then Resource Monitor will choose a bright color to draw attention to it. For example, the outbound network I/O on the fourth host of our LASR cluster is shown as a purple rectangle and we can see from the legend that it represents a value beyond the range at which the network interfaces are operating on the other cluster hosts.

The data shown in Resource Monitor is live or collected moments ago while the Resource Monitor was online. These charts are reinitialized with each invocation of the Resource Monitor. So for historical views of past resource usage, the SAS Environment Manager is a better tool to use.

Usage Reports

SAS Visual Analytics Administrator offers an automated collection of reports that can help with the administration by reporting on the actual usage of reports, objects, data sources, and LASR.

Figure 9.15 SAS Visual Analytics Administrator provides usage reports

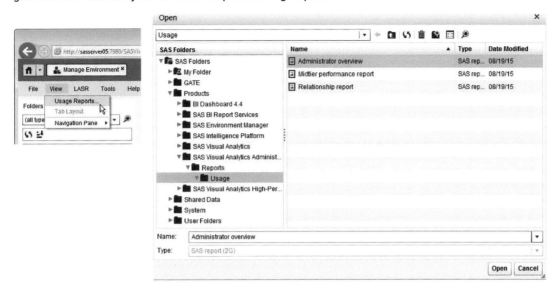

In particular, the Administrative Overview report is interesting. It generates a SAS Visual Analytics report with multiple tabs that show usage statistics by report, by user, by data source and much more.

Figure 9.16 The LASR Server tab in the Administrator Overview usage report

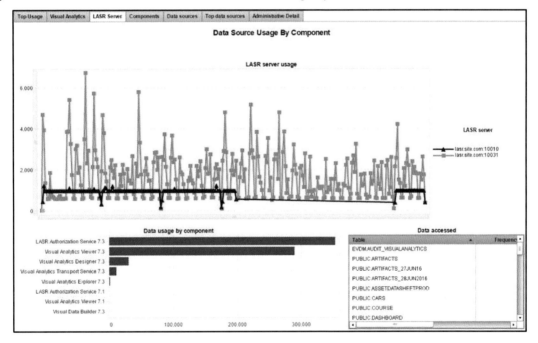

Understanding how your SAS Visual Analytics solution is being used is important to ensure that the correct resources are available. And this understanding can provide justification to continue using those resource as well as acquiring more if needed.

To make full use of all of the SAS Visual Analytics Administrator Usage Reports, you will want to enable the SAS Environment Manager Extended Monitoring functionality – often referred to as the EMI Framework. When activated the EMI Framework will create and maintain a data mart of usage statistics gathered by the SAS Environment Manager. That data mart then supports extensive reporting on how the SAS solution deployment is used.

SAS provides much more information about deploying and using SAS Environment Manager Extended Monitoring and the EMI Framework in the *SAS Environment Manager: User's Guide* available on http://support.sas.com.

References

So far we've just given you a taste of the flexibility and power available when administering the LASR Analytic Server in support of SAS Visual Analytics. You are likely to be eager to learn more. SAS provides a lot of documentation to help you out. So polish up your administration skills by referring to the following SAS documentation online at support.sas.com:

SAS Institute Inc. 2016. *SAS Visual Analytics 7.3: Administration Guide.* Cary, NC: SAS Institute Inc.

SAS Institute Inc. 2016. *SAS LASR™ Analytic Server 2.7: Reference Guide.* Cary, NC: SAS Institute Inc.

SAS Institute Inc. 2016. *SAS Environment Manager 2.5: User's Guide, 3rd edition.* Cary, NC: SAS Institute Inc.

SAS Institute Inc. 2016. *SAS 9.4 Intelligence Platform: System Administration Guide, 4th edition.* Cary, NC: SAS Institute Inc.

SAS Institute Inc. 2016. *SAS 9.4 Intelligence Platform: Security Administration Guide, 3rd edition.* Cary, NC: SAS Institute Inc.

chapter ten

performance considerations

SAS Visual Analytics was built for speed. This design goal was strongly applied to the SAS LASR Analytic Server, which is an in-memory analytics engine. Working with the full set of data placed in RAM allows LASR to crank through large numbers of records at dizzying velocities. And while LASR is certainly central to the performance of the overall SAS Visual Analytics solution, there are also other areas that you'll want to consider when planning a new deployment or attempting to squeeze the most out of the deployment that you've already got.

This chapter will look at several deployment options that can have significant impact in performance of SAS Visual Analytics at your site.

LASR performance

Did you know that when the technology for the SAS LASR Analytic Server was originally built, it was expressly designed for operation in massively parallel processing (MPP) environments? That is, LASR was designed for maximum scalability right from the start.

Over time as LASR matured further, the minimum system requirements to support a LASR Analytic Server were reduced until now they are:

- Distributed LASR in MPP environments requires a minimum of 4 server hosts with a total of 16 cores (4 servers × 4 cores) with a combined 256 GB of RAM (16 GB per core).

Figure 10.1 A distributed LASR Analytic Server acts as a single service while running in parts across multiple host machines

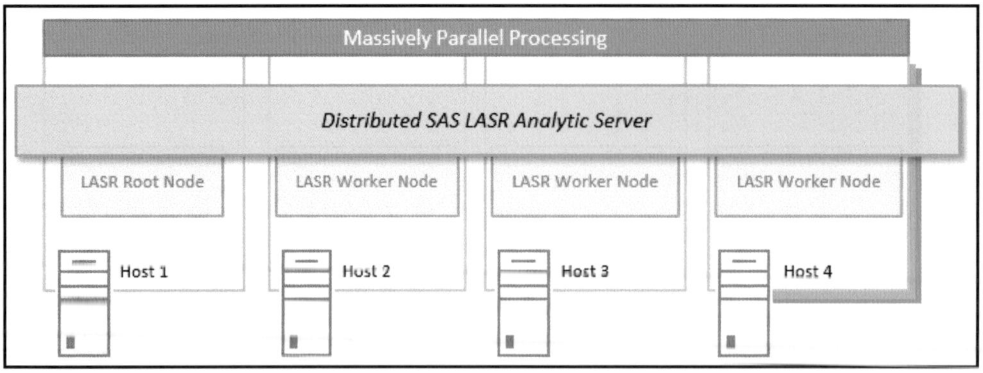

- Non-Distributed LASR in symmetric multi-processing (SMP) environments requires a minimum of 1 server host with 4 cores and 16 GB of RAM per core.

Figure 10.2 A non-distributed LASR Analytic Server runs on a single machine as part of a SAS deployment

Non-Distributed LASR (SMP)

A non-distributed SAS LASR Analytic Server runs using the SMP compute model. In other words, it runs on a computer like most other applications with which you're familiar.

This means that an instance of non-distributed LASR Analytic Server can only scale up as far as the host hardware will allow. If your data sets grow in size over time, they might eventually exceed the size limit of what can be adequately processed by a non-distributed LASR Analytic server on your host machine. If possible, you can add more RAM onto your host machine to extend the LASR working size. But using this approach means that eventually the host machine will reach a maximum amount of RAM it can hold. If your data set continues to grow, then you need to look at buying a whole new server – a higher class with larger RAM capacity – or consider upgrading to Distributed SAS Visual Analytics and the distributed LASR Analytic Server, which can scale much higher by running across multiple machines simultaneously.

Scaling up in size using this SMP approach can get expensive very quickly. Shop around on the various retail sites for server hardware vendors, and you can see that moving up from one machine to another with twice the CPU and RAM can cost three, four, or more times as much.

Distributed LASR (MPP)

MPP offers a much longer path for scalability than SMP. The idea with an MPP approach is to use smaller machines that are relatively cheap and more cost-effective. Then as your computing power needs increase, add more of those cheap commodity machines to your environment and extend the software cluster to run on them. In this way, there is effectively a much, much higher limit on the number of CPUs and the amount of RAM that can be thrown at your computing tasks.

Distributed SAS LASR Analytic Server was built from the ground-up specifically to get the most out of the MPP compute model.

When data is copied into a distributed LASR server, it is broken up into chunks and divided across the multiple servers that are hosting LASR. The LASR components that hold and process this data are known as the LASR Workers. Their actions are coordinated on another host machine known as the LASR Root Node. In this way, when a request comes to LASR for analytic processing of the data, the LASR Root sets the LASR Workers to task. Each LASR Worker acts independently on its chunk of the data and sends the resulting answer back to the LASR Root. Once all LASR Workers have reported back, the LASR Root will finalize the answer and provide the response back to the requestor. In a properly configured environment, SAS has demonstrated that LASR can process a billion records in just a few seconds. Because of this incredible speed, LASR does not cache any results. Every request that comes in is fully acted on the entire in-memory data set every time.

Load balancing by data distribution

When data is loaded into a Distributed LASR Analytic Server from SAS, the LASR Root Node accepts the incoming data, and then evenly distributes it across all of the LASR Workers.

Figure 10.3 LASR distributes incoming data equally across the LASR Workers

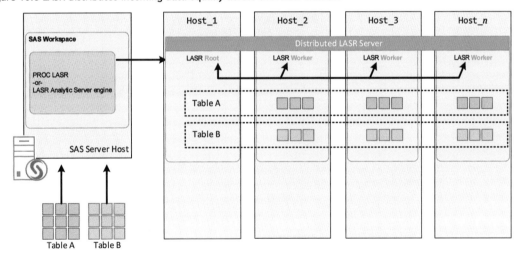

This approach to load balancing – that is, equitable data distribution to achieve similar workloads – is predicated on the assumption that each of the machines hosting the LASR Workers have equivalent hardware specifications as well as similar workload that is not related to LASR.

For example, let's suppose that server Host_3 in Figure 10.3 above is running some other process that consumes 50% of its CPU and that the other three LASR Worker hosts are comparatively idle. Now a request comes into LASR to run some big number-crunching on a table that already resides in memory. The LASR Root will direct the Workers to perform that task. But the LASR Worker on Host_3 only has 50% of the CPU left to work with. Therefore, in the race to complete the analytic task, the LASR Worker on Host_3 will return its results to LASR Root last. Of course, LASR Root cannot respond to the incoming request until all of the answers are received. So the delay from Host_3 has affected the overall LASR response time. This example illustrates that LASR is only as fast as its slowest node.

Keep this consideration in mind when planning your SAS Visual Analytics software deployment in association with other SAS and third-party software required by the enterprise.

High-volume access to smaller tables

Not all of the data tables in your enterprise environment are large in size. And yet you still might want to put some of this smaller data into your Distributed SAS LASR Analytic Server. With relatively small data volumes, it can be inefficient to break it into chunks and distribute them across multiple hosts for MPP processing. This is because the communication and coordination between nodes will consume a significantly larger percentage of LASR's overall response time. In those situations, you might see faster response times if that data is placed into a non-distributed LASR Analytic Server because having the entire table in one place eliminates the multi-node coordination necessary for a distributed LASR Analytic Server.

Figure 10.4 Smaller tables copied to non-distributed LASR Analytic Server for more efficient processing

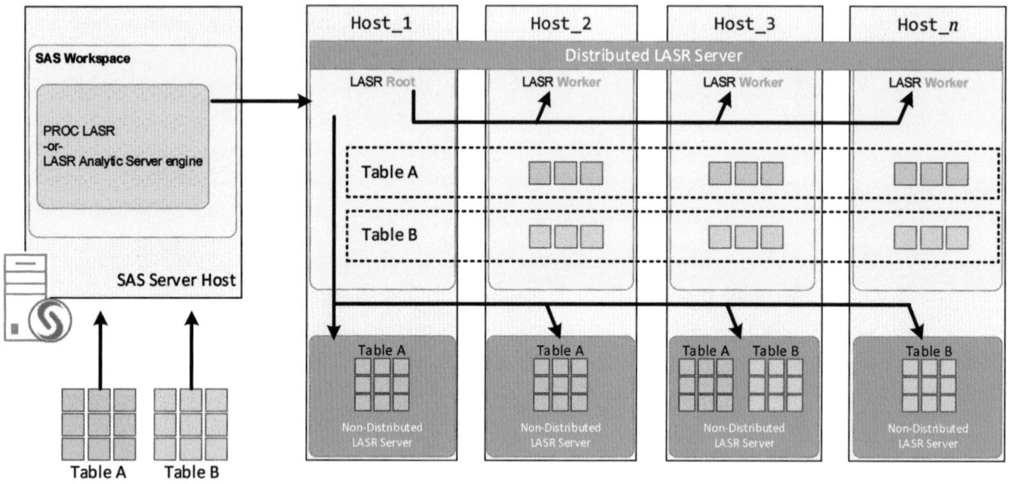

What is a small table in terms of size? That answer varies depending on factors, but generally any table less than 2 GB in size is likely to be an ideal candidate for this approach. Tables ranging in size between 2 GB and 20 GB are possibly good candidates, depending on the current workload, the available RAM to each host, the number of nodes, and so on. Tables that are over 20 GB in size are probably best served in a distributed LASR Analytic Server.

To meet this need, a distributed LASR Analytic server can also support running individual non-distributed LASR Analytic Server instances within the cluster as well.

There are two approaches for enabling this high-volume access to smaller tables:

1. LASR Libraries

   In the SAS metadata, create a LASR library dedicated for hosting smaller size tables, and set the extended attribute called VA.TableFullCopies. The VA.TableFullCopies attribute takes a positive integer as its value, which represents the number of copies to create in the cluster.

Figure 10.5 Enabling full copies of smaller tables in a distributed LASR Analytic Server

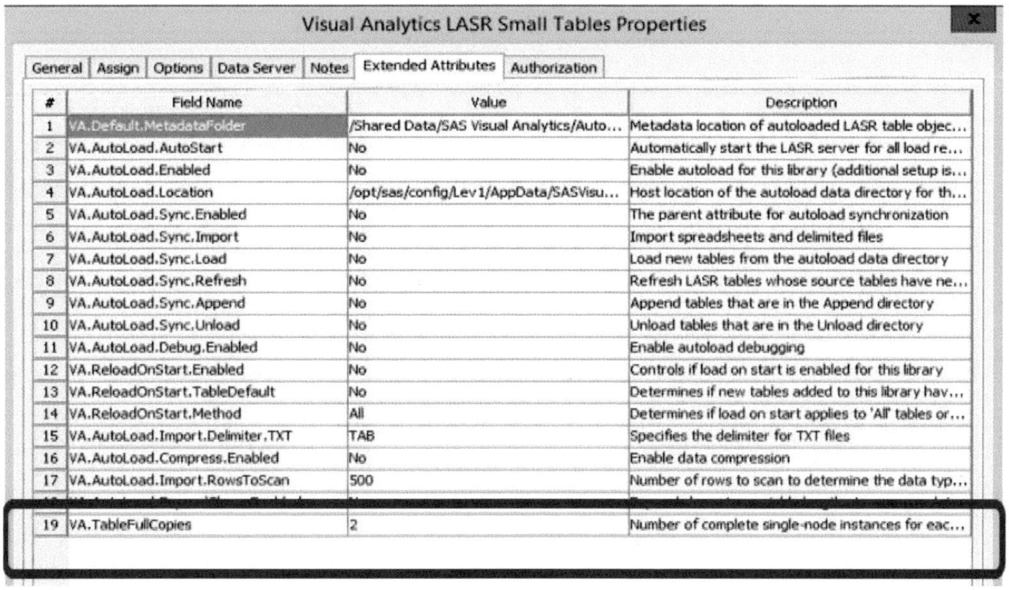

Visual Analytics LASR Small Tables Properties

#	Field Name	Value	Description
1	VA.Default.MetadataFolder	/Shared Data/SAS Visual Analytics/Auto...	Metadata location of autoloaded LASR table objec...
2	VA.AutoLoad.AutoStart	No	Automatically start the LASR server for all load re...
3	VA.AutoLoad.Enabled	No	Enable autoload for this library (additional setup is...
4	VA.AutoLoad.Location	/opt/sas/config/Lev1/AppData/SASVisu...	Host location of the autoload data directory for th...
5	VA.AutoLoad.Sync.Enabled	No	The parent attribute for autoload synchronization
6	VA.AutoLoad.Sync.Import	No	Import spreadsheets and delimited files
7	VA.AutoLoad.Sync.Load	No	Load new tables from the autoload data directory
8	VA.AutoLoad.Sync.Refresh	No	Refresh LASR tables whose source tables have ne...
9	VA.AutoLoad.Sync.Append	No	Append tables that are in the Append directory
10	VA.AutoLoad.Sync.Unload	No	Unload tables that are in the Unload directory
11	VA.AutoLoad.Debug.Enabled	No	Enable autoload debugging
12	VA.ReloadOnStart.Enabled	No	Controls if load on start is enabled for this library
13	VA.ReloadOnStart.TableDefault	No	Determines if new tables added to this library hav...
14	VA.ReloadOnStart.Method	All	Determines if load on start applies to 'All' tables or...
15	VA.AutoLoad.Import.Delimiter.TXT	TAB	Specifies the delimiter for TXT files
16	VA.AutoLoad.Compress.Enabled	No	Enable data compression
17	VA.AutoLoad.Import.RowsToScan	500	Number of rows to scan to determine the data typ...
19	VA.TableFullCopies	2	Number of complete single-node instances for eac...

2. SAS Program Code

   The LASR Procedure provides a FullCopyTo option which, when used to load a table into LASR, specifies the number of copies to create of the smaller table in the cluster. A simple example:

   ```
   proc lasr add data=hdfs.small_table1 fullcopyto=3 port=10010;
   run;
   ```

When using the full copy functionality for small tables with a distributed LASR Analytic Server, considerations to keep in mind are the following:

- In some cases, the Distributed LASR Server must also have a copy of the small table. Tasks that use more than one input table (such as the SCHEMA and the SAVE statements) run on the distributed server only. If the table exists only on a non-distributed server, then the table is copied to the distributed server before the requested processing begins.

- Table requests are load-balanced across machines that are hosting full table copies.

- Full table copies are read-only. UPDATE and APPEND statements will return an error.

The following administrative actions are recommended when working with full copy tables in LASR:

- Start with a small number of copies, which represent less than the total number of LASR Worker hosts and then incrementally increase as needed

- Train users to use the LASR library (or the FullCopyTo option for PROC LASR) with care because inadvertently loading a very large table in this way could quickly consume all RAM resources on affected hosts.

- Non-distributed LASR servers continue to run until the distributed LASR server is stopped.

- If logging is enabled, only the distributed LASR server will capture activity. The non-distributed LASR servers do not log any activity directly.

Fast loading of data to distributed LASR Analytic Server

The SAS LASR Analytic Server can be loaded with data from any source that Base SAS in your environment has access to. Base SAS comes with the built-in ability to work with data from sources such as the following:

- Local text files
  - Formatted, like CSV
  - Raw, like log files
- SAS data sets
- SAS Scalable Performance Data Engine (SPD Engine) data tables
  - On direct-attached storage
  - On HDFS

Furthermore, Base SAS can be extended to with optional SAS/ACCESS engines for native access to third-party data providers such as Oracle, DB2, SQL Server as well as storage based on Hadoop, such as Hive, Impala, Spark, and more.

All of these data sources have one thing in common: The Base SAS instance acts as a data proxy that connects to the source data, siphons it out, and then sends it to LASR. Data transferred in this manner is all sent directly to the LASR Root Node, which then distributes it across the LASR Workers.

Figure 10.6 SAS supports a wide variety of data sources for serially loading data into LASR

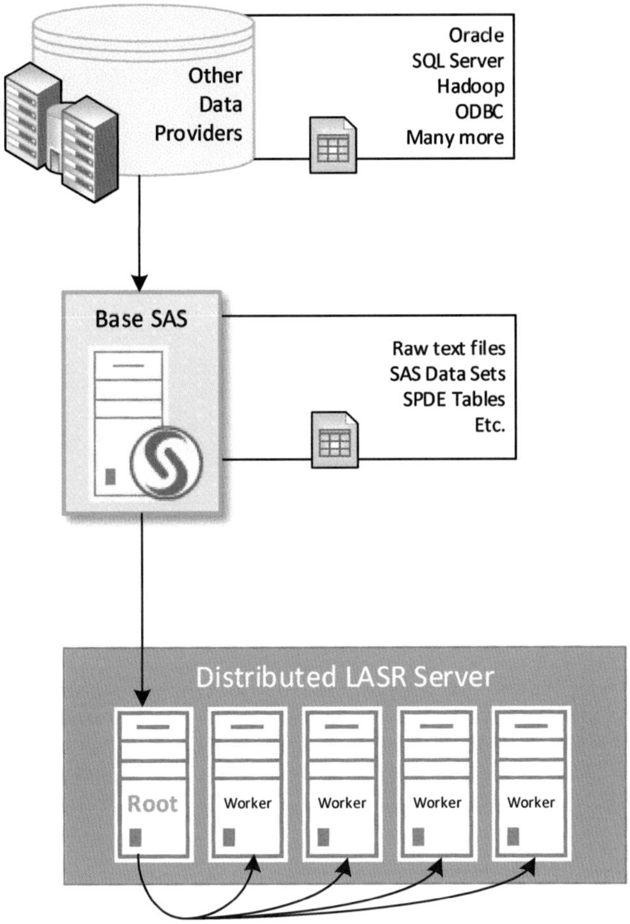

While this approach works well in support of a very wide array of supported data providers, its performance is constrained by the serial distribution points: Base SAS and the LASR Root Node. For better throughput, it is possible to load data using multiple parallel streams directly to the Worker Nodes of a distributed LASR Analytic Server. The architecture and deployment of software in your environment determines exactly which of these parallel loading techniques are supported.

LASR and a remote data provider (asymmetric)

Chances are that, after deploying Distributed SAS Visual Analytics at your site, there is a data provider elsewhere in your environment that hosts data that you want in LASR. The serial loading technique illustrated in Figure 10.6 above will certainly work, but for a large volume of data, it might take a long time to complete the transfer.

For supported data providers, SAS offers In-Database technology. This technology delivers the ability to parallel load data from multiple nodes of the remote data provider directly to each of the worker nodes of a distributed LASR Analytic Server. To gain this ability, your site will need to license the appropriate SAS/ACCESS product and deploy the SAS Embedded Process into the remote data provider.

One benefit of keeping the data provider separate from LASR is that it enables you to customize each environment for their specific service objectives. Each environment can scale independently of the other and each one can have its own maintenance operations with minimal impact to the other.

LASR symmetrically co-located with HDFS

At some sites, the distributed LASR software is placed on a cluster of machines that are also hosting Hadoop. In that case, LASR is said to be co-located with Hadoop. If we take this concept a step further and carefully deploy the distributed LASR service components alongside their equivalent Hadoop Distributed File System (HDFS) counterparts (that is, place the LASR Root with the HDFS NameNode together on the same host as well as a LASR Worker with each of the HDFS DataNodes on their hosts), then LASR is symmetrically co-located with HDFS.

With a symmetrically co-located deployment of distributed LASR with HDFS, then a symbiotic relationship between those services is possible:

- LASR can save in-memory tables directly to disk in HDFS on each Worker Node in the SASHDAT format (and plain text comma-separated values files, CSV).

- LASR can read SASHDAT format (and CSV) directly from HDFS.

SASHDAT Tables

SASHDAT is the SAS high-performance data structure optimized for MPP environments. The SASHDAT format is binary, compressible, and encryptable. It explicitly avoids fractional rows (which is a challenge for most HDFS-stored items). As a rule, SASHDAT provides the fastest and most efficient way to (re-)load data into LASR.

SASHDAT is provided as a function of the distributed LASR server. So it is not a feature provided directly by Base SAS or any SAS/ACCESS engine. Also, SASHDAT is not available for non-distributed LASR Analytic Server because it is expressly designed for MPP environments. Notice that we wrote "(re-)load" above – data must first be loaded directly through in-memory LASR from an external source before it can write the data down to SASHDAT on HDFS.

SASHDAT is not intended to act as a primary data store. This is due in part to the typical limitations you deal with when working with files stored in HDFS. Because HDFS takes an immutable approach to file state, it's not possible to modify the contents of a file. Only appends are allowed. If you need to delete a single line from a file in HDFS, the resulting action is to basically write a new copy of the entire file, minus that one line, and then delete the old file. This makes HDFS slow and ponderous for transactional update actions. Therefore, SASHDAT is better positioned as a staging area to aid in the rapid (re-)loading of data into a distributed LASR Analytic Server. If your environment must drop some in-memory tables to make room in RAM for others and then later swap back, then having fast, efficient SASHDAT to cut down on transition time can be a real help.

LASR co-located with dedicated HDFS and loading data from remote HDFS

The SAS LASR Analytic Server is an in-memory analytics engine that relies heavily on RAM. The Hadoop Distributed File System relies heavily on disk. They both use CPU and network when performing most actions.

So if your site is currently using Hadoop services such as HDFS, MapReduce, Spark, Hive, and more, then you probably will not want to co-locate a distributed LASR Analytic Server in the same cluster because it will just compete for resources which you've already allocated in support of Hadoop. So with your Hadoop services running in one cluster of machines, it's likely you'll want to procure a new set of servers to host the distributed LASR Analytic Server. That way, you can have some manageable control over resource allocation for Hadoop and LASR since you've physically separated them.

But then what about SASHDAT? Since SASHDAT offers the fastest, most efficient way to (re-)load data into LASR, it is a pretty tempting feature. It'd be great if we could keep it to use as needed.

So then you can symmetrically deploy a co-located instance of HDFS to the cluster of hosts where the dedicated LASR Analytic Server is running. This second instance of HDFS should be dedicated to only hosting SASHDAT files for LASR as a staging area.

Figure 10.7 Dedicated HDFS for storing SASHDAT

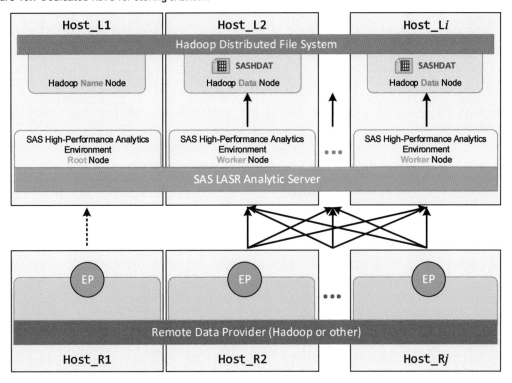

In this way, your primary deployment of Hadoop (or other remote data provider) can be optimized to best perform for your enterprise. The LASR cluster will be optimized for super-fast, in-memory processing, and the LASR cluster can provide a secondary service acting as host to SASHDAT files in HDFS. Any supported distribution of Hadoop can be used for storing SASHDAT files.

References

When dealing with a software solution like SAS Visual Analytics, which offers new levels of speedy performance, there is much information to consider and many decisions to make. After acquainting yourself with the topics illustrated here, you'll find more details about your exact situation in the SAS documentation which is available online at support.sas.com:

SAS Institute Inc. 2016. *SAS Visual Analytics 7.3: System Requirements*. Cary, NC: SAS Institute Inc.

SAS Institute Inc. 2016. *SAS Visual Analytics 7.3: Administration Guide*. Cary, NC: SAS Institute Inc.

SAS Institute Inc. 2016. *SAS LASR Analytic Server 2.7 Reference Guide*. Cary, NC: SAS Institute Inc.

SAS Institute Inc. 2016. *SAS 9.4 Supported Hadoop Distributions*. Cary, NC: SAS Institute Inc.

part four

SAS Visual Analytics 8.1

This part of the book takes you into the newest release of SAS Visual Analytics, which is on SAS Viya. These chapters introduce you to the new environment and show you how to navigate and use the Visual Data Builder and Visual Analytics applications.

The chapter provides an overview of the SAS Viya environment and managing your environment with the SAS Environment Manager.

This chapter takes you into an overview of the SAS Visual Data Builder that comes with SAS Visual Analytics on SAS Viya. You learn about the new interface, how to extract and load data to CAS, and how to use the new features to transform your data sets.

In this chapter, we take the dive into the reporting and analytics section of SAS Visual Analytics on SAS Viya. You learn how to import data into the tool along with how to build reports and get a deeper look into your data with the new interface. There are many new features that let you quickly get to actionable insight.

chapter eleven

introducing the SAS Viya platform

In 2016, SAS introduced its new SAS Viya platform. SAS Viya is a completely re-imagined approach to delivering powerful SAS analytics using the latest technology in services deployment. The promise of cloud computing is being realized today, and SAS has designed SAS Viya to capitalize on the flexibility of elastic infrastructure.

SAS Visual Analytics 8.1 is based on the SAS Viya platform.

Overview of the SAS Viya platform

The Viya platform is made up of many different pieces, but they can be summarized in just a few categories:

- **CAS In-Memory Analytics Server**: The CAS server is the next generation of in-memory analytics. Built on the lessons learned from previous in-memory analytics such as the SAS LASR Analytic Server, CAS extends its operational goals beyond just speed. While SAS software is a natural client for the CAS server, it also offers open programming APIs for clients other than SAS, such as Java, Python, and the R programming language.

- **Microservices**: Each microservice has a singular goal and is focused on delivering just that. Consider the SAS Metadata Server, which does not exist on the SAS Viya platform directly. Instead, its many roles have been given to individual microservices. One of the many benefits of this approach is that SAS microservices no longer require a rigid, structured start-up and shut-down order. They are designed to act intelligently in dealing with up- and down-stream dependencies.

- **Stateful services**: A handful of SAS software services must be continuously present and deliberate in their interactions. These stateful services are critical infrastructure for the SAS Viya platform since the other services rely on them to understand the environment as well as to act upon incoming directives. One example is Consul, which acts as a service registry. All of the microservices contact Consul to register their availability as well as to find out where the other microservices, which they require, are listening.

Altogether, the pieces of the SAS Viya platform can be visualized in following illustration:

Figure 11.1 SAS Viya Platform

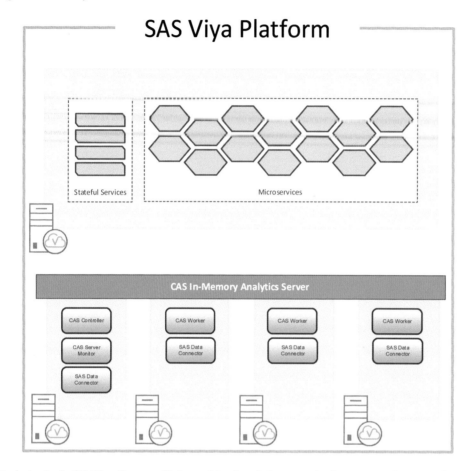

As is typical of SAS software offerings, this view is just one deployment option out of many that are possible. Here, we see that the stateful services and the microservices all reside together on a single host machine and that the CAS In-Memory Analytics Server is deployed in a massively parallel processing (MPP) configuration across a minimum of four host machines: one acting as the Controller and the others as Workers.

Alternatively, the simplest deployment of the SAS Viya platform would consist of all software running on a single host machine where the CAS server would run as a single instance in single machine, symmetric multiprocessing (SMP) mode. Or you could choose to deploy in support of a large enterprise and run on even more machines than illustrated here. The usual advice follows at this point: When sizing an environment for your site, contact the SAS Enterprise Excellence Center for assistance to ensure that all considerations are weighed so that sufficient compute resources will be available for your needs.

Understanding the CAS In-Memory Analytics Server

To fully realize the new capabilities of the CAS server, it's helpful to understand the journey that SAS has taken to develop in-memory analytics over the last several years.

Introducing massively parallel analytics

The first iteration of SAS in-memory analytics using an MPP approach was the SAS High-Performance Analytics Server offering. Still available today for the SAS 9.4 platform, the SAS High-Performance Analytics

Server showed just how incredibly powerful SAS analytics can be when performed completely in memory, without using disk during interim calculations. The SAS High-Performance Analytics Server only runs on demand. This means that each invocation of the SAS High-Performance Analytics Server required loading data into RAM. Once the requested in-memory analysis task completed, the SAS High-Performance Analytics Server released the memory and shut down. To perform a follow-up calculation on the same data requires repeating the entire process. Reloading the data with each request can be tedious, especially if you are not using a fast and efficient parallel loading mechanism.

Adding persistence

The second major iteration of SAS in-memory analytics is the SAS LASR Analytic Server. Where the SAS High-Performance Analytics Server is on-demand only, the SAS LASR Analytic Server offers a persistent service that loads data into RAM and keeps it there until directed to release it. For multiple-step analysis operations on the same table, this is a huge performance improvement since data needs to be loaded only once. But with that capability, came more responsibility. Persisting large tables in memory means that someone must actively monitor and administer the environment to ensure that the correct tables are loaded when needed. Multiple LASR Analytic Servers could be started to provide flexibility in data availability and access control. But this compounds the issue of overall monitoring and administration. Furthermore, as LASR Analytic Server takes on an increasingly important role in the enterprise, IT organizations began demanding more automation of data management, failover support, and more.

Providing more flexibility

The SAS CAS In-Memory Analytics Server is the next major leap forward. Speed is still one of the foremost goals of CAS, and its internal structure has been optimized to surpass LASR in key areas. But speed is no longer the only primary objective. CAS offers a slew of improvements to how data is managed internally. For example, CAS can now understand the active data source for a specific table. When that table is needed in-memory (for example, when a SAS Visual Analytics user opens a report for the first time), then CAS can load that data automatically – without direct involvement of the administrator. In order to work automatically with data in this way, CAS uses a new memory management model that can actively cache data to disk and/or memory map at the source. This model enables CAS to seamlessly work with more data at once than LASR could in an equivalent environment. Failover is also a major goal, and the first release of the CAS server shipped with support for CAS Worker failover. If a CAS Worker goes down, then the other CAS Workers can pick up the lost node's data and complete its analysis tasks.

The CAS server also offers new levels of openness and integration with how SAS users and their IT organizations prefer to operate. SAS currently offers programming APIs to direct CAS actions that enable users to work in programming environments (other than SAS), which they are already familiar with. So besides SAS languages, coders accustomed to working in Python and Java can use those languages to perform analysis in CAS. SAS will soon offer programming API for the R language and others as well.

Furthermore, the CAS server supports an all-new approach to loading data over parallel channels: DNFS. DNFS, which is an acronym for distributed network file system, refers to the ability to connect your CAS server hosts to a high-performance storage solution where data can be stored in CSV (text-delimited format), standard SAS data sets, and the new SASDNFS file container.

Figure 11.2 CAS accessing SASHDAT data using DNFS

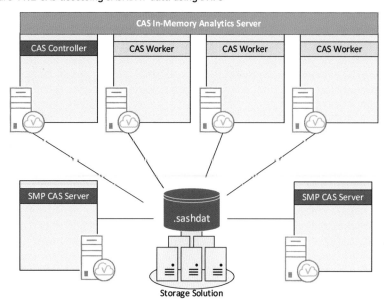

So in addition to parallel loading of SASHDAT files stored in HDFS or using the SAS In-Database Embedded Process, users of the SAS Viya platform with the CAS server can now parallel load from standard high-performance storage offerings that your IT organization might be familiar with or otherwise prefer.

Notice also in this figure that SMP CAS servers can access the exact same SASHDAT data as MPP CAS. This is yet another way in which CAS offers new flexibility and capabilities for your analytics efforts.

SAS Viya and SAS 9.4 together

SAS Viya is an all-new platform that has been developed from the ground up. However, SAS Viya is still relatively new in its lifecycle. As such, it does not offer the full breadth and depth of capabilities that are offered by the software of the mature SAS 9.4 platform.

SAS Viya can operate independently and offer a suite of capabilities that are sufficient for delivering analytics. For a wider range of options, deploy the SAS 9.4 platform software as well. SAS 9.4 is integrated to work with the SAS Viya platform through the use of SAS/CONNECT software. For example, the CAS server provides Data Connectors, which can connect directly to third-party data providers. However, the range of Data Connectors is not yet as extensive as those provided by SAS/ACCESS products. So in a situation where your data resides somewhere available to SAS/ACCESS but not yet to the CAS Data Connectors, use SAS 9.4 products to get that data and then deliver it to SAS Viya using SAS/CONNECT. In this way, SAS 9.4 helps extend the reach of SAS Viya beyond its currently built-in capabilities. Currently, development of SAS 9.4 solutions and SAS Viya solutions is performed along parallel tracks.

Managing the SAS Viya environment

SAS Environment Manager has become the heart of the system administration. Using the SAS Environment Manager from SAS 9.4 M3 as the basis, SAS rebuilt this application. The goal was to have a unified way to administer the system and reduce complexity. To that end, the new application combines SAS Management Console, Visual Analytics Administrator, and Deployment Manager with the capabilities of the SAS Environment Manager.

Opening the application

There are two ways to open the application, from the SAS Home navigation panel by selecting the SAS Environment Manager link. SAS Environment Manager allows you to access different application features from the shelf-menu (or navigation pane) on the left. When you open SAS Environment Manager the top-level dashboard appears similar to the following figure.

Figure 11.3 SAS Environment Manager

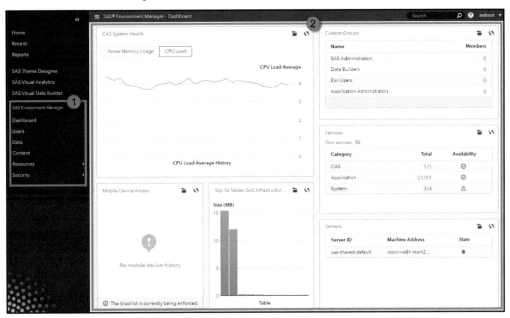

This Dashboard page (shown with a 2 in the preceding figure) provides an overview of the environments connected to your SAS Visual Analytics application. You can quickly understand your deployments, custom groups, services, and servers. There are also metrics to help you understand the system health, mobile devices, and the PostgreSQL database.

From the shelf menu shown with a 1 in the preceding figure, you can access the following application areas:

- **Dashboard**   top-level page that provides an overview of the system.

- **Users**   Allows you to manage users and groups.

- **Data**   Allows you to manage the CAS content.

- **Content**   Allows you to manage the metadata associated with the environment.

- **Resources**   Allows you to manage system resources and configuration.

- **Security**   Allows you to control the capabilities, domains, and mobile devices.

Managing users and groups

You can manage users and groups from the Users page. A big improvement was changing the way users and groups are administered in the system. SAS Environment Manager links to a corporate directory service using LDAP. During the deployment, you can determine which groups are displayed in the tool. Note that none of this data is stored in SAS Environment Manager.

You can create custom groups for the application. Custom groups are ones that do not exist in the corporate directory. You might want to have custom groups to limit features or to better control the application security. This information is stored and managed by the application. There are some default custom groups available with the application.

By selecting Custom Groups from the top-left menu you can review all of the custom groups. When you click on a group name, the right pane shows information about that group. The SAS Administrators group, which is similar to the Unrestricted user in SAS Management Console, has the most abilities in the system. The fewest number of users are in the group. You can use the Edit icon in the corners to make changes to the group or its members.

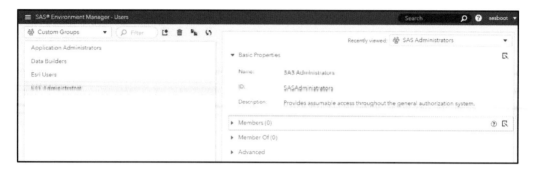

Managing data

One of the most important items to manage in the system is the data. From the Data page, you can use the drop-down menu to manage the Loaded Tables, Libraries and Servers.

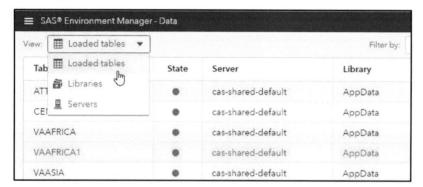

Each of these pages provides a different view of the data:

Loaded tables	See a detailed view of the tables loaded into the system and their state.
Libraries	See all libraries and load data.
Servers	See CAS servers.

Viewing data tables

The Loaded tables page lists all data tables in each server and library. For each table you can review the state, location, and source table. You can also see the row and column count for the table to better understand the size. You can search and sort the columns.

A table has multiple states. If the table is loaded into the CAS server, then it has a green icon. If the table is not loaded, then the icon is red. You can click on the table name to review the table properties or to control and change the authorization.

Figure 11.4 Viewing tables

Viewing libraries

Libraries provide logical groupings to store data. Libraries are associated with servers. You can have multiple libraries for each server. The following figure shows the libraries.

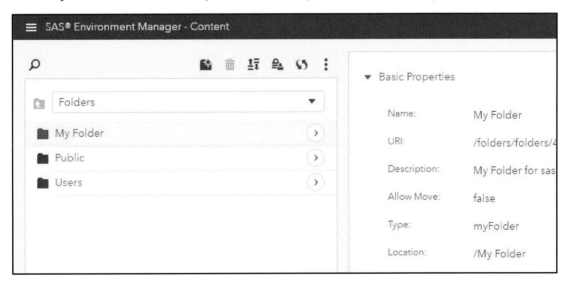

Managing content

You can use the Content tab to create directory structures for the reports and data. When storing reports and data tables in SAS Visual Analytics, you need a logical structure. You want users and consumers to locate content quickly. You may also want to isolate contents from certain users. For instance, not everyone needs access to personnel data that might contain salaries or other sensitive information.

If you are familiar with the SAS 9.x folder structure, then you will find a similar methodology here. Each user has their own private folder area called My Folder, where they can store individual reports.

From the Content area, you can navigate the folder structure. When you click on a folder name, the property information appears in the right pane. You can use the icons along the top to add folders, remove folders and control folder access.

References

SAS Institute Inc. 2016. *Differences in the SAS 9 and SAS Viya 3.1 Platforms*. Cary, NC: SAS Institute Inc.

chapter twelve

wrangling your data

SAS has always been known for its ease of data preparation. Starting with the DATA step, gathering and altering your data has been a simple process. With the SAS Visual Data Builder 8.1, SAS has taken those principles and given them a fresh interface with some updated techniques.

In SAS Visual Data Builder 7.3, the interface and query building were focused around how the programming language, SQL, works. That made it easy for anyone with an SQL background to understand. But the whole SAS Visual Analytics application is also meant for non-technical users. So with the new development, SAS switched gears and focused on ease of use as priority number one.

In this section of the chapter, we are going to explore SAS Visual Data Builder 8.1 and the differences from SAS Visual Data Builder 7.3 that you need to know. We lead you through the new, modern user interface. There are now more options for joining tables and transforming columns. Also, working with the new platform has changed how you develop and execute changes on the new data sets.

Introducing a modern user interface

With the updated look, the process of loading data has changed as well. One of the first things that you'll notice when heading to the data builder is that you are greeted with a welcome window. This window lets you decide between opening up a data source, creating a new plan, or opening an existing plan. Plans are similar to queries and will be covered later in this chapter.

Figure 12.1 SAS Visual Data Builder Welcome Mat

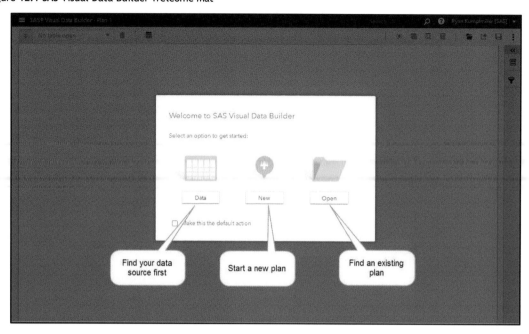

Importing data

When you select the Data option in the welcome mat window, it brings you to the Open Data Source window. This window is very similar to the loading data feature in the Report Designer that was available in SAS Visual Analytics 7.3. In Chapter 2, we reviewed the Report Designer. When you add data, you had the ability to import directly from local files, servers, and social media. In Report Designer 8.1, that option is now available in the Data Builder as well. In the previous Data Builder, you could only access tables and libraries that were registered into metadata. Updated functionality also enables you to drag files from your desktop or folders right to the window.

Figure 12.2 Open Data Source Window

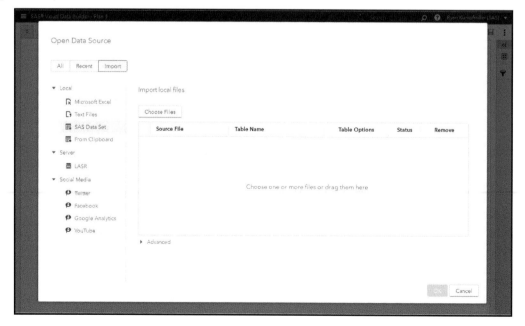

The **All** tab shows you which data sets are available to you in the CAS server. The **Recent** tab lets you see any data sets that you have worked on recently, and the **Import** tab is where you can access data in other areas. The LASR option under Server lets you pull data from previously used versions of SAS Visual Analytics.

Viewing the data

Once you have selected your data source, you are brought to the application where your data appears on the screen. This is one of the more noticeable differences for users between versions. Instead of working with columns names and then previewing the data, you are now looking right at the data and can visualize the changes to the data as transformations are made.

Figure 12.3 Open Data Source Window

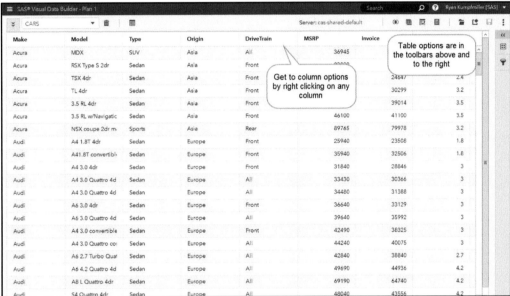

In this view it is easy to structure how you want the output data set to look. You can remove and rename current columns by right-clicking on them.

Profiling your data set

Not only has the new Data Builder increased your data preparation ability, but it also gives you a new look regarding the details about your data. While looking at your data table, there has been a down-arrow in the top left corner that we haven't explored yet. When you click that icon, you get metadata information as you can see in Figure 12.4.

Figure 12.4 Table Profile

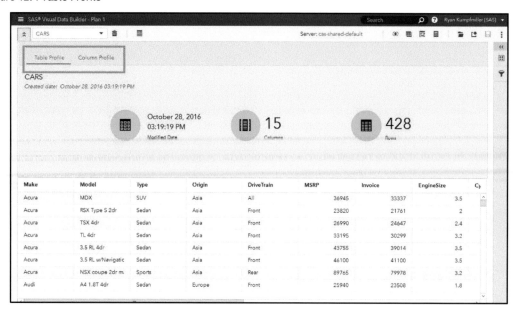

There is a **Table Profile** tab and **Column Profile** tab to choose from. On the **Table Profile** tab, you are given a small dashboard that tells you when the table was created and last saved as well as the number of columns and rows in your data set. This can be useful when validating when the data set was last changed or when checking how large a table might be. Click the **Column Profile** tab to go to another level of statistics about your data items.

Figure 12.5 Column Profile

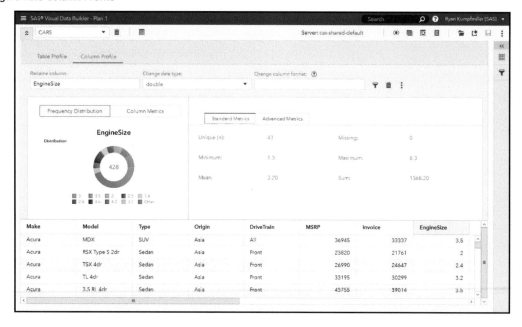

In order for the details to show up, there must be a column selected from your table at the bottom. For character data items, Frequency Distribution shows the number of times each unique value is in a row. Standard Metrics shows you the total number of Unique values. The Column Metrics and Advanced metric are used for numeric data items only and show various statistics about the data item such as what the maximum, minimum, and mean values are for the whole data item.

In the top bar below the **Column Profile** tab, you can see that this is also the location where you can rename the data item (same process as if you right-clicked the column name), change the data type, and change the format.

It's a good practice to make sure that all of your data types and formats are set here so that you don't have to do any more data prep work in the report designer part.

Creating a new data item

If you want to add a column, there is a calculator icon in the top toolbar on the right side.

Figure 12.6 Add Calculated Column Window

This window gives you all the tools to do calculations for new data items. The two tabs on the left let you access all of your current data items and operators that help you manipulate numeric, character, and date items. There's also options in the top right corner where you can select what type and format the resulting data item is supposed to be. Once you are done, you can even use the **Preview** button at the bottom to make sure the column you just created is what you want. Clicking the Accept button at the bottom adds the column to the dataset.

Using in-memory joins

This version of the data builder has made joining tables as simple as possible by making the join more visual. Even if you do not completely understand the difference between inner, outer, left, and right joins, being able to see the columns and data gives you the understanding of what is going into the resulting table from the join. To access the Join Tables window, click the icon in the top right corner that is grouped with the Calculated Column icon.

Figure 12.7 Join Tables Window

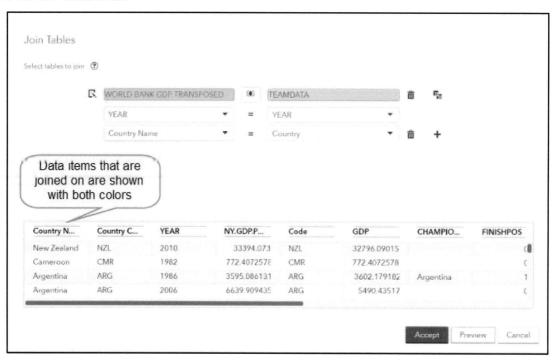

In Figure 12.7, we have brought in our two tables. The columns from the first table are shown in the tabular view below. When you first open the join window, you will have your first table on the left and then a **Select Table** button on the right. The Select Table option brings you to the open data window that you saw at the beginning of this chapter. In this window, you can find other data sources. Notice how the tables are color-coded at the top.

The data items that we want to join are listed below the tables. As you can see from this example, we can have multiple keys joining the tables. When we click **Preview**, the color scheme from the tables is used to label each data item to show you what your new table looks like and which table those data items are coming from.

Figure 12.8 Preview a Join

The colors that outline the column names represent which data items come from each table. For the data items both tables have in common, the colors are split. This makes it very easy for a user to visualize how their data is coming together. There is also a button icon between the two tables that lets you select which type of join you want to use to combine the tables.

Plans and tables

Another aspect of the Data Builder that differs from that in SAS Visual Analytics 7.3 is the concept of plans. In the earlier version, you created queries that brought in tables, joined and manipulated data items into a final data set, and then sent that data set to a location. In the new version, plans are similar to queries except they are shown as a set of instructions.

Figure 12.9 View Plan instructions

In Figure 12.9, you can see an example of a Plan. It contains instructions on joining tables that was done in the previous section as well as renaming a column.

Figure 12.10 Saving a plan

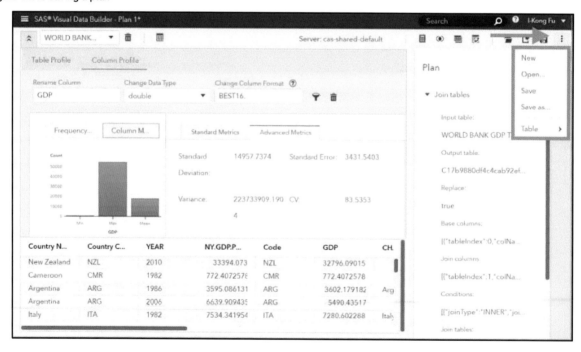

At the top right corner of Figure 12.10, we have selected the icon that gives us our options to save. The difference between the plans and queries is that there is no running of the plan in order to get your data where it needs to be. Instead, you have the option to save a plan or save the table. Saving a plan is like saving a query; you are storing the steps needed to get your create your data set. This does not execute anything, and you can easily pick up where you left off by just saving the plan. Saving the table is like running the query. All of your steps have already been accepted and executed on the table. Now, you are just moving the new table to a specific location.

New features

To go along with a brand new interface and process in constructing your data sets, SAS has also introduced some new features that give you more ways to prepare your data. These features include the following:

- Transformations – Includes ways to manipulate data items using built-in SAS functions
- Transposing tables – A way to reorganize tables based on certain data items
- Filtering – Limits rows in the table by choosing values of data items to exclude

Transformations

A part of the new functionality is the ability to transform your data on the spot with all of your favorite SAS functions. By right-clicking any of the columns, you are given a drop-down list that enables you to perform different data manipulation functions right on the spot.

Figure 12.11 Data Manipulation Functions

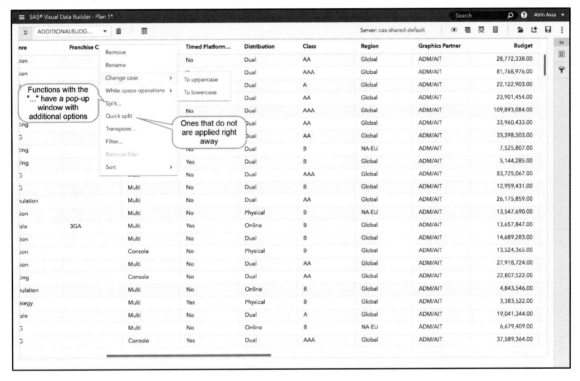

On the drop-down list, you find the options to do a variety of things with the column. Along with the column properties table that we covered in the last section, you can also rename the column here. You can drop columns by clicking the **Remove** option. There is also an option to filter out values; this option takes you to a window with all of the column values.

Two of the more useful options are **Quick Split** and **Split**. These can be used to parse out a character field. When you click **Quick Split**, you get a result like you see in the figure below.

Figure 12.12 Quick Split Example

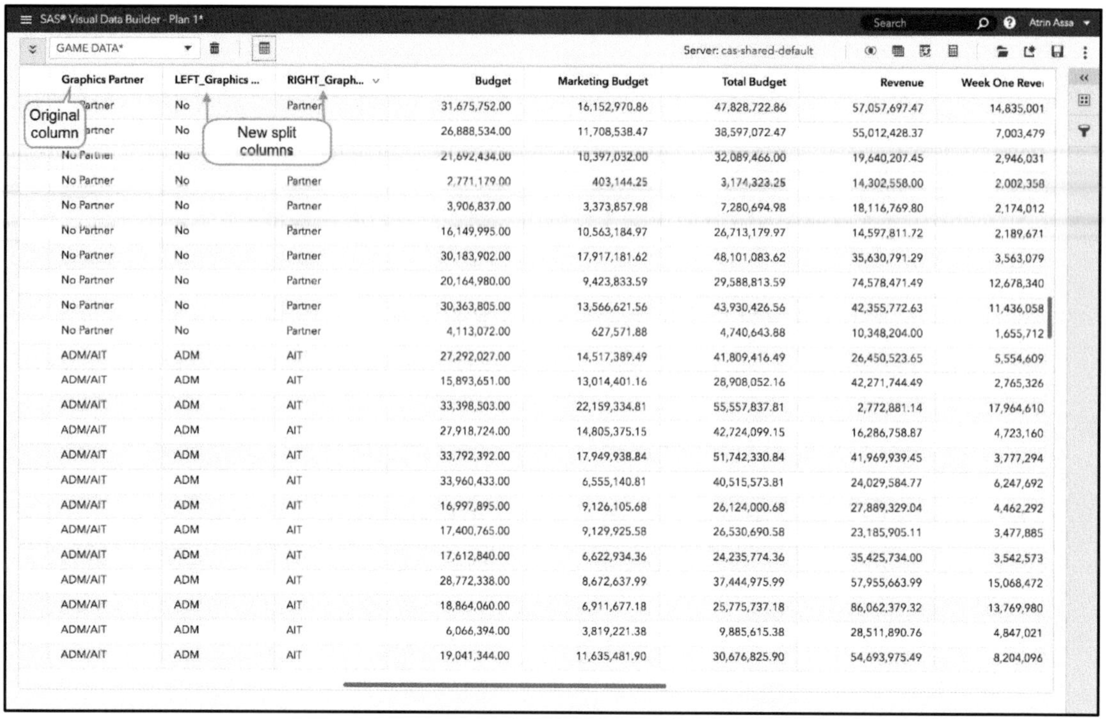

Graphics Partner	LEFT_Graphics ...	RIGHT_Graph...	Budget	Marketing Budget	Total Budget	Revenue	Week One Reve
artner	No	Partner	31,675,752.00	16,152,970.86	47,828,722.86	57,057,697.47	14,835,001
rtner	No		26,888,534.00	11,708,538.47	38,597,072.47	55,012,428.37	7,003,479
No Partner	No		21,692,434.00	10,397,032.00	32,089,466.00	19,640,207.45	2,946,031
No Partner	No	Partner	2,771,179.00	403,144.25	3,174,323.25	14,302,558.00	2,002,358
No Partner	No	Partner	3,906,837.00	3,373,857.98	7,280,694.98	18,116,769.80	2,174,012
No Partner	No	Partner	16,149,995.00	10,563,184.97	26,713,179.97	14,597,811.72	2,189,671
No Partner	No	Partner	30,183,902.00	17,917,181.62	48,101,083.62	35,630,791.29	3,563,079
No Partner	No	Partner	20,164,980.00	9,423,833.59	29,588,813.59	74,578,471.49	12,678,340
No Partner	No	Partner	30,363,805.00	13,566,621.56	43,930,426.56	42,355,772.63	11,436,058
No Partner	No	Partner	4,113,072.00	627,571.88	4,740,643.88	10,348,204.00	1,655,712
ADM/AIT	ADM	AIT	27,292,027.00	14,517,389.49	41,809,416.49	26,450,523.65	5,554,609
ADM/AIT	ADM	AIT	15,893,651.00	13,014,401.16	28,908,052.16	42,271,744.49	2,765,326
ADM/AIT	ADM	AIT	33,398,503.00	22,159,334.81	55,557,837.81	2,772,881.14	17,964,610
ADM/AIT	ADM	AIT	27,918,724.00	14,805,375.15	42,724,099.15	16,286,758.87	4,723,160
ADM/AIT	ADM	AIT	33,792,392.00	17,949,938.84	51,742,330.84	41,969,939.45	3,777,294
ADM/AIT	ADM	AIT	33,960,433.00	6,555,140.81	40,515,573.81	24,029,584.77	6,247,692
ADM/AIT	ADM	AIT	16,997,895.00	9,126,105.68	26,124,000.68	27,889,329.04	4,462,292
ADM/AIT	ADM	AIT	17,400,765.00	9,129,925.58	26,530,690.58	23,185,905.11	3,477,885
ADM/AIT	ADM	AIT	17,612,840.00	6,622,934.36	24,235,774.36	35,425,734.00	3,542,573
ADM/AIT	ADM	AIT	28,772,338.00	8,672,637.99	37,444,975.99	57,955,663.99	15,068,472
ADM/AIT	ADM	AIT	18,864,060.00	6,911,677.18	25,775,737.18	86,062,379.32	13,769,980
ADM/AIT	ADM	AIT	6,066,394.00	3,819,221.38	9,885,615.38	28,511,890.76	4,847,021
ADM/AIT	ADM	AIT	19,041,344.00	11,635,481.90	30,676,825.90	54,693,975.49	8,204,096

The Quick Split option was used on the column Graphics Partner. This gives us two new columns, LEFT_Graphics Partner and RIGHT_Graphics Partner, which have split the Graphics Partner column after a space in the first value and a forward slash in the second value. The Quick Split option looks through your data for the first possible delimiter and splits your column from there. This, however, is not our desired result. We wanted the Graphics Partner column split at only the forward slash, so now we can go into the Split option instead.

Figure 12.13 Split Column Window

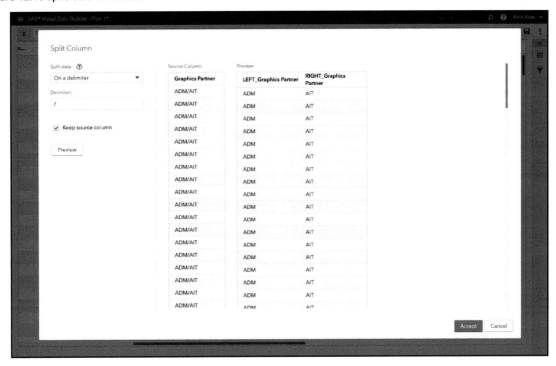

Instead of the automatic split, now a window appears where we have multiple options to parse our character data item. The options in the drop-down list are shown below:

- On a delimiter

- On fixed length

- Before a delimiter

- After a delimiter

- On multiple delimiters

These options give you a lot to work with when you need to get a certain character string of a data item.

Transposing tables

The Transpose option on a column comes from PROC Transpose that can be used with the SAS programming language but it is completely new to SAS Visual Analytics and the Visual Data Builder. With this feature, you can easily change the structure of a data set from a wide spreadsheet format to more of a relational data table. An example of how the restructuring is done is shown in Figure 12.14.

Figure 12.14 Transpose Diagram

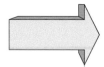

Grp	ID	Tps1	Tps2	Tps3
A	C	10	50	100
B	C	1	2	3

Grp	New	C
A	Tps1	10
A	Tps2	50
A	Tps3	100
B	Tps1	1
B	Tps2	2
B	Tps3	3

With transposing in the Visual Data Builder, we classify our data items into three categories:

- Group By (Grp)
- ID Columns (ID)
- Transpose (TPS)

In Figure 12.14, the value C from data item ID now becomes a variable with the values from the TPS variables. Each value from the TPS data items now has its own row. Transpose Data items are the data items that you would like to now have their own individual row. For our example in the Data Builder, we are going to transpose a dataset about countries' yearly GDP.

Figure 12.15 Transpose example

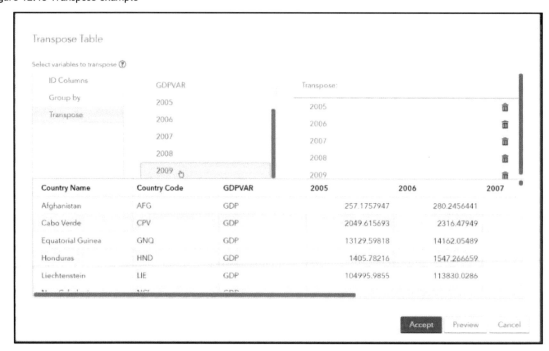

Each of the years has its own column, but we want each year to each have its own row instead. The year columns are our Transpose data items.

Figure 12.16 Transpose data items

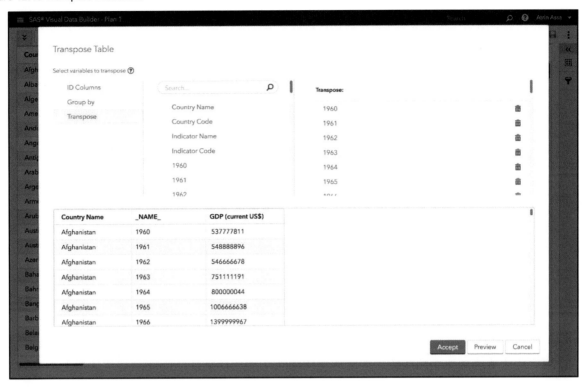

The Group By data items are your keys for the table. Each set of these variables combined with the Transpose columns are on their own row. For this example, that would be Country Name.

Figure 12.17 Transpose Table Window

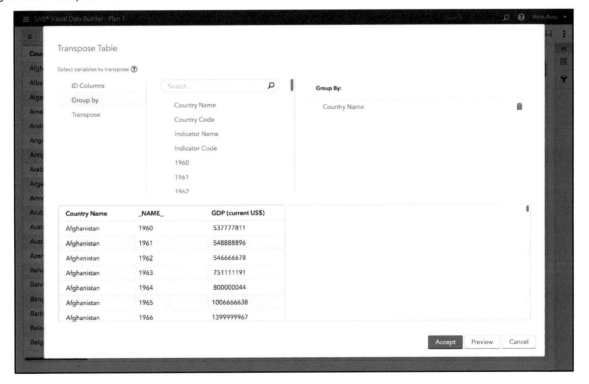

The ID Columns are the data items onto which you are transposing. The values in this data item now become a data item with the value from the transpose data items. In this example, the ID column is Indicator Name.

Figure 12.18 Transpose Table Window

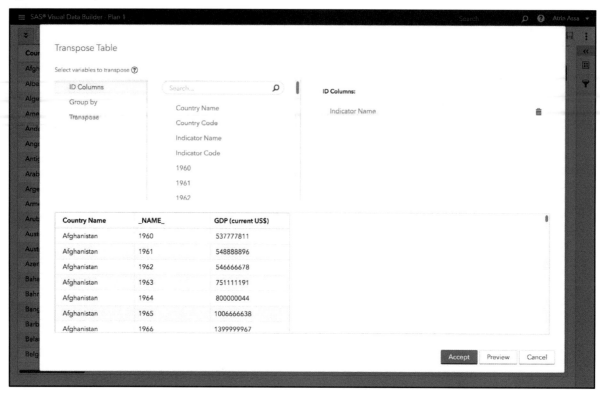

After clicking preview, we now get our transposed data set. The value GDP from the GDPVAR table is now a new column with all of the values from the transpose data items. The names of the transposed data items are now in a new column _NAME_. This is a new column that was created in the process and can be renamed once you accept the new data set.

Figure 12.19 Final transposed data set

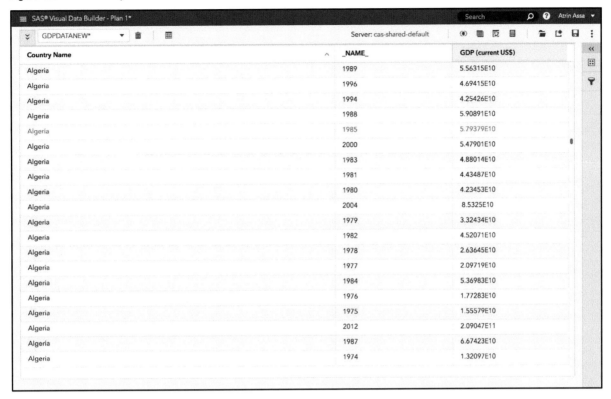

Filtering data

Sometimes you don't want to bring in all of the data from a table. There might be some rows that contain a certain value, category, or date range that you have no need for in your analysis. You can remove that data in the Data Builder by using the Filtering option. This option, similar to the transpose and split options, is available when you right-click the column head of a data item. When you click the filter option, the filter panel on the right side will open.

Figure 12.20 Filter Example

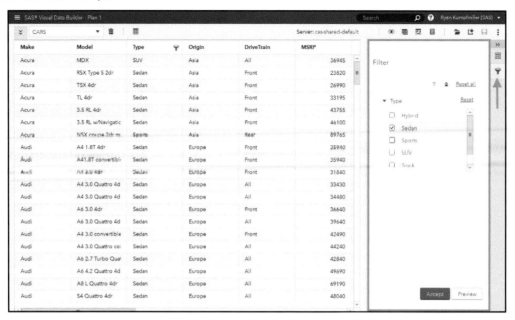

The panel will update with a selection of values from the data items that were selected. If the data item was a category, then a list box will be shown with all of the distinct values available to include. If the data item was a measure, then you will be given a range control bar where you can select which range of numeric values you would like to keep in the data set. When doing multiple filters on a data set, the filter panel will show all of them at once so that you are aware of what data items are filtered.

References

SAS Institute Inc. 2017. *SAS Visual Analytics 8.1: User's Guide*. Cary, NC: SAS Institute Inc.

SAS Viya Communities. https://communities.sas.com/t5/SAS-Viya/ct-p/sas-viya

SAS Visual Analytics. https://communities.sas.com/t5/SAS-Visual-Analytics/bd-p/sas_va

visualizing and exploring your data

In the previous chapter, we walked you through the modern interface of the SAS Visual Data Builder. That same look has also been applied to the SAS Visual Analytics section for the version on SAS Viya. This new appearance gives you more space to work with and easier navigation of features, resulting in more control over your reporting and data analysis capabilities.

The architecture of the application has also been updated. Some parts that were previously split between sections are now combined into a unified application. Since this is an update, there are added features to the application as well. In this chapter, we explore this new version of SAS Visual Analytics and explain what has been added.

Introducing the new layout

The new layout of SAS Visual Analytics has a structure similar to the one from previous versions, but a new look and feel to it. Two of the major changes are the panels and top toolbar.

In Figure 13.1, a blank report is shown in SAS Visual Analytics 8.1.

Figure 13.1 SAS Visual Analytics layout

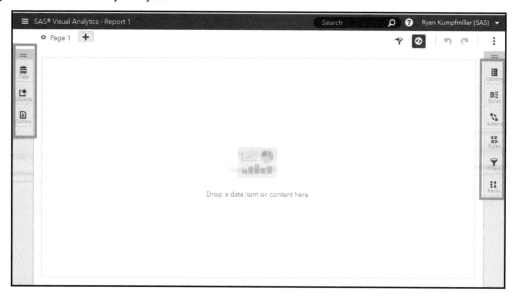

In the top left corner of the report, you can see that we have Page 1. This shows the tabs of the report, which are called pages. You can click the plus sign to create multiple pages for a report if you would like. If you have used any of the previous versions of SAS Visual Analytics, you should be able to recognize the panels that we have here as well as some added icons.

You can access your data and objects from the left panel. If you click the **Data** tab, it opens a panel with your data set and all of its data items. The **Objects** tab shows you all of the objects within the application that you can use for reporting. Within both of these tabs, the drag-and-drop functionality lets you easily drag data or objects to the canvas. The **Outline** tab outlines the structure of your report so that you can see the pages that you have created and the objects in each one of them.

The right panel lets you control your objects. The **Options** button gives you the choices to customize the object, changing titles, backgrounds, layout, and other data options. The **Roles** tab is where you can see and add data items to your object. With the **Actions** button, you can set up interactions between objects or links to other pages. The **Filters**, **Rules**, and **Ranks** tabs let you customize your object to your requirements.

An important aspect of this new layout is how the panels are minimized. If you click one of the tabs, it opens, and you can use it as needed. But once you are done, you can close the tabs and have an open white space to work in while you are building a report.

Top toolbar

The toolbar at the top that sits across from the pages of the report contains some new features that make reporting even more convenient. The first icon that looks similar to the filter in the right panel controls the display for the report and page prompts. When this icon is clicked, two bars appear at the top of your page, as shown in the following figure.

Figure 13.2 Report and page prompts

You can drag data items or control objects into these sections, which filter out data according to which one they are in. The **Report** prompt section filters data for all pages, and the **Page** prompt filters data for all objects on that page.

The next icon is the auto update. This is turned on by default so that when you make changes to the data within objects, the objects update automatically with the new results. If you're working with large data sets that can take a few moments to process, you can turn this feature off to build reports quicker.

You should recognize the next two icons on the toolbar: **Undo** and **Redo**. You might find this new part of the interface to be the most convenient of them all. Not only does the **Undo** button keep track of your last action, but it also keeps a history of them, as shown in Figure 13.3 below. Left-click **Undo** to revert your last action; right-click to see the history of your actions. Now mistakes can more easily be corrected compared to previous versions.

Figure 13.3 Undo button

Starting a new report

When you click SAS Visual Analytics from SAS Home, you are immediately brought to a window with options to go to your data sources, create a new report, or open a saved report. This is the welcome mat of the application and lets you choose where you want to start in the application.

Figure 13.4 SAS Visual Analytics welcome mat

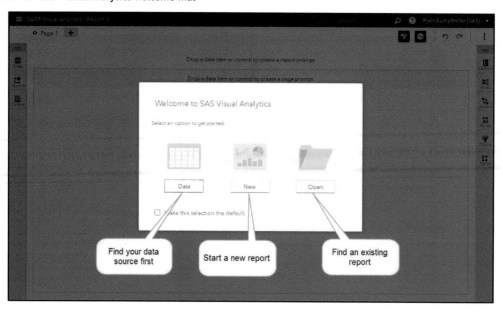

There is a check box at the bottom where you can default to a certain selection so that you do not get this welcome screen each time you log in. The options to open a report, create a new one, or load data are all available in the application as well.

Importing data

If you selected data from the welcome screen, you are brought to the Open Data Source window. You can also reach this window by selecting **Add** and then **Add data source** on the **Data** tab.

Figure 13.5 Open Data Source window

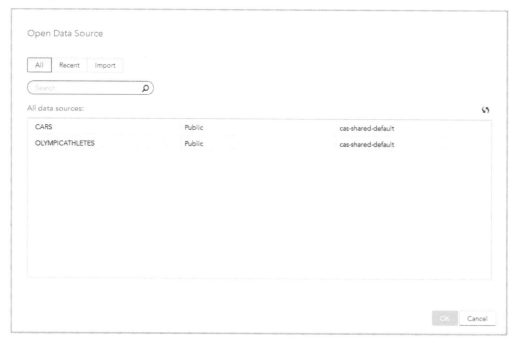

In this window, under the **All** tab is where you can find all of your data tables that are loaded into the CAS Server. The **Recent** tab shows all the data sources that you might frequently use, and the **Import** tab is where you can pull in data from other servers or your local machine. When under **Import**, there is an option **From Clipboard** in the local options. This option lets you paste data from places such as a web page.

Exploring data

From Figure 13.5, we are going to select the OLYMPICATHELETES data set and open in the application. After you click **OK**, the report canvas appears with the **Data** tab open.

Figure 13.6 Data panel

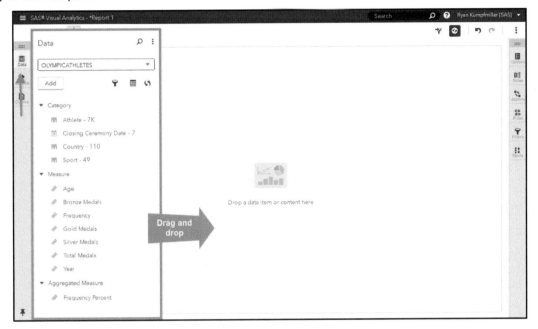

This panel is very similar to the one from previous versions. You can find your data source in the top drop-down bar. If you have imported multiple data sets, this drop-down bar is where you can switch between them. Down in the panel is where you can find your Category (character and datetime type), Measure (numeric), and Aggregate Measure data items. Right below the table name is the **Add** button. This is where you can access the options for creating hierarchies, new calculated items, custom categories, and parameters. The icons across from the **Add** button let you filter the whole data source, get to measure details (covered later in this chapter), and refresh the data.

Adding objects

Under the **Data** tab, is the **Objects** tab, which opens to a panel with an inventory of all of the available objects.

Figure 13.7 Objects panel

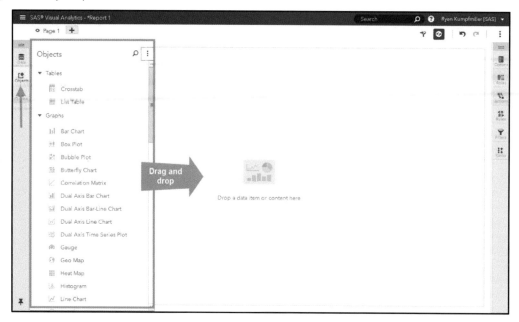

If you are familiar with previous versions, you notice that this is similar to the older objects tab with a few additions. As the instructions on the canvas mention, you can simply drag content to the canvas. For this example, we are just going to start with a list table.

Figure 13.8 Adding an object

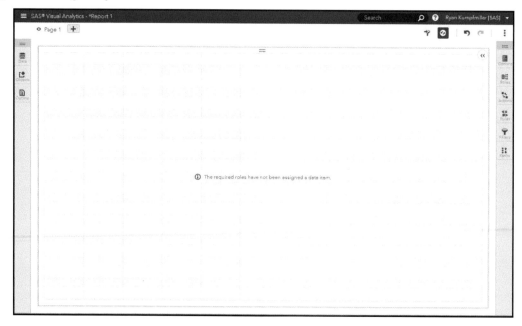

The canvas is updated with the list table, but we still do not have any data added. So a message sits in the middle of the object letting us know that data has not yet been assigned to the required roles. In order to add those roles to your object, you can drag data items from the data panel to the object or you can go to the **Roles**

tab like we have in the figure above. When you click the **Add** button, a window appears like the one in the figure below.

Figure 13.9 Adding roles to an object

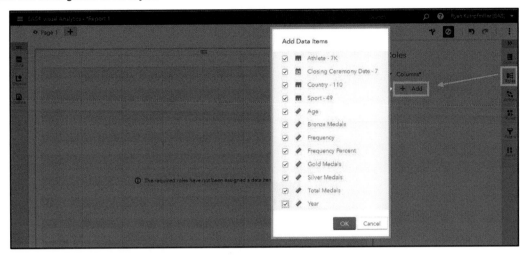

If the specific role that you are populating can take multiple data items, then a check box list appears. If the role only takes one type of measure or category, then you are given a choice of the ones that fit that required role. For the ones with possible multiple selections, you can select the first one and hold down the Shift key to select all or as many as you like. With our Olympic Athletes data set, we want to pull everything over first so that we can a look at all the data we have available. Here's what the page looks like after we click **OK**.

Figure 13.10 List table with data

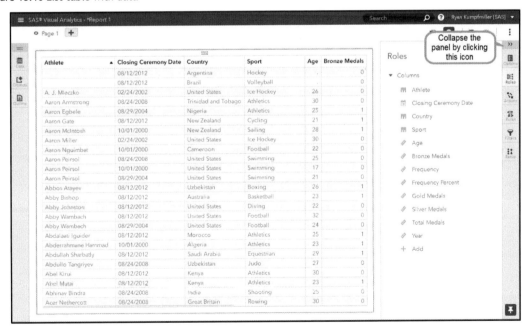

The Roles panel shows us that all of the columns have been added to the list table and are in order according to how they appear in the table. All of the data items cannot fit on the screen. But there is an invisible scroll bar at the bottom that you can use to see the rest of the items. It appears as your pointer moves to the bottom of the table.

If you want to add another object, you can go back to the objects panel and drag another object to the canvas. While you're still dragging, there are blue highlights on each side of the canvas indicating where the object is going to appear when you have finally dropped it. When you do drop, the canvas divides the space between your old object and the new one that was added. In Figure 13.11, we dragged a bar chart and added Country as our category and Total Medals as our Measure.

Figure 13.11 Adding multiple objects to the canvas

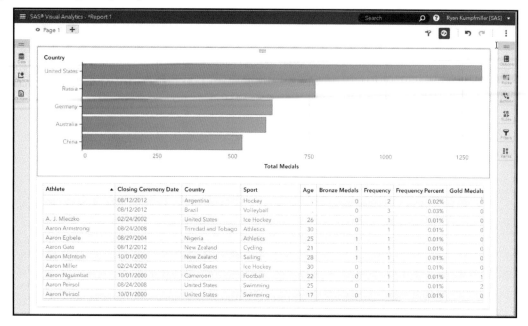

All-in-one application

In Chapter 2, we walked you through the designer part of SAS Visual Analytics and how to start building out reports. Then in Chapter 7, we showed you how to create visualizations in the explorer section of the application. The explorer section had quite a few features that you could not use in the designer. In this section we are going to show you where you can find them in SAS Visual Analytics 8.1.

Auto-chart and changing objects

One of the big differences between the report designer and explorer in previous versions was that in the explorer you could drag data items to the visualization area and then the application would automatically determine a chart to use. From there, you could change that chart if you would like through a drop-down menu. This feature has been merged into SAS Visual Analytics 8.1.

Figure 13.12 Dragging data items to a blank canvas

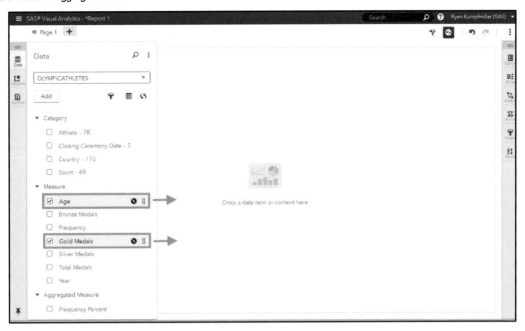

You can see in Figure 13.12 that we have selected Age and Gold Medals as measures from our Data panel. We can then drag those two items to the canvas to the right. By just dragging any data item to the canvas space, your data is automatically charted into a graph depending on what type of data it is.

Figure 13.13 Using the auto chart

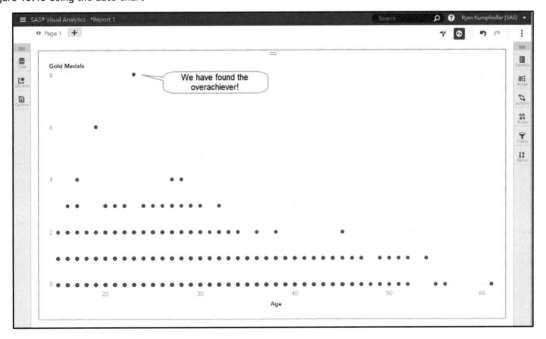

After dragging those fields over, a scatter plot appears with our data. The automatic chart feature determined that this was the best visual to display the fields that we gave it. With the scatter plot, we get a visual that plots the data of the two measures against each other. We seem to have an outlier at the top with someone winning 8 gold medals at the age of 23—wonder who that could be?

If you would like to add more fields, you can go back to the Data panel and continue to drag more into the object. Since we are still in the auto-chart feature, your object might change depending on the data item that you add. You can also select an option at the top of the report that shows which other types of charts are available for the data items that are in the report.

Figure 13.14 Changing the auto chart object

This is a cool feature that lets you change objects when you know you have the right set of data items to analyze. So with the data items that we currently have in the Scatter Plot, the **Change Auto Chart to** icon at the top lets us know that we can also look at it in a Bar Chart, Correlation Matrix, Crosstab, Histogram, List Table, and Word Cloud. Switching among all of these quickly gives you many different views of your data. Doing this might uncover a better object to visualize your data than you initially conceived.

Getting more measure details

When trying to learn more about a data item, you might put it into a table or bar chart so that you can better understand the values that it contains. In SAS Visual Analytics 8.1, the Measure Details feature from the Explorer in SAS Visual Analytics 7.3 has been brought in to give you all the information that you need to know about each of your measures. At the top of the **Data** tab, where the name of your data set is, click the Table icon to open a window that contains information about each measure in your data set.

Figure 13.15 Measure details for a table

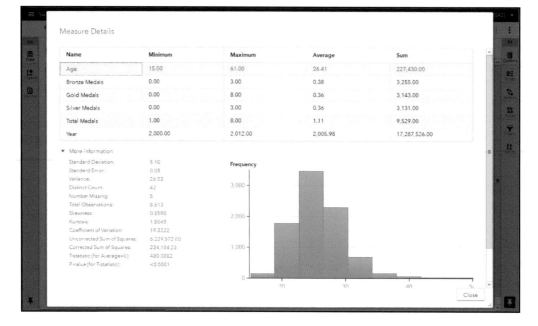

The top table shows your minimum, maximum, average, and sum for each measure. In Figure 13.15, we have Age selected for the **More information** section at the bottom. But you can select any of the measures from the top table and the bottom then updates. The bottom statistics show many advanced metrics for an individual measure ranging from distinct counts all the way to a value for skewness. The advanced metrics update by clicking on any of the measures in the table at the top.

Objects and Data Analysis Features

In previous versions, since the Explorer section was meant for more data analysis, it was packed with a few additional objects and features that you could not get to in the designer. Now that there is only one application, all of those have moved over. You can find heat maps, correlation matrices, word clouds, and many more objects in the objects panel in SAS Visual Analytics 8.1. Also, the data analysis features have migrated. Forecasting is available in the Time Series Plot, and fit lines are available in the Heat Map and Scatter Plot.

Rearranged features in SAS Visual Analytics 8.1

You might notice some other changes to the objects when comparing SAS Visual Analytics 7.3 and 8.1. For example, the Scenario Analysis in forecasting is now called What-If Analysis. Also, text analytics is now its own object (called Text Topics) instead of being a mode of the Word Cloud.

Figure 13.16 Forecasting feature in a line chart

Launch into analytics with visual statistics objects

While you're analyzing a set of measures, you might want to look deeper into your data. Getting into the more advanced objects can be done through the launch option, which is similar to how you change the chart type. You can find the explore option in the small object toolbar in the top right corner, where you can change the chart.

Figure 13.17 Launch option

With the measures that you have in the current object, any of the advanced objects that require a similar set of measures are now available. You can see in Figure 13.17 about that the Cluster object is available for us to use. When we click this, we are taken to a whole new object that segments our data into clusters providing another perspective of our data.

Figure 13.18 Cluster analysis

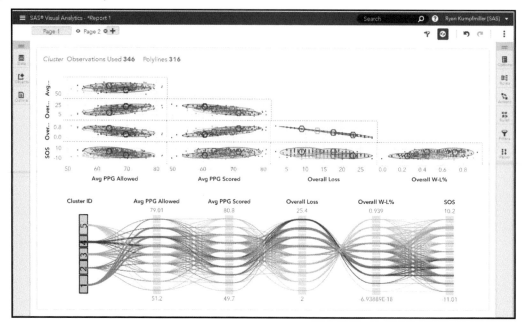

Additional features

To go along with the new interface and everything that we have covered so far, there are also plenty of other new features added into SAS Visual Analytics 8.1. These include hiding a page, a new look to the pie chart, padding, and web fonts.

Hiding pages

This new feature lets you hide a page so that you can only view it when editing the report. If you share it or go to the viewer mode, that page does not show up. This can be very useful when in the process of developing pages in a report. Now you can just hide the pages that are a work in progress instead of having two versions of the report. You can set a page to be hidden by just clicking the eyeball icon that shows up right next to the page title when it's open.

Figure 13.19 Hiding a page

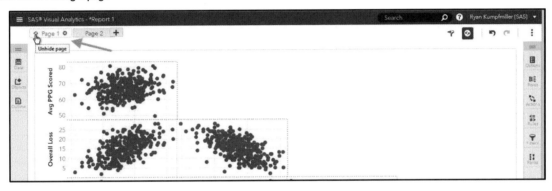

Adding the donut chart

A popular visualization object, this SAS Visual Analytics 8.1 version has revamped the Pie Chart to look more like a donut by just having an outer ring that divides the values that you are looking at. Additional options have been added so that you can choose where the chart starts, and you can also change the ring width. If you prefer the original pie chart, there is an icon in the options tab to revert.

Figure 13.20 New pie chart with donut style

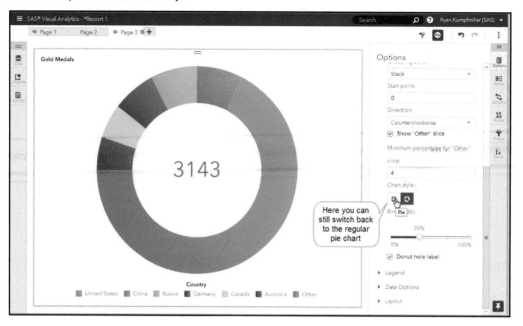

Add padding to objects

Sometimes it can be hard to get your labels to fit correctly on your charts. With the new padding option on the **Options** tab, you can give yourself more or less space between the border of the objects and where the text and chart of the object starts.

Figure 13.21 Padding feature on the options tab

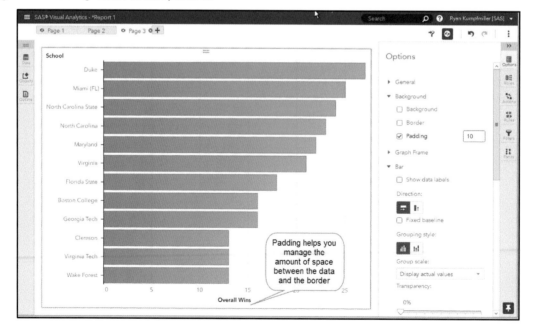

Keeping fonts consistent

The number of fonts available to use in this version has actually been reduced to just a few common fonts that are universally accepted on all platforms. In this way, when you export and share reports you know that your viewer has the same look and feel that you have.

Figure 13.22 Fonts available in SAS Visual Analytics

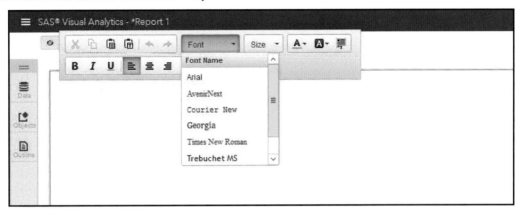

References

SAS Institute Inc. 2017. *SAS Visual Analytics 8.1: User's Guide*. Cary, NC: SAS Institute Inc.

SAS Viya Communities. https://communities.sas.com/t5/SAS-Viya/ct-p/sas-viya

SAS Visual Analytics. https://communities.sas.com/t5/SAS-Visual-Analytics/bd-p/sas_va

Ready to take your SAS® and JMP® skills up a notch?

Be among the first to know about new books, special events, and exclusive discounts.
support.sas.com/newbooks

Share your expertise. Write a book with SAS.
support.sas.com/publish

sas.com/books
for additional books and resources.

§.sas.
THE POWER TO KNOW.®

Printed in Great Britain
by Amazon